The Bankers in Bolivia

A Study in American Foreign Investment

"Cuba, the Philippines, and Hawaii are but the *hors d'oeuvres* to whet an appetite for an ampler banquet."

—J. A. HOBSON, *Imperialism: A Study.*

"The wise man looks for the cause of war not in Nietzsche's gospel of the Will to Power, or Lord Roberts's far blunter gospel of the British Will to Conquer, but in the custom house."

—G. BERNARD SHAW, in the Introduction to Woolf's *International Government.*

The Bankers in Bolivia

A Study in American Foreign Investment

By MARGARET ALEXANDER MARSH

AMS PRESS
NEW YORK

Reprinted from the edition of 1928, New York
First AMS EDITION published 1970
Manufactured in the United States of America

Library of Congress Catalog Card Number: 79-99250
SBN: 404-04190-6

AMS PRESS, INC.
NEW YORK, N. Y. 10003

EDITOR'S INTRODUCTION

WHAT is usually known as modern economic imperialism is one of the most characteristic and important historical developments of contemporary times. It is not only a leading phase of modern commerce and investment, but has also profoundly affected other and non-economic aspects of our life. In the field of politics it has involved: (1) the development of a foreign policy conditioned by overseas ambitions and colonial dominion, and (2) the reaction of this type of foreign policy upon the domestic political institutions of those states which have participated to any extensive degree in imperialistic ventures. As L. T. Hobhouse long ago made clear, no country can expect to devote a part of its energy and resources to the acquisition and domination of lands and peoples overseas and still expect to keep its domestic politics free from the responsibilities and handicaps imposed by overseas dominion. In the field of social institutions far-reaching modifications have been produced both at home and abroad through the contact of widely different cultures. Likewise, culture and intellectual life have been deeply influenced by that interaction of divergent cultures upon each other which has been produced through the contacts promoted by modern imperialism. Therefore, it may be contended with full assurance of accuracy and with a sense of moderation that one who fails to acquaint himself with the nature and achievements of contemporary imperialism will have ignored one of the most significant phases of contemporary civilization. Inattention to contemporary imperialistic activity not only marks one out as deplorably ignorant of vital issues but also renders one incapable of coping intelligently with many of the more pressing and baffling problems of present-day politics and international relations. It represents a type of ignorance which is not only humiliating but positively dangerous. Almost worse than blank ignorance, however, is that Pollyanna attitude of benign trust and cosmic complacency which is born of acquaintance with the issues of modern imperialism solely through the medium of those conventional journals or party channels which assure us of the unmitigated benevolence of investors and of the deaf ear which foreign offices and state departments turn to all appeals to put the force of an imperialistic nation behind the appeals of interested investors and merchants.

It is obvious that the particular manifestation of contemporary imperialism most interesting and relevant to Americans is the expansion of American capital and colonial power beyond the ancient boundaries of the United States. It has often been stated by patriotic orators that the United States is the one state which has resolutely stood aloof from the general imperialistic orgy of the last half century. Yet the truth would seem to be that we were conceived in imperialism and dedicated to the principle of expansion. Founded as a phase of the first great period of imperialism and colonialism, we have always been an imperialistic country from the standpoint of development of control over new areas and the subjugation of lower peoples. The growth of our country has been, in one sense, the record of imperialistic efforts and successes. The history of the United States from 1607 to 1890 is the record of a continually expanding frontier, during which process we brought the original Indian population under our control and conquered most of a great continent. This stage ended about 1890, at the very time when we had just passed through the most important period of the Industrial Revolution and had for the first time acquired a considerable volume of excess capital and developed a greater need for markets overseas. In other words, we needed to expand our boundaries at the exact moment when we had the resources to do so and were under the control of a political party that was to a peculiar degree dominated by American industry and finance.

It was natural that we should first turn to Latin America, justifying our action in official rhetoric on the ground of advancing the cause of human justice and material culture, but not failing in the process to increase the facilities for investment and to acquire under favorable conditions the valuable natural resources of the lands occupied. Our intervention in Cuba was not in any sense a novel or cataclysmic affair. We had aided the movement for Cuban independence from Spain and considered intervention at various times for more than half a century before 1898. At the close of the century things shaped up in such a way that we took the final step. From Cuba we extended our economic penetration and political pressure into other parts of Latin America: Mexico, Haiti, Santo Domingo, Nicaragua, Honduras, Panama and the Virgin Islands. During the same period we turned to the Pacific and entered the Hawaiian Islands, the Philippines and China. With the outbreak of the World War came our remarkable investments in Allied bonds and the subsequent European loans which have made us the most powerful factor in European finance. With the discovery of rich petroleum resources in Asia Minor and Mesopotamia we have interested ourselves in the Near East. There is no discernible limit to the nature or extent of our future investments in overseas areas.

There have been much heat and dogmatism developed in the efforts to define and describe contemporary imperialism. Some regard it chiefly as an economic process, others as extension of political domination. By some it is judged to be a benevolent civilizing process; to others it seems the most brutal and heartless manifestation of modern capitalism and the spirit of acquisitiveness. To the writer it appears that it is best to abandon, for the time being, any of the old single-track dogmas concerning imperialism and make a careful study of the actual facts, in order that we may find out just what contemporary imperialism really amounts to. In so doing we may find that some of our older dogmas are completely discredited while other assumptions may be verified and extended. We have conventionally assumed that the imperialistic process is essentially the following:

1. Merchants and bankers recognize the opportunities for pecuniary gain in certain relatively backward political and economic areas.
2. Their penetration is followed by appeals to the foreign offices of their respective states.
3. These requests lead immediately to military intervention and the political administration of such areas.

Such a sequence, while not uncommon, is by no means inevitable. In many cases there is no political or military intervention at all because the bankers and merchants feel that they can carry on their activities to better effect without the embarrassment of political friction.

Hence, what is most needed is a series of concrete studies of imperialism in action. This does not imply that we shall emerge as eulogists of imperialism. We may end by formulating a more vigorous indictment of imperialism than that conventionally offered by socialistically inclined writers or we may discover that in some respects the imperialistic process is mitigated by the achievements. What we need is the facts before we can construct either a convincing condemnation or a telling defense of imperialism. After all, the most useful definition of a thing is a description of what it does.

Further, we need to relinquish the somewhat simple-minded hypothesis of the conscious, overt and undeviating diabolism of contemporary imperialism. There is no doubt that, as society is organized today, we have certain definite economic needs which can only be met by obtaining markets overseas and by securing raw materials from foreign areas. We have accumulated a large surplus of capital for investment which will inevitably seek an outlet beyond our national boundaries. We have to consider frankly such economic realities. We are likely to be faced for a long time with the problem of the contact of higher and lower cultures, of so-called superior and inferior economic systems. As long as the prevailing types of political organizations and economic systems continue, we shall have to confront this issue of economic penetration and political dominion. If we desire to modify or eliminate this situation we shall have to operate, in part at least, indirectly in the way of changing the nature of the economic, political and social organization of humanity. Yet we need not accept the naive belief that with the progress of socialism, imperialism will immediately disappear. If we could have a world wide socialistic revolution which successfully carried into immediate execution the transition from an acquisitive economy based upon private profit to one founded on the objective of production for social service, then, indeed, imperialism might disappear rapidly. It is probable, however, that if socialism triumphs it will be a gradual process in which the socialistic states will have to face hostile and greedy capitalistic polities. Under these conditions the socialistic commonwealths can scarcely surrender meekly to their capitalistic rivals these indispensable raw materials and markets essential to the happiness and prosperity of their citizens. Imperialism would not forthwith disappear with socialism, but would constitute one of the knotty problems with which socialism would have to deal in order to remain consistent with its theoretical pretensions. One fact is certain, namely, that socialist and capitalist alike, if honest and intelligent, must unite in desiring the facts in the situation, and that is what this series of studies in modern imperialism has been designed to produce.

The American Fund for Public Service is engaged in the process of employing a considerable sum of money for the purpose of advancing in diverse ways the cause of human enlightenment and social justice. It was conceived, and probably justly, that one way in which this goal could be attained would be the appropriation of an adequate fund to allow the prosecution of studies into American expansion and investment. The organization rendered substantial aid in the process of compiling and publishing the notable books by Dr. Nearing and Mr. Freeman on *Dollar Diplomacy* and by Mr. Dunn on *American Foreign Investments.* It was further decided to carry out three initial investigations of typical examples of American imperialism under the general direction of the present writer. Cuba, Santo Domingo and Bolivia were selected for this purpose. Cuba provides the example of a theoretically independent state which has become in fact an economic protectorate and also occupies a peculiar political status owing to the Platt Amendment and the consequent ability of the United States to protect economic investments by periodic political interventions. Santo Domingo is a representative case of forceful intervention to protect American investors. Bolivia presents an instance where the penetration has thus far been purely economic, and in which the engagements of the government of the state occupied have been made primarily to the private bankers who have floated the requested loans.

For the execution of these studies in American Investments Abroad three highly competent investigators were engaged. Dr. Melvin M. Knight, a trained historian and economist, a professional student of contemporary economic history, and a specialist in the subject of imperialism, was selected to study Santo Domingo. Dr. Leland H. Jenks, likewise trained equally in history and economics, and a specialist who has demonstrated his competence in this field by producing the foremost work on the migration of British capital overseas, has been entrusted with the task of dealing with the Cuban situation. Margaret Alexander Marsh, long well known for her interest in international affairs, for a considerable period Executive Secretary of the American Association for International Conciliation, and a specialist for the Federal Council of Churches on American investments in Mexico, was chosen to investigate the situation in Bolivia. It is to be hoped that other studies will be added from time to time, until the chief Latin American areas have been dealt with.

Mrs. Marsh has prepared a monograph which may be regarded as a model of method in studying modern imperialism. She has drawn a broad historical, geographical, ethnographic and economic background for the picture of the intrusion of foreign capital into Bolivia. She has started with no pre-conceived theories to prove, but has clearly indicated the economic and political conditions in Bolivia which invited exploitation by foreign capital and support by foreign loans, and has made it plain how these circumstances have conditioned the financial intrusion from abroad. The book is amply documented and presents adequate factual details dealing with the financial and industrial situation. Yet this paraphernalia of scholarship and information does not obscure the outlines of the story or prevent the narrative from possessing clarity and force. Her work may be offered to the American public as an exhaustive but absorbing study in the economics, politics and foreign relations of an area too little known to the majority of Americans.

Northampton, Mass. HARRY ELMER BARNES.
February, 1928.

CONTENTS

MAPS AND TABLES

THE BANKERS IN BOLIVIA

CHAPTER I

INTRODUCTION

TIN and the bronze race[1] are the two most significant elements in Bolivia today. The tin quotations from London are watched in La Paz, the nation's capital, with close interest as an index of the country's prosperity; a third of the national revenue and more than half of the total customs in 1925 were derived from tin; in short, that humble but indispensable metal is the hub around which Bolivia's economic life revolves. Racially Bolivia is an Indian country. About half of the two and a half million inhabitants are pure Indian; some twenty-five to thirty percent is mixed breed or *cholo,* as the Bolivian mestizo is called; the white group, in whose hands the wealth and the political power of the country is centered, numbers approximately 375,000 all told, a mere handful. A raw material of great importance to modern industry, and a primitive, poverty-stricken and inarticulate native population—these are the primary facts upon which the structure of society in Bolivia and the economic status of the republic are based, and prognostications as to the country's future, if sound, must take them both into consideration. The tin deposits of Bolivia, second largest in the world, represent great natural wealth, and invite development. Tin is, moreover, of great importance to the United States, both because we consume more tin than any other country and because it is one of the raw materials essential to war which we lack and over which, according to Mr. Hoover, a foreign power exercises some measure of monopoly control. But Bolivia's mineral riches are offset by the weakness of her human resources. The country is vastly underpopulated, immigration is practically nil, about eighty-five percent of the population is illiterate, and some fifty percent is desperately poor, either living in a state of peonage or eking out a miserable existence on the bleak plateau of highland Bolivia, without spirit or initiative to change their living conditions, which have altered little since the days of the Incas. To understand the implications of Bolivia's external debt, which United States' citizens hold almost in its entirety, and of our growing investments in Bolivian tin, oil and other minerals, it is necessary to look at them against the background of these two determining components of Bolivia's economic and social life. This has been attempted in the chapters that follow.

After a brief description of the geographical setting of the country, the climatic contrasts and the topographical idiosyncrasies which to a large extent condition its development, a chapter on the Indian will indicate the role of this silent and submissive laborer in the life of the country and the limitations imposed on Bolivia's growth by the preponderance in her population of a beaten and submerged race. Following that is an estimate of the importance to Bolivia of her mineral resources, more especially of tin, which now assumes the prominence that silver once occupied in the history of Upper Peru. In this chapter will be discussed the meager returns to the country of a purely extractive industry like tin-mining, in which the controlling capital is held abroad and the profits largely exported, resulting in a thoroughly illusory favorable trade balance and a steady draining of the country's most valuable resource. Bolivia's transportation problem, and the share of North Americans in developing and constructing her railway system, is the subject of the next chapter. With this introduction to the country it will be possible to analyze the loan made by North American bankers to Bolivia in 1922, the most important single factor in Bolivian finance today, following closely the course of the negotiations, checking the stringency of the terms against the essential conditions of Bolivian life and credit, estimating its effect upon the future development of the country, studying the degree of interference it involves in the administration of the nation's affairs, and attempting to evaluate it as either a sound investment or a speculation, upon which last two points rests its importance as a potential problem in economic imperialism.

The stuff of which spheres of influence, protectorates, economic imperialism in short, are made, is to be found in Bolivia: a country rich in raw materials that are indispensable to modern industry; a sparse and backward population ruled, in spite of the theoretically democratic basis of its government, by a small minority of whites which is divided into two camps that swap control by methods not accepted in the best political society; a lack of domestic capital to develop the country's resources and to construct the necessary public works; and an inefficient and at times corrupt administration of the country's all too inadequate revenues, resulting in a chronic case of unbalanced budgeting and in the need of foreign financing to keep the government in operation. Add to this a growing interest of citizens of the United States in Bolivia in the shape of private mining ventures, investment in government bonds, and Bolivian imports, which have come increasingly from the United States since Bolivia started to turn to New York for her foreign credits, and the stage is set for action if these interests should be endangered.

Investments of United States' citizens in Bolivia approximate $100,000,000: something over forty million dollars in government bonds and the balance principally in mining and petroleum development. Our exports to Bolivia in recent years have been in the neighborhood of six million dollars a year, a very small fraction of our total export trade but exceeding those of any other country and steadily on the increase since 1922.

To the public debt, external, internal and floating, Bolivia has already hypothecated eighty percent of the country's revenues; more than fifty-eight percent of the total national income in 1925 was pledged to the American refunding loan of 1922 alone; over forty-six percent of the revenues for that year were required for the service of the national debt. A balanced budget is almost unknown in the history of Bolivian finance, 1924 being an abnormal year in that respect. Although the gold standard was adopted in 1908, her bank notes have been inconvertible since 1914. The boliviano, the unit of currency, with a legal par value of 38.93 cents U. S. currency, has fluctuated in value since the beginning of the war in 1914, and is now quoted at around 34 cents.*

---

* The following terms, frequently used in this book, are given below with their American equivalents so that their values may be more quickly understood:

The standard value of the *pound* (£), the gold monetary unit of Great Britain, is $4.8665. For quick calculations it is convenient to think of it as approximately equal to $5.00.

In 1922 an autocratic and irresponsible government saddled the country with a heavy debt, much of which was unproductive, with the result that Bolivia's debt capacity has been reached, if not exceeded, without producing sufficient capital for railways, roads and other much-needed improvements. This fact, combined with the high interest rate paid for the foreign credits and the encumbrance of most of the country's revenue with liens, leaving only second mortgages or liens available for future loans, led the Liberals, the opposing political group in Bolivia, seriously to consider at one time the repudiation of the 1922 refunding loan in case a shift of political fortune should put them in office. The wiser policy, of maintaining the country's credit reputation at all costs, prevailed, and, much though this loan is criticized in Bolivia as illegal, burdensome, and not in keeping with the sovereignty of an independent nation, the observance of most of its terms is regarded as inevitable, although a desire and a hope for modification of some of the provisions of the contract still exists. Any deliberate default on the bonds of this issue was carefully guarded against by the bankers in the provision for a Permanent Fiscal Commission of three members, two to be nominated by the bankers, which should during the twenty-five year life of the loan collect Bolivia's taxes. Repudiation, then, or default, except through *force majeure*, is not likely.

The *Boliviano* (Bs.), the silver monetary unit of Bolivia, is equal to \$.3893, or approximately 2½ bolivianos to an American dollar.

A *Centavo*, 1/100 of a boliviano, is equal to about \$.004.

The standard value of the *Franc*, the monetary unit of France, is \$.193, or approximately one-fifth of an American dollar. This value has varied, however, and it is now equal to about \$.04.

A *Hectare*, the metric measure of area, containing 100 ares, or 10,000 square meters, is equal to 2.471, or approximately 2½ acres.

A *Kilometer*, the metric measure of length, 1,000 meters, equals 3,280.0 feet, or nearly ⅝ of a mile.

The real danger lies in the possibility of a drop in the price of tin to a point where the country might face actual bankruptcy. Tin quotations are at a high point now, reaching in the fall of 1926 well over £300 a ton, a higher level than at any time in the history of the industry except for the war period when metal prices were very much inflated. There is some talk at present of stabilizing the price at this figure, but let it drop to the low figures the metal was bringing in 1922, when the average was £159 a ton, or let some substitute for tin be discovered, and the Bolivian Government, which counts heavily on the production and export taxes on this mineral for revenue, would be hard-pressed to serve its debt and carry on its normal functions. How much truer would this situation become if Bolivia's obligations abroad should be still further increased. Foreign bonds are now so active in the American market, and the high price of tin has made Bolivian bonds appear such a good speculation, that Bolivian 8's of 1947 are now selling at several points above par. But the country operates on too narrow a margin, and dependence on a single resource, with a fluctuating and externally fixed value, is too precarious to make unbridled optimism regarding the country's future justifiable.

Bolivia has so far a clean debt record, and the United States has had as yet no cause to wield the big stick in that country. "Strong representations" on the part of the State Department when Bolivia, hoping to secure changes in the contract for the refunding loan, refused to sign the permanent bonds, and the proposal, put forth early in the negotiations for this loan, that one member of the Permanent Fiscal Commission be nominated by our Secretary of State, are, so far as is known, the sole associations of the United States Government with

Bolivian affairs—beyond, of course, a full cognizance of the negotiations and a negative approval of the loan.

There has been as yet no imperialist move in Bolivia, for the situation has not called for one—and a recent writer's comment on the refunding loan of 1922: "And so another Latin American state, this time south of the equator, slips its neck into the noose of American financial control. Was Mr. Champ Clark wrong when he said that our bounds extended to Tierra del Fuego?,"[2] was in its inference the statement of an apprehension rather than a fact. But let trouble break loose in Bolivia and the political implications of our growing investments in that country would come home to roost on the steps of the State Department. The tactics employed in the Caribbean countries might then be extended to the Southern continent, and the nations of South America would come to have more than an academic fear of "Yankee imperialism."

CHAPTER II

BOLIVIA, A LAND OF CONTRASTS

THE danger of explaining the civilization or development of a people in terms of any one factor, such as climate or race, having, as any determinist theory has, the attraction of simplicity, is very great. If geographical determinism leaves many questions unanswered so does racial determinism. The key to the mystery of contrasting cultures is not so easily found. Yet, in seeking to understand why Bolivia is, next to Paraguay, the most backward country in South America, two permanent elements of Bolivian life command attention: the geographical handicaps under which the country labors and the racial character of the Bolivian people. According to Bolivia's last census, about fifty percent of the population is pure Indian, while the white element constitutes less than fifteen percent of the whole.[1] Thus the Indian, who is the most picturesque figure in Bolivian life, is also, because of his preponderance in the population, his economic position as laborer of the country, and his educationally and socially backward state, the country's most important domestic problem. But to understand the Bolivian Indian it is necessary to know something of the land he lives in.

Bolivia combines the bleakness of Labrador with the enervating warmth of the Yucatan jungle. Its early history as *audiencia* of Charcas under the Spanish colonial system[2] and, even before that, as Upper Peru in the Inca Empire, established the dour Andean plateau as the center of political and industrial activity, and there three-quarters of the population now live, although some two-thirds of the country lies to the east of the mountains.[3] This eastern country, the northern part fed by tributaries of the Amazon, the southern by the waters of the Paraguay and Pilcomayo Rivers, is very fertile, and if properly cultivated and provided with transportation facilities to make marketing profitable, could be made to produce enough food to meet all of Bolivia's needs and still yield a surplus for export. Unfortunately for Bolivia, the Indians, using the most primitive farming methods, get from the soil less than half the produce that more efficient methods would yield; only about a twentieth of the cultivable land of the entire country is under development;[4] and any great efforts at increasing output are discouraged by the lack of markets, a condition which only railways and good roads can alter. An underpopulation of the country results; capable of supporting from twenty-five to thirty million people,[5] the present population is well under three million; and the remoteness of the fertile land on the one hand and the barren nature of the plateau on the other make it unattractive to colonists. *Falta caminos! falta gente!*"* is the cry of the Yungeño [6] and of the ambitious Bolivians even farther east.

The high mountain system which runs like a spine in a generally southerly direction throughout the American continent, creates from Mexico to Chile an almost incredible contrast in climate and living conditions in regions within a few miles of each other. This condition is intensified in southern Peru and Bolivia by their

*We need roads! we need people!

proximity to the equator and by the extraordinary height of the Andean plateau. East of the Andes lie the tropics with all the ease of life associated with those regions; west of the Cordillera Real is a high and almost perpetually wintry desert some five hundred miles wide where life is an eternal struggle for the barest necessities. The highland Bolivian is always cold, except when he is under the full rays of the sun, for the plateau or altiplano is over 13,000 feet high, and mining and agriculture are carried on at even greater heights. This Alto, as it is commonly called, a continuation of the Peruvian plateau, stretches from Lake Titicaca to the Chilean and Argentine borders—a vast plain, the northern half furnishing grazing lands for sheep and llamas and yielding millet, barley and a great variety of potato, which is indigenous to this Andean country;[7] to the south, salt and borax marshes and waste desert. The wealth of the plateau, paradoxical as it may seem, lies in the mountains which, rising from this 13,000-foot table land to as high as 23,000 feet, give the sandy and rocky stretches of the altiplano the appearance of sea level.* Here are the

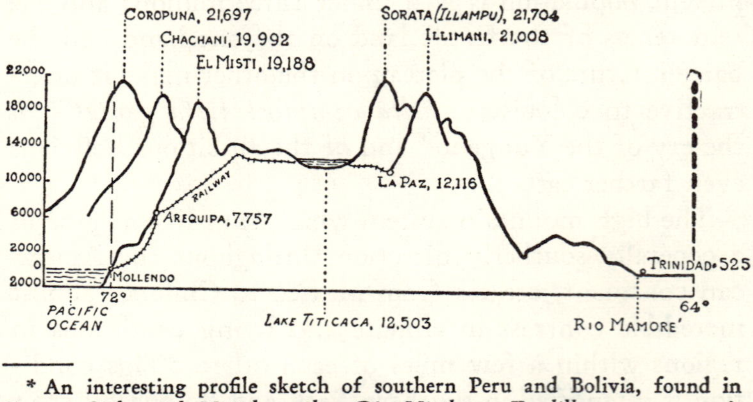

* An interesting profile sketch of southern Peru and Bolivia, found in Sievers, *Süd- und Mittelamerika: Die Mittleren Kordilleren*, p. 315, is reproduced here in the rough. Heights given in feet.

second largest tin deposits in the world, the famous silver mountain of Potosí and other silver mines that made Bolivia the richest part of old colonial Peru, as well as gold, copper, lead, bismuth, antimony and tungsten. There is no coal, a hardship in a country so perpetually cold and without trees within practical reach for fuel, and the principal oil deposits lie to the east of the Andes barrier. Nevertheless, although smelting and refining in Bolivia is impossible, mining is the important industry of the country, and the only one of significance to foreigners.

Yet in spite of the rich mineral deposits in the mountains, upon which the country and the few cities of the plateau largely depend for revenue and support, the highland Bolivian is distinctly agricultural and pastoral.[8] The last census showed thirty-two percent of the population engaged in agriculture as against less than eight percent in mining,[9] an inaccurate and arbitrary classification, it is true, but one that is roughly indicative of the general situation. The best lands naturally were taken by the Spanish and are still held in large estates or *fincas* by their descendants. With the land, under the Spanish colonial system, went the Indians who cultivated it, and the value and size of a finca is today told in the number of its *colonos* or peons rather than in acres or hectares. The peon is compelled to work from two to four days a week on the finca with no other compensation than free rent and a small patch of land which he can cultivate as his own. In addition he is required to render a certain amount of personal service to the owner of the land.[10] Besides the big estates with their peon labor, there are high up on the hill sides, in the stoniest parts of the plateau, and in the isolated but fertile level patches around the lake, free Indian holdings, sometimes individual, more often communal,[11] where the Indians utilize the poor lands left them and all available water painstakingly and cleverly. They scratch and terrace the steep slopes right up to the snow line, leaving the lower and more level stretches for grazing. Their methods and implements are exceedingly primitive, however, and fertilization of the soil or rotation of crops are practically unknown, the only treatment of the soil being to allow it to lie fallow on an average of four years in every five.[12] There is a Government project afoot to introduce modern agricultural methods and machinery through colonization of the altiplano.[13] No public lands are left on the plateau [14] but the Government proposes to purchase some land, preferably along the railway, and by a system of farm credits induce American or other immigrant farmers to settle in the country and show the highland Bolivians how the land should be cultivated. Even if upon investigation the soil should be found sufficiently fertile to make farming there pay,[15] it is a question whether foreigners would be willing to go through the painful adjustment to the rigors of the climate which the Indian, who has been born to them, does not mind. Up to the present the foreigners who have gone to Bolivia have been interested either in commerce or mining, and their stay has been only temporary. Farming is another matter and calls on the settler to send down his roots into the soil and to grow up with the land. Here is a chance for pioneering and a frontier, but these with less hardship can be found elsewhere, as the Italian emigrant has discovered in the Argentine and in Uruguay.

The poverty and the simple tastes of the Indian make him self-sufficient,[16] but for the whites and for the mestizos with more highly developed living standards flour and rice must be imported from Chile and the United States, although both could be, and to some extent are, grown in the fertile Cochabamba valleys and in the low-lying lands to the east.[17] So difficult is communication between the plateau and eastern Bolivia, however, that under present conditions they hardly seem part of the same national unit, logically—and, in fact, there exists in the east country a strong spirit of separatism. This is the potentially rich area where the future of the country will lie when the minerals are exhausted and the plateau is left as bare as an abandoned Arizona mining town. In the Yungas provinces to the east of La Paz, at an average elevation of three to four thousand feet, oranges grow in abundance and for lack of any market sell, when they are not given away, for fifty centavos[18] a hundred. Here are the coca plantations where that staple of the Indian, not of nourishment but of stimulation, is grown. This region also produces excellent coffee and bananas, and some sugar cane and rice. Plentifully watered and naturally very fertile, with the development of transportation facilities and the introduction of colonists it could be made very productive. As it is, it is divided into large fincas in the hands of absentee landowners who entrust the cultivation of their holdings to mestizo overseers, while they pursue the universal occupation of the *blanco* in Bolivia, politics.[19] This system makes for carelessness and inefficiency,[20] and yet, thanks to the peonage system of free Indian labor, the sale of coca and of distilled liquor, for which the greater part of the sugar cane is used, these fincas net their owners a fair income. The largest of them, the Cañamina estate, covering some 300,000 hectares, especially adapted to the growing of sugar cane, has recently been purchased by some North Americans,[21] but American land ownership or development in Bolivia is so rare as not to be a factor at all in the country's agrarian situation. Except for the La Paz-Yungas Railway which, crossing the mountains and descending to an altitude of some 10,000 feet, could not be completed for lack of funds, the only communication with this country is by long and painful trails over a 14,000 foot mountain pass by mule back or burro, or on foot.

To the north and east of the Yungas is the Beni country, watered by the river Beni and other branches of the Amazon river system, where quinine and rubber are the most important products. The outlet for this region is either thousands of miles to the east along these Amazon tributaries, which in Bolivia are not always navigable, or by mule or burro over the high mountains to Lake Titicaca and thence out by rail to the Pacific.

Bolivia del Oriente as far as the Brazilian frontier, and southeastern Bolivia bordering on the Argentine and on the disputed region known as the Chaco, is rich agricultural and cattle country,[22] but so removed from markets of any kind that a good steer sells there for $2 or $3 and private lands in the neighborhood of Santa Cruz can be bought for from five to ten cents an acre.[23] The city of Santa Cruz, which is roughly the center of this region, is twelve days on muleback from Cochabamba, the rail head for La Paz and the plateau.[24] Mule trails connect it with the Beni River system to the north, with Puerto Suarez on the Paraguay, and through the oil country with Yacuiba and Embarcación in the Argentine. There is a great deal of agitation for railways from Cochabamba and from the south into this part of Bolivia, which the Government recognizes as a political as well as an economic necessity, but the necessary capital is not available. Colonization of the public lands, which according to Bolivia's land and immigration laws can be purchased for ten centavos a hectare (about 1½ cents U. S. currency per acre),[25] has been proposed a number of times,[26] and by 1924 concessions for over sixteen million hectares had been granted with little benefit to the state in the way of settlement or development.[27] A British company, of which Sir Martin Conway, the famous explorer, is a member,[28] early in 1926 secured a concession for over 120,000 square miles,[29] which it shows signs of developing.[30] Of the two American enterprises one seems to be a deliberate hoax,[31] the other a dismal failure,[32] and both illustrate the impracticability of attempting to colonize these remote regions without strong financial backing—sufficient means at least to provide a means of communication with the world outside so that the colonists can market their produce and overcome the isolation which is otherwise their inevitable and unenviable lot.[33] Colonization of the fertile Bolivian country east of the Andes is, as the Government recognizes,[34] a thing of the future when railroads and highways will have brought the Beni country, the Santa Cruz section and the Bolivian Chaco in touch with the navigable rivers flowing to the Atlantic, and with the railroads of the Argentine and of the Bolivian plateau. Not until then can the different parts of Bolivia supplement each other and that "tripod—agriculture, cattle-raising, and mining—on which the collective prosperity and the political and economic independence of the Republic must rest" [35] become a reality. In contemplating the irony of these fertile regions so necessary and yet so useless to highland Bolivia, where the life of the country centers, one is reminded of Doughty's description of the Moabite country in his superb *Travels in Arabia Deserta*: "Here are very fertile corn fields, ploughed to a hand depth by the Kerakers; a few pounds will purchase a great field, and grain is in their town almost as the sand that it cannot be sent abroad, for the excessive cost of camel carriage, which is as much as half the load to Jerusalem."

Not only does Bolivia suffer this disadvantage of being cut in two by almost the highest mountain range in the world, so that the people of the plateau can only with the greatest difficulty communicate with their countrymen to the east, but she labors under the additional handicap of having no outlet to the sea. The country once had a coast line with the Pacific port of Antofagasta as her commercial outlet, but the war with Chile in 1879 cost her this territory. Since the Treaty of Ancón in 1883 the country has been landlocked, although by treaty agreements with Chile and Peru the ports of Antofagasta, Arica and Mollendo are free for Bolivian exports and imports. The port question is naturally, therefore, a prominent one in Bolivia today,[36] the students and younger generation in a spirit of irridentism clamoring for the return of Antofagasta, the older men, with a more practical sense of what can be hoped for, looking towards Arica, an ambition which Secretary Kellogg's proposal that Bolivia purchase the provinces and thereby end the long-standing dispute between Chile and Peru, has naturally reenforced.

Following the old Indian caravan trail from the plateau to the coast, the Arica-La Paz Railway provides the shortest outlet for the rich mineral section around Oruro and has been since colonial times the natural port for this whole region. As far back as 1545, when the Cerro de Potosí, rich in silver, was discovered, the *Caja Real* or Spanish administrative office for the collection of taxes on mining products and the shipments of gold and silver to Spain, was established at Arica, and by 1570 the port had grown so that Arica was given the rank of city. When the struggle for independence from Spain was over, Bolivia tried to get Arica, which had been included in Peru, from the latter country in exchange for some territory around Lake Titicaca and for a small money payment, but Peru refused.[37] The effort to get possession of Arica was renewed in 1895 when a secret treaty was signed with Chile, who since the War of the Pacific had been occupying and administering the Tacna-Arica provinces, by which Chile agreed to turn over Tacna and Arica to Bolivia in case the plebiscite provided for by the Treaty of Ancón resulted in favor of Chile. This treaty the Chilean Congress refused to ratify.[38] "History, geography and economics," says Señor Rojas, "drive us fatally and invariably towards 'el Puerto Potosí' [the port of Potosí], whose only reason for existence was and will be Bolivia." [39] And if it were not for the Antofagasta and Bolivia Railway's control of the roads supplying the all-important mining section of the country, he would be right. Unfortunately, this control makes it possible by means of preferential rates to deflect most of the mineral shipments to Antofagasta, and very materially reduces Arica's importance to Bolivia.[40] Doubtless the loss of her littoral has intensified Bolivia's natural isolation and probably checked her progress somewhat, but it is fair to ask whether with three free ports on the Pacific through which to ship her exports and imports there are not other problems whose solution would contribute more powerfully to the country's development than the port question. National prestige might be increased by an outlet to the sea, and, as is sometimes alleged, Bolivia's credit abroad might be improved if international bankers could advertise the country as having an excellent port on the Pacific and so many miles of seacoast, thus satisfying prospective purchasers of Bolivian bonds that the country no longer stood in danger of being bottled up in case of war between Chile and Peru or with either of them. But it is exceedingly doubtful whether such tenuous advantages are worth either the cost of a war with Chile, which the hot-headed youth of the country in their zeal for the restoration of Antofagasta are prepared to contemplate, or the burden of an enormous foreign debt, probably more than twice the amount the country is already carrying, which is what purchase of Tacna and Arica might conceivably involve.[41]

Here, then, is the third largest country in South America walled in from the Pacific by the western Cordillera of the Andes and thousands of miles from the Atlantic, with three-quarters of its population grubbing out a miserable existence on a bleak and unfertile plateau, and the Cordillera Real, the highest range of the Andes, setting up a natural cleavage between the Alto and the rich, hospitable country to the east. As a result, the two regions, the one rich in minerals but destitute of water and fuel and yielding a grudging harvest of foodstuffs, the other thickly-wooded, moist and fertile but sparsely inhabited and lacking the means of communication with the highlands, do not supplement each other as they should. The cattle of eastern Bolivia, if shipped to the plateau at all, must either go out through Brazil or the Argentine and thence by a most circuitous rail and water route, or walk for weeks over difficult trails with great loss of life.[42] The potentially rich oil region of southeastern Bolivia can never serve Bolivia directly, for if production once starts, the oil will be piped to the Paraguay River and shipped to

Buenos Aires, a pipe line over the Andes being out of the question. Lumber is imported from Portland, Oregon, for use in the railway and mining construction on the plateau, although there are dense forests right over the mountains in Bolivia del Oriente. Foodstuffs are imported into western Bolivia which grow or could grow in abundance in the east.[43] Such interchange of products between the plateau and the east as exists is largely carried on by means of the weekly and annual fairs that characterize the central Andes which, though on the decline, "are still of dominant commercial importance in the eastern valleys and must continue so while mule and llama caravans account for so much of the traffic."[44] Through this mediaeval form of trading, "grain comes from Tupiza and Sucre and other upper valley regions, wine from Cinti, fruit and coca from the warmer valleys such as Mizque, sugar, rice, brandy from Santa Cruz. From the altiplano itself come woolen fabrics, wrought silver, *chuño* (the frozen potato), and vicuña and chinchilla skins from the desolate region of Lipez, southern Bolivia. The larger towns, La Paz, Oruro, Potosí, send European goods."[45] But an exchange commensurate with the productivity of the east and with the needs of the plateau cannot be brought about through such a slow and inadequate means of communication.

The solution of such geographical difficulties lies in railroads and highways, which call for capital, and since there is very little available capital in Bolivia, foreign loans or foreign enterprise are the only recourse. But the soundness of investment in Bolivia depends upon a number of factors in international credit, important among them being the human resources of the country. An educated and enterprising population, on the increase either because of its birth rate or through immigration, is one of the best securities a country has to offer in seeking foreign capital, for such a population makes for stability and steady and progressive development. To pile up foreign investments in a country that is underpopulated, where fifty percent of the inhabitants lack initiative, can neither read nor write, and are to a large degree practically slaves, means either encouraging exploitation of the country's resources with little permanent benefit to the country, or saddling the country with an external debt which there is little indication it will ever be able to meet. Such seems to be the case with Bolivia. But to make this point clear something must be said of the characteristics and habits of the Bolivian Indian, who constitutes the great bulk of the population.

CHAPTER III

A LICKED PEOPLE

BOLIVIAN census statistics are so faulty that it is difficult to know just what the population of Bolivia is at present but the usual estimate is between two and a half and three million.[1] The extreme altitude at which the majority of the people live may explain the lack of fecundity;[2] the rigorous climate and inaccessibility of the country have so far prevented any extensive immigration; the result is a practically stationary population.[3] Racially it is, as has been pointed out, predominantly Indian and mestizo.[4] Thorough scientific knowledge of race is so slight that assertions as to the superiority of any one race over another are absurd, and conclusions as to the inferiority of any of the colored races based upon the correlation of color and culture as the white race sees it are likely to involve grave fallacies. To point out that Costa Rica, once called the Athens of Latin America, is eighty-five percent white, and Nicaragua, where revolutions are rife, only one percent, is to state an interesting fact, if it be such,[5] but to conclude that race were the sole explanation of the difference in the political stability of the two would be hazardous. The remains of Aztec, Maya and Inca civilization, and the pre-Inca ruins at Tiahuanacu in Bolivia, traces supposedly of an old Aymará Indian culture, are demonstration enough that there is nothing inherent in the

Indian race to prevent marked cultural achievement and a high degree of civilization.

It seems to be a fact, however, that the countries in the western hemisphere where the Spaniards settled, conquering the native peoples, subjecting them to slavery and oppression, and intermarrying sufficiently to develop a large mestizo element in the population, seem to have suffered a kind of arrested development. A caste system has been developed, based upon the notion that physical labor is degrading and upon the presence of a subject race to carry on the menial work; the problem of popular education has been neglected to the point where illiteracy prevails among great masses of the people; in short, the Spanish conquerors and, after independence, the group that inherited political control in the Spanish-American countries, failed utterly to create conditions in which an effective democracy would work. A submerged Indian population and political instability characterize practically all the nations of Spanish America from the Rio Grande to Bolivia's southern frontier. Argentina and Chile followed the method adopted in the United States of killing off the Indian, so that in those comparatively advanced countries he is not a significant element of the population. The little inland country of Paraguay is largely Indian, and thoroughly backward according to modern western standards of civilization and progress. Unquestionably, circumstance has made of the Latin American Indian, where he predominates in the population group, a drag on the nation's development, and for this not race but such social evils as peonage and a lack of education are largely to blame.

The theory has been set forth by an Argentine sociologist, Sr. Ernesto Quesada, that, contrary to Spengler, a new cycle of civilization will have its origin among the autocthonous races of America, probably among the Bolivian Indians, who are now passing through a quiescent period,[6] but who will in the future, the inference is, reassert themselves and revive the prestige of the old Indian empires of this continent. In refuting this argument, Sr. José Ballivián, a Bolivian who is acutely conscious of the sufferings of the Indians but not blinded by his sympathy to their limitations, contends that the race is not resting but degenerate, reflecting the permanent injury caused by cocaine poisoning and undernourishment, and, moreover, completely lacking the leaven of the ideal of regeneration. "A race," says Ballivián, "which is the victim of physiological poisoning, is overwhelmed by exploitation, and lacks ideals will never wake up, any more than fallow land when irrigated with salt water will yield a harvest."[7] Who knows? The same might have been said of the Mexican Indian of less than a quarter of a century back, and in view of the regeneration which has come about since the Revolution of 1910, would now need to be unsaid. The future of the Bolivian Indian is, of course, a matter of conjecture; facts can be brought forth to support one guess as well as another; and a dogmatic assertion would be futile as well as dangerous. Even the effects of the coca leaf which the Indian chews incessantly in the belief that it relieves his fatigue and lessens the pangs of hunger are disputable for want of any careful scientific study. But the undernourishment of the Bolivian Indian, the starvation point at which the majority of the plateau Indians, at least, live, and the mental inefficiency and spiritual inertia that result are facts.

This condition is the inevitable result of the meager diet upon which the most strenuous Herculean labors are performed. Parched corn, dried beans and frozen potatoes[8] are the staples, made palatable by the use of chili or aji for seasoning, and supplemented by the indispensable coca. On these the Indians work long shifts underground in the mines or walk from dawn to nightfall over rough mountain trails carrying huge and heavy burdens, sometimes as much as a hundred pounds, on their backs. Climate is to some extent responsible for these starvation rations among the Indians of the altiplano, who live in perpetual fear of frost and drought. Primitive farming methods the country over account in part for the scanty yield of the soil: ploughing by hand with the crudest of ploughs, threshing by having either oxen or the Indians themselves tread out the kernels, winnowing by tossing the grain in the air to let the wind sort out the chaff. The custom of letting the land lie fallow, sometimes as much as thirty years,[9] to restore its fertility, keeps much of the farm land idle a great deal of the time and necessitates, too, cultivation of the most inaccessible land at precipitous angles and at the cost of tremendous human effort and discomfort. Absentee owners and mestizo administration of the large fincas or *haciendas* (plantations) increase the inefficient cultivation of the soil, and further reduce the output. Lastly, inadequate transportation facilities and high freight charges, setting far too high a price on imported foodstuffs to bring them within reach of the Indian, are an added reason for the monotony of his diet. The Indian is of necessity self-sustaining, and that meagerly. Whether free Indian or peon his lot is much the same. The latter, especially in the lower-lying and more hospitable valleys of the Yungas, is often better off, physically at least, than the Indian who ekes out a scant living working in the mines for a dollar or less a day, carrying goods over the steep and difficult trails either on burros or llamas or on his own back, as the *fleteros* do, or farming the miserable lands that were left to the community Indians which, difficult as their lives are, they cling to tenaciously.[10] Perpetual cold with only llama dung or the resinous shrubs growing on the altiplano for fuel, rarefied air, and a niggardly soil are the relentless enemies of the Indians living in the bleak highlands of Bolivia.

Agriculture and the herding of animals are the Indian's chief occupation. When he leaves to work in the mines or on the railroads his wife and children carry on these labors, while he frequently returns for the harvest season. The children of an Indian family are a great asset as they can assist in the care of the animals which, as with all primitive peoples, play a big part in the Indian's life as beasts of burden and as wool-givers.[11] The free Indians of the plateau supplement the scanty returns from the soil by fishing, weaving, and serving as carrier for a country where either no railways exist or where freight rates are so high that the iron horse has never actually become a rival of the stately llama, the patient burro and the stubborn, surefooted mule.

When the Bolivian Indian changes his bright-colored poncho for the drab clothes of civilization his parents are said to mourn him as dead and at the same time to rejoice at the sufferings he will be spared in the new life of which the strange clothes are a symbol; his fellow-villagers despise and likewise fear him for turning "*gente*", as the phrase goes, for they see in the change a renunciation of agricultural labor and the delivery of one more of their race into the ranks of the mestizos, their hated oppressors. The transformation is genuinely more than a change of garment. In Bolivia clothes proclaim the man's and woman's economic and social position at least. The mark of distinction between an Indian woman and a *chola*[12] is found in her footgear rather than in her face; and the mournful attire of the clerk or petty office-holder seems deliberately to emphasize the emancipation of its wearer from the ranks of the Indian laborer. To quote one of Bolivia's modern writers: "Rare destiny of a race, whose social evolution depends in great measure on the tailor's scissors."[13]

The mestizo group, almost thirty percent of the population, constitutes the small merchant and artisan of the community. The cholo, owing to his greater initiative and superior intelligence,[14] is the foreman in the mines, the sub-official of the Government in the villages,[15] and the major-domo of the finca, all of them positions of authority over the Indian, a fact which, added to the tendency of the mestizo along with the whites to absorb the free Indians' land, explains somewhat the Indians' hatred and fear of him. His small trading and his natural ambition are leading to an accumulation of wealth which will make him an increasingly important figure in Bolivia's industrial and commercial affairs. The great mass of the voters are cholos, and the mestizo element in politics is becoming more and more a factor to be reckoned with. The descendants of the Spanish conquerors are relatively few in the country; inevitably, as in Mexico today, the mestizo will dominate. It is unfortunate for Bolivia that he should demonstrate so few superior qualities beyond ambition, initiative and a certain mental alertness. A lack of dependability, cruelty, drunkenness, and some thoroughly vicious traits are frequently mentioned as characteristics of the Bolivian cholo, but such generalizations are dangerous and more often than not worthless.[16] As yet, however, the mestizo group in Bolivia has shown few signs of any cultural expression,[17] nothing comparable to the admirable paintings of Diego Rivera in Mexico with their underlying proletarian philosophy, nor has the cholo developed any such social idealism as the present ruling group in Mexico has voiced and is carrying out. When he rises to political or economic prominence he emulates the Bolivian *blanco* and carries on the traditions of the "*gente descente*". It is for this reason that the Indian looks upon him as an enemy, and fails to find in him an ally at court.

For the ways of government and of the modern world are a mystery to the Indian. Shut in by the Cordillera —which, as Bowman points out,[18] is not a barrier to him because he has no vision of a world beyond it—, his way of living and his mental equipment differing little from the Indian's of Atahualpa's day, life consists of the same superstitions and struggles, with the added injury of hopeless submission to the white man's power and authority, a passive pessimism which is the inheritance of Spanish misrule and exploitation and which the juster and more benign Inca rule, tyranny though it was, seems to have spared him. Indian outbreaks occur at times, and the mestizo major-domo alone on a finca with some hundred or so *colonos* has been known to express fear of the time when the Indians might assert their rights to the land once theirs. In the spring of 1927 there was an uprising of some fifty thousand Indians in the departments of Potosí, Cochabamba and Chuquisaca, against the powerful land-owners and unscrupulous government officials of those regions. McBride, in speaking of the free Indians' jealous guarding of their cherished land, says:[19]

"The Indian well understands how his white neighbors covet his lands. He is always suspicious of any visitor in the neighborhood of the community. Occasionally he enters an emphatic protest against the persistent pressure of whites upon the border of his inherited domain, and the Bolivian people live in ill-concealed fear of a general uprising. Only a few years ago alarming rumors were circulated throughout the highlands of a carefully prepared insurrection by which the Indians hoped to regain their lost lands. There was ground for the rumor, for the owners of many farms were either threatened or actually attacked by their own tenants, and a considerable army of Indians gathered on the hills overlooking the city of La Paz. Troops were required to quell the uprising, and some hundred or so of the most audacious spirits were rounded up for a few months of prison life, which proved sufficient to smother the threatened outbreak.

"But the unrest still exists both among the communities and on the large farms where the Indian lives attached to the estate as a kind of serf. For there is no matter that so vitally concerns the aborigine of these highlands as the little parcel of soil which has come down to him, either as an individual or as a member of the clan, from uncounted generations of his fathers."

Fear of a general Indian uprising may, in part, account for the ignorant state in which the Indian is kept, fortified probably by the suspicion of the Bolivian landowner that education might provide the bootstraps by which the Indian could lift himself out of his state of peonage. This was one of the explanations offered for the failure of the Pro-Indio Crusade launched by the

Catholic Church in Bolivia during 1926.[20] Questionable as the "crusade" may have been, it at least had the merit of calling attention to the Government's neglect of the problem of Indian education. The share of the national budget devoted to education is shockingly small,[21] averaging slightly over nine percent of the total in the last ten years. The total number of primary schools in the country is 450, fewer even than in Haiti, in Santo Domingo and in Salvador.[22] The rate of illiteracy practically coincides with the percentage of Indian and mestizo in the population, the number of those who can neither read nor write being about eighty-five in every hundred.[23] By this inadequate educational appropriation and program the Indian profits little if any. As a result superstition, always the side partner of ignorance, prevails. Natural phenomena—frost, drought, illness—are always the work of evil spirits, and magic and sorcery is still a recognized and revered profession, as well as a source of individual profit, in Indian communities.[24] The medicine man or *callahuaya,* though somewhat losing his hold, can still be found exercising his trade.[25] The Roman Catholic Church here, as elsewhere, has utilized these age-old superstitions to strengthen its hold on the Indians, and whether the fires that burn on the hilltops on St. John's Day, which happens to come at the time of the winter solstice, are to celebrate the Christian saint or are supposed by the force of imitative magic to induce the sun to turn south once more,[26] is an open question. According to Paredes, the friar is considered by the Indian a necromancer who, through his occult powers, is supposed to make off with the Indian's food, "leaving the poor Indian to die for lack of it, his stomach sticking to his spine."[27] Symbolically, this may apply to the numerous fees and charges for masses demanded by the *curas* which eat into the Indian's small surplus and only intensify his poverty.[28] The natural desire of the Indians to break the monotony of their lives by occasional festivity is encouraged by the priest who exhorts the villagers to celebrate the day of their patron saint,[29] and sometimes appoints the *alferez* (a sort of master of ceremonies) whose responsibility it is to make the celebration a success by providing the drinks and costumes at a ruinous expense to himself.[30] Bowman, in speaking of this mixture of primitive and Christian worship, says: "The old rites of the Indians are grafted upon a new principle, often with but a change in name and not in symbol. The spirit of the old prayers for abundant rivers and rich harvests breathes through the new devotions, and the quaint, melancholy songs of the ancient Quichua or Aymará tribes often follow upon a fiesta in which the rites of the Christian religion are but new form for an old and pathetically simple speech. The rivers and the harvests are the forms in which they understand the Deity. It is hard to teach men new faiths or religious or moral niceties whose first and only prayer has always been for the daily bread fairly wrung from a stubborn earth."[31] The coincidence of some of the Christian and pagan festivals aided the clergy in their attempt to graft a new religion on the old, as for example Corpus Christi which, falling about the end of May, coincides with the *chuño* festival of the altiplano. Even the annual fairs, which in the early days of missionary effort presented opportunities for converting the Indians, still in many cases preserve their religious character, falling usually on the day of the patron saint of the town. Especially is this true of the famous six-day fiesta at Copacabana, where the sacredness attaching to the traditional place of origin of the Incas, the Children of the Sun, was exploited by the erection there of the shrine, Our Lady of Copacabana.[32] These fiestas, which are so prominent in the Indian's life, though ostensibly celebrating a Christian feast or national holiday,[33] are in reality Bacchanalian debauches. The dancing and drinking is continuous, day and night, for at least three days, and in some of the remoter villages lasts for a week or more. The hideous masks and elaborate costumes testify, too, to the barbarity of the occasion.

Such orgies are also a demonstration of the physical endurance of the Indian. To dance for three days and nights, full of hard liquor, at an altitude of 13,000 feet and over, is no mean accomplishment and calls for an organic adaptation to altitude which only centuries of living in such rarefied air could develop. The highland Indian's sensibilities seem different from those of people who have lived in easier climates. He can walk barefoot through snow, provided his ears are covered, and stand exposure on his long journeys over the high mountain trails which would kill less rugged natures. He can cover the seventy-five miles from La Paz to the heart of the Yungas in two and a half days with a hundred pounds on his back, a journey in which the altitude ranges from over 14,000 feet to 3,000, and a day begun next a glacier will end under an orange tree. For such exertion he requires no other food than some parched corn, the never absent coca, and such fruit as he may find along the way. In one of the mines in Potosí the Indians work on thirty-six hour shifts, remaining underground during that entire period and living while at work on nothing but dried corn and coca. This dried leaf, from which the drug cocaine is extracted, is thought to lessen his hunger and fatigue, and is said by its enemies to dull his mind, but as yet it has not robbed him of the physical traits which made the *chasquis*, the messengers of Inca days, so renowned.

It is a great pity that such endurance is not coupled with strength of spirit, confidence in his destiny and a fearlessness to struggle for relief, from the grind of incessant poverty and oppression. But the Bolivian Indian is for the most part licked. Except for the spasmodic exhibitions of spirit mentioned above, he is subservient and accepts his position of underdog with an acquiescence that is born of lethargy and fear rather than content. The very plodding, obedient and sedentary characteristics that distinguished the Indian of Inca days from our own North American Indian and rendered possible the development of the fine type of agricultural civilization that existed in the land of the Incas, made the Peruvian and Bolivian Indian an easy prey to conquest and exploitation by the Spaniards, and developed in the indigenous population of the high plateau this self-effacing humility and lack of ambition which, coupled with a sense of defeat, make fully half of Bolivia's people sluggish in mind and spirit. Bolivia needs nothing so much as a spiritual cathartic which would rouse her Indian population to a sense of personal dignity and independence. A Bolivian who has studied the Indian's superstitions and beliefs paints a black picture of his mental outlook:[34]

> "His suspicious and profoundly pessimistic spirit doubts everything, and in everything supposes a greater possibility for evil than for good. It seems as if the eyes of the Indian had no vision except for the dark side of things, and his heart no feeling except for sorrow. He understands more

> readily sinister than joyful or beneficent projects. He walks in a world full of deceptions and possessed of a terrible fear. In every step that he takes he fears to meet an enemy who will harm him, or someone who will gratuitously injure him in his own interests, and in every act he performs through his own will he looks for an unfavorable result. Doubt and fear have taken possession of his spirit in such a way that it is impossible for his being to develop fully; doubt and fear have eaten into the roots of his will. It is for this reason that he has greater confidence in the counsels of sorcery than in his own impulse. Faith in the miraculous is a sign of the weakness and intellectual backwardness of a race. One seeks out a sorcerer when one does not understand what one should do, nor rely on one's own strength. Such is the case with this unhappy race. The sadness of the poor existence of its members is reflected even in their withered faces, in their miserable living conditions, and in their readiness to respect sorcery and magic, to submit themselves to those whom they believe to be dispensers of the supernatural."

Indians have risen to prominence, and will again, but they are the exception. Ignorance and superstition, dumb brute strength and a licked spirit, characterize about fifty percent of the Bolivian people. With the human resource, the primary requisite of national development, so weak, no matter what the natural wealth of the country, a rapid advance toward stability and prosperity cannot be expected. Without this, the piling up of a huge long-term external debt with any expectation of safety to the investor is not warranted.

CHAPTER IV

TIN AND OIL IN THE NATIONAL ECONOMY OF BOLIVIA

TIN

THE major-domo of a Bolivian finca was once said to be praising the great natural wealth of his country to a European diplomat. "The whole Cordillera of the Andes is a mass of gold and tin. Here where we stand we are treading pure gold, and you will sleep tonight on a bed of gold." In relating the anecdote the diplomat commented, "The man who was walking on gold had no shoes and his bed was made of mud. In the words of an old philosopher, 'Rich country, poor people.' "[1]

A large share of the Bolivian population, as we have just seen, lives on the verge of starvation; yet, exceeded only by the United States and Mexico, Bolivia ranks third among all the countries of the Western hemisphere in mineral wealth. The barefoot cholo who was bursting with pride in his country's treasures was impressed most by that rare and romantic metal that is the symbol of fortune and prosperity the world over. Gold and silver were the magnets that drew the Spanish adventurers to Upper Peru, and it was the precious white metal that led to the growth of a city at the foot of the famous Cerro de Potosí three times the size of the Potosí of today.[2] A system of forced labor made it possible for the Spaniards to carry on a feverish campaign of prospecting and mining,[3] and the thousands of abandoned mines in Bolivia and southern Peru bear witness to the Spanish zeal in pursuing this lucrative activity, relentlessly disregarding the cost in Indian lives and suffering.[4] But it is no longer on these precious metals that the economic life of Bolivia depends, nor even on her deposits of copper, lead, bismuth, antimony, and wolfram, valuable as these are. The mainspring of Bolivian industrial activity today is tin. The second largest tin deposits in the world lie hidden in the Eastern Cordillera of the Bolivian Andes[5] and the day may not be very far distant when, the alluvial deposits of the Straits Settlements having run out,[6] Bolivia will have no rival in supplying the world with tin.

In modern life tin is an indispensable raw material. Its uses are so obvious they hardly need recounting. In tin cans, toothpaste tubes and tinfoil it makes its appearance daily in every modern household. Armies live almost entirely on canned goods, so that it becomes of the utmost necessity in time of war. In solder, in such alloys as bronze and babbitt, in the automobile industry, in the manufacture of silk, as well as in other manufacturing processes, tin is used.[7] The commonest use to which the metal is put is in the manufacture of tin plate, the thin steel sheeting coated with tin of which the ordinary "tin" can is made. The McKinley Tariff, which levied heavy duties on the import of tin plate, gave a great impetus to this industry, with the result that the United States, and in particular the United States Steel Corporation, is the greatest consumer of tin in the world.[8] Over fifty percent of the world's output comes to this country. In 1925 the United States consumed 76,445 tons out of a total production of approximately 142,000 tons.[9] Our tin imports for the first eleven months of that year were valued at more than $85,000,000,[10] out of a total import of raw materials for the year of under one and a half billion dollars.[11] Yet practically no tin is to be found in this country or in any of its possessions.[12] The United States is, therefore, dependent upon outside sources for a raw material that is highly essential to her industries and indispensable in time of war.[13]

This situation is aggravated by the British control of tin, which in effect amounts almost to a monopoly. The tin deposits of the world, as has been suggested, have been concentrated chiefly in two areas: in the Straits Settlements in the Malay Peninsula and the neighboring Dutch East India islands, and in Bolivia. Their relative importance is indicated by the production figures for these regions for 1925:[14]

Federated Malay States	46,000 tons, fine tin
Bolivia	36,602 tons, fine tin
Dutch East Indies	31,000 tons, fine tin

The Federated Malay States produce almost one-third of the world's output, Bolivia approximately one-quarter. Cornish tin, once important, has dwindled practically to insignificance. Great Britain's control of the tin market is due to her large Eastern deposits and to the British monopoly of tin-smelting. This latter has a three-fold explanation: the differential export duty on tin ore shipped from the Malay States to any but British ports; the high costs of smelting in the United States; and natural conditions in Bolivia, particularly lack of fuel, which make smelting in that country impractical. An additional factor lies in the impurities in Bolivian

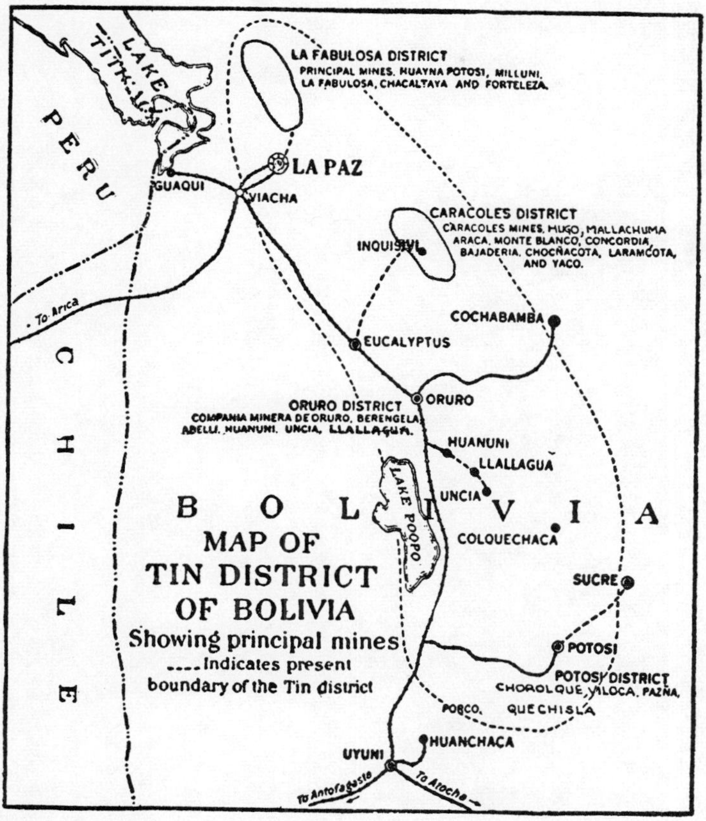

Reprinted, with permission, from *Bolivia, a Quarterly Survey of Bolivian Activities,* December, 1926, Vol. I, No. 2.

tin which make it less desirable for some purposes than Straits tin.[15]

The large tin smelters near Liverpool, most important of which are those controlled by the Williams-Harvey Corporation, are assured of a supply of concentrate[16] by means of a differential export duty, similar to that levied on manila from the Philippines. On tin ore from the Malay States not destined for British smelters Great Britain levies an *ad valorem* tax of 40 percent.[17] Such a restriction necessarily handicaps tin smelting in the United States. During the war it was attempted, however, and Bolivian tin was in great demand. During the short space of time, from 1915-1923, when the plants of the American Smelting and Refining Company and the Williams-Harvey Corporation at Perth Amboy and Brooklyn were operating, Bolivian tin exports to the United States jumped enormously, closely rivalling those to Great Britain.[18] But tin smelting in the United States was not financially successful, and in 1923 the attempt was abandoned.[19] Bolivian tin once more, therefore, must be carried by rail to a Pacific port, there shipped through the Canal to England to be smelted, and then as a metal recross the Atlantic, to be made into tin plate in the factories of the United States Steel Corporation or put to other manufacturing or industrial uses. Smelting in Bolivia is out of the question at present. Attempts have been made, once at La Paz in 1917 and again at Arica, but both failed,[20] and the small amount of ore reduced in the native smelters at Potosí is so insignificant as to be hardly worth mentioning. The principal reasons are, of course, the lack of coal and the high transportation costs which make it impossible to operate a smelter profitably at some central point where the output of the scattered mines could be sent for reduction. If any tin mines were discovered in Bolivia comparable in size to the Braden or the Chuquicamata copper mines in Chile, the incentive to discover a means of smelting in Bolivia would be stronger, but the known deposits are relatively small and very much scattered. If, moreover, the streams that flow down the east slopes of the Andes could be converted into electric power,[21] the waste of shipping ore with a metal content, on an average, of not more than 60 percent tin could be eliminated, but as yet hydro-electric power within economical reach of the tin mines does not exist to any degree. For all of these reasons, then, the Williams-Harvey Corporation, which is controlled by the Williams-Harvey Company of Liverpool, the National Lead Company of New York and Simón Patiño,[22] maintains an almost complete monopoly of the tin-smelting industry.

Mining in Bolivia encounters the difficulties attending any complex technical activity in a remote and primitive country. The longitudinal railway system that connects Lake Titicaca with Buenos Aires, with branches connecting the plateau with the Pacific Coast at Arica and Antofagasta, although close enough to the mining districts to serve as a practical outlet for the products of the principal mines, actually reaches very few of them. The rich Llallagua mines which are connected with the main railway system by Patiño's private line, the Machacamarca-Uncia Railway, the Corocoro copper mines, linked to the Arica-La Paz Railway by a short Government-owned spur, the Huanchaca silver mines near Uyuni, and the Aramayo-Francke mines at Atocha on the newly-finished connection with the Argentine, are the exceptions. In most cases either machinery and provisions for the mines and the outgoing minerals must be packed on the backs of mules and slowly and with considerable cost and difficulty transported to or from the railway, or, as the Guggenheims have done in connection with their Caracoles plant, the mining companies must build motor roads, often at very great expense, to put the mines into practical touch with the railroad. In either case transportation is an exceedingly difficult problem. Due to the inaccessible character of the mining country and the inadequate railroad facilities, there are still many valuable mineral deposits untouched, especially on the eastern slopes of the Andes, although the absence of any thorough mineral survey of Bolivia makes it impossible to say how extensive they are.

Lack of fuel is another big handicap in exploiting Bolivia's mineral resources.[23] Almost as ironical as the barrenness of the West Coast country that yields two of the chief natural fertilizers—nitrate and guano—is the absence of any combustible in a region so rich in minerals that it fairly cries aloud for fuel to develop them. To the insult of depriving Bolivia of coal, nature has added the injury of setting her treasures at such an altitude that locomotives and Diesel engines lose a good share of their efficiency,[24] so that the fuel imported at so great a cost does considerably less work than it would at a lower level. The mines placed on the eastern side of the Cordillera, like those at Caracoles and Araca, and even the big Patiño mines on the altiplano make use of water power by damming the small streams and conserving the rain and the melting snow from the mountains in artificial lakes, but in the dry season even these plants are forced to resort to the costly oil-burning Diesel engines or to reduce the scale of their operations and consequently their output. Some of the mines on the dry plateau use llama dung or *taquia* for fuel, and to supply the needs of the United Corocoro Copper Mines, which consume more than fifty tons of *taquia* daily, on an average of 3,000 llamas enter the city every day, each carrying a sack of this make-shift fuel which contains about one-eighth the heat value of good coal.[25]

Cheap labor offsets somewhat the heavy expenses involved in meeting these problems of transportation and fuel, but low wages, when the labor is inefficient, do not necessarily mean low operating costs. Nor is mine labor in Bolivia plentiful.[26] Aside from the white technicians and the cholo overseers, the mining community is almost entirely Indian, as only the native Indians can stand living and working at an altitude of 15,000 feet and more.[27] The free community Indians, from whose ranks the miners are principally drawn, are often so reluctant to leave their humble farming for the mines, especially when the plants are situated at extremely high altitudes and far from any village or town, that highly questionable methods are sometimes employed to secure laborers. At the time of the fiestas advantage is taken of the prevailing state of intoxication to bind the Indian to a mine by signing him up and advancing him some pay, which being promptly drunk up, the Indian is in the debt of the company and must work in the mine to pay it off.[28] It has been officially estimated that at the end of 1924 the number of laborers employed in mining in Bolivia was 27,340,[29] some 5,000 of whom were at the Patiño mines, Llallagua and Uncia, and another thousand at the Guggenheim's Caracoles plant. The scarcity of labor is a constant stimulus to the substitution of mechanical devices and installations. An excellent case in point is the concentrating mill at Caracoles which, though capable of handling from 350 to 400 tons a day, as few as twenty men can operate.

Wages and the length of the working day vary considerably in the different mines. The Bolivian labor laws provide for an eight-hour day. This is observed at Caracoles where the miners work on two shifts, day and night, from 7 to 4:30, with a half hour off to chew their coca and an hour later for the noon or midnight meal. In the intervening time between shifts the mine is blown out with compressed air to clear the air of the dust and fumes of dynamiting. In another American mine, a small one where prospecting for copper and lead was being carried on, a nine and a half hour day and a seven day week were found in the summer of 1926 to be the rule. At the same time, in the mill at Atocha of the Aramayo Mines (*Compagnie Aramayo de Mines en Bolivie*), a British-Swiss company, the Indian laborers, men and women, were working twelve hours a day. Schurz, writing in 1921, says that the hours for mine labor vary from nine to eleven.[30] The record for inhuman hours is that of a mine near Potosí where the Indians work on a thirty-six hour shift, with a little time off at intervals for food and coca, the pay being on the basis of eleven days pay for a seven day week. Nor can it be said that wages are dependent upon the number of hours worked. At Caracoles the common laborer gets from $0.50 to $1.00 (U. S. currency) a day, depending upon the rate of exchange of Bolivian currency; semi-skilled workers, such as mechanics' helpers, get $1.00 to $1.50; carpenters, mechanics, and other comparatively skilled workers, are paid $1.50 to $3.00. At the Laurani mines, the small American enterprise mentioned above, wages for common labor ranged from 1½ to 4 bolivianos a day, the men in the mines not getting less than two. At Llallagua, the big Patiño property, 5 bolivianos per day is fairly customary for work in the mines. In the Aramayo mill the women were receiving 2 bolivianos, the men

4.50 bolivianos for their twelve-hour day.[31] The women and children, who are quite generally employed at sorting ores, receive from less than one boliviano to two bolivianos a day. Such low wages are in keeping with and, of course, tend to perpetuate the poverty scale on which the free Indian throughout the plateau lives, and have been adjusted to a society in which it is possible to hire a *fletero* to trek seventy-five miles over a period of two and a half days, with a hundred pounds of coca on his back, for from six to eight bolivianos.

The Indian miner is often a migratory worker, as has been pointed out in the last chapter, leaving his farm in the off season to work in the mines, and returning for the planting and the harvest. This is not always the case, however, and communities grow up around the mines in regions which, for the most part, would be considered uninhabitable. Free living accommodations are usually provided for such families, and amusing incidents occur in the attempt to raise the standard of living of the Indian by the introduction of such generally accepted necessities as windows and stoves. Provisions, as in isolated mining camps throughout the world, can be purchased at the company store, or *pulpería*, frequently at cost plus the expense to the company of running the store, but sometimes at exorbitant prices. The mines are usually so high and the surrounding country so bleak, that the miner or his family can carry on very little farming, if any, unless he be one of those transitory workers with whom mining is but a seasonal occupation.

Undernourishment and bad living conditions, ignorance, and the periodic drunken debauches which are an inescapable phase of the mining game in Bolivia, make for considerable inefficiency in the Bolivian miner. The

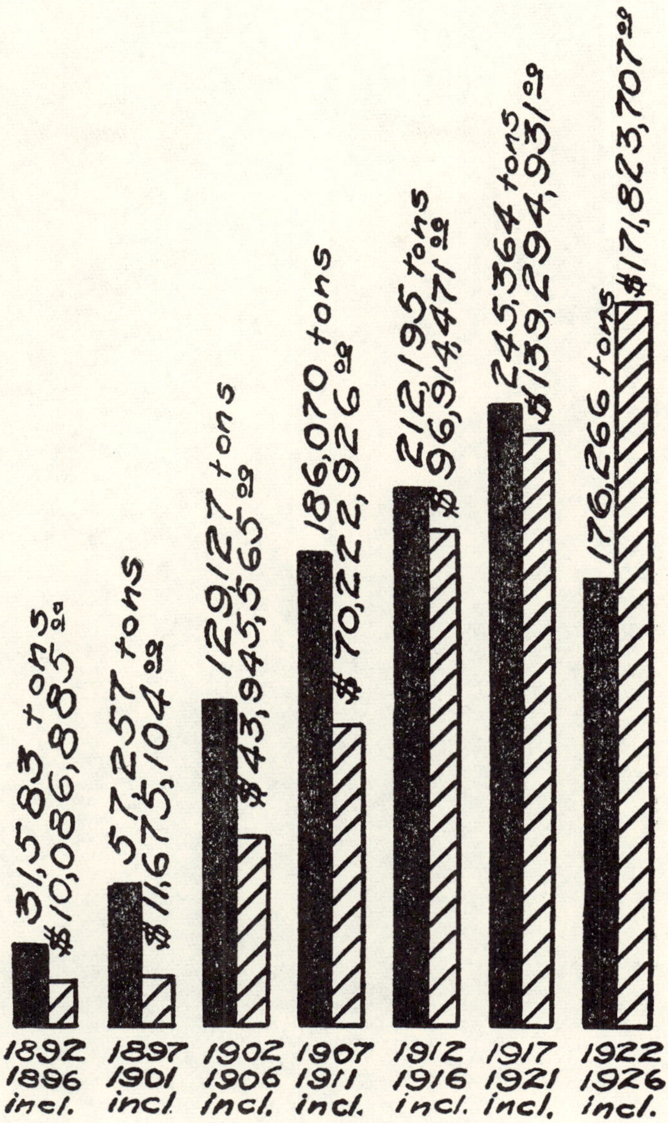

Bolivian Tin Production
1892-1926
2000 lb tons

Indians can, however, learn and master mechanical processes; at work requiring patience they are without equal; and except for the regular periods of intemperance, they are dependable. They are, moreover, the only people, probably, who could endure the hardships of mine labor and of life in a mining camp at such extreme altitudes. The only mines to experience labor difficulties on any large scale are the Patiño properties at Llallagua and Uncia, where a big strike occurred in 1919.[32] The strikers were quite summarily dealt with, and the miners' union broken up. Although the railroad workers are organized and a General Labor Federation exists in Bolivia, there is very little labor organization in the mining camps.

The high cost of fuel, heavy transportation charges, the necessity of importing practically all machinery, mining materials and provisions, the inaccessible character of the country, and other lesser causes combine to make mining in Bolivia a fairly costly process. It is difficult to give a reliable estimate of the cost since the grade and quality of the ore, a factor that enters heavily in determining the production costs, varies greatly in the different mines,[33] the cost of materials fluctuates considerably, and the export duties levied by the Bolivian Government are based on a sliding scale dependent on the price of tin in the London market. Probably a fair general average, including all costs from the time the ore is mined until it is actually sold on the market—that is, operating expenses, transportation charges, export duties and smelting charges—is thirty-five cents, United States currency, per pound. The total costs on the 6,837 tons of tin sold by the Patiño Mines and Enterprises Consolidated in 1925 amounted to $833.70 a ton, or 37 cents a pound. With tin selling in that year at an average price of £260 per ton it is not difficult to understand the company's report of earnings of $5.08 per share and of dividends of $3.15, or over fifteen per-cent.[34] At the rate at which tin prices are soaring at present, the profits for 1926 and 1927 should be even more substantial.

Thus it can be seen that the ball of profit-making, once started rolling in Bolivia, gathers plenty of moss, but capital is needed to give it the initial push and this, with one remarkable exception, Bolivia for the most part lacks. Such difficulties as mining in Bolivia presents, call, moreover, for a genius for organization and for a high degree of initiative, which the traditional social position of the Indian and the political interest pattern of the whites have not developed. The Indian as an independent miner is often pretty skilful, and in prospecting he seems to be a very divining-rod for minerals. Not infrequently the free Indians of the plateau, owning small and insignificant claims, will work by hand the tailings or dump of an old mine or open up an abandoned Spanish mine, and, treating the ore by a primitive but effective process, will often produce as high a concentrate as the most efficient and best-equipped mill can turn out. A good deal of independent gold-washing is done by the Indians of Bolivia, too. They then sell their findings to some of the big mining companies or to metal-buyers. The Spaniards were, of course, indefatigable in exploiting the minerals of the New World, and to a slight extent the mining tradition, though not the zeal, is carried on by their descendants in Bolivia. But, except for Sr. Simón I. Patiño, the Bolivian tin magnate, who, by a singular stroke of good fortune,[35] became possessed of probably the richest vein of tin ore in the world and is without question the leading figure in the Bolivian tin industry, the development of Bolivia's minerals is largely in foreign hands. At the end of 1924, of a total capital investment in the Bolivian mining industry of Bs. 323,754,620, practically two-thirds was foreign.[36] Of this, 22 percent was said to be Chilean, although as Schurz points out,[37] a large part of the capital invested in Bolivian mining companies organized in Chile is owned elsewhere. The reorganization of the Patiño enterprises in 1924 considerably increased the participation of North Americans in this largest of Bolivian mining companies, although the actual degree of American control is still probably fairly small. This, combined with the growing investment of the Guggenheims in Bolivia and with the smaller North American companies of which there are a number, gives citizens of the United States a big stake in Bolivian mining. Among the foreign companies operating in Bolivia[38] there are many British enterprises as well. Unquestionably the lion's share of the seventy million dollars[39] of foreign capital invested in Bolivian mines is concentrated largely in American, British and Chilean hands.

The five most important tin companies in Bolivia, to judge from the statistics of their output and exports during the year 1925,[40] are, in the order named, Patiño Mines and Enterprises Consolidated, Caracoles Tin Company of Bolivia, Compañía Minera y Agrícola Oploca de Bolivia, Empresa de Estaño Araca, and Compagnie Aramayo de Mines en Bolivie. The last of these, as has been indicated above, is a British company, organized in Switzerland, and need not therefore enter into this study of American investments in Bolivia. The Araca mines have recently been purchased by Mr. Patiño, and are now a part of his holdings in Bolivia, although not included in the Patiño Mines and Enterprises Consolidated. In the Oploca mines both Patiño and the National Lead Company of New York have a big interest. The Caracoles Tin Company is owned outright by the Guggenheim Brothers.

Before 1924, the principal Patiño properties were the extremely rich Llallagua and Uncia mines, situated not far from the city of Oruro and connected with the main railway system by a privately-built line fifty-seven miles in length. In 1922, at the instance of Sr. Patiño, the National Lead Company purchased stock in the Llallagua company and acquired an interest in the Oploca mines, investing $1,500,000 in Bolivian tin properties at that time.[41] Shortly thereafter the Llallagua and Uncia mines, appraised at over six million pounds sterling, and the Machacamarca-Uncia Railway, valued at something under a million pounds,[42] were combined in a new American company, Patiño Mines and Enterprises Consolidated, which was incorporated in Delaware in 1924. A capital stock of $50,000,000 was authorized, of which $30,000,000 in shares of $20 par value was issued.[43] About four percent of this was taken by the National Lead Company,[44] and Mr. Edward J. Cornish, president of the National Lead Company, was made a director of the new company. The Patiño and National Lead Company interests further overlap in the Williams-Harvey tin smelting concern, which is one-third owned by Sr. Patiño.[45] The formation of Patiño Mines and Enterprises was hailed as assuring to American interests a control over a very large share of Bolivia's tin production.[46] Since this single company produced in 1925 over forty-two percent of Bolivia's entire output and more than eleven percent of the world production for the year,[47] the significance of the increasing control of the enterprise by North Americans can be understood. The floating of 200,000 shares of its stock in the New York market in December, 1926, marked the first offering to the American public of Bolivian tin securities of any consequence. *The New York Times*[48] greeted this transaction as a step in support of the Hoover policy of combating foreign control of the prices and supplies of raw materials that are essential to American industry.

The mining properties held by Patiño Mines and Enterprises Consolidated on December 31, 1925 covered an area of 4,591 acres, with titles to 608 more acres in the course of being perfected. In addition it holds surface rights to 1,770 acres for mills, dams, etc., exclusive of its franchise and surface rights for the Machacamarca-Uncia Railway. The company has a concentrating mill with a capacity of about 650 metric tons per day, or 210,000 per year. At this rate of production the present ore reserves, estimated in 1926 at 1,061,000 tons of ore averaging 4.74 percent tin, would last about five years. In addition to tin, the ore carries a small amount of bismuth which the consulting engineers that examined the properties[49] stated might be safely counted on to yield an average net profit of $1.37 per ton milled. Recent improvements provide for a supply of hydroelectric power throughout the entire year, eliminating the Diesel engines which up to the present have had to be relied on half the time.[50]

Whether Patiño's other mining properties in Bolivia will be absorbed later by the new corporation is not known, but it has been suggested that the Araca and Oploca mines might be included in the combine, a rumor that was sufficient to send the Araca £1 shares up to £7 and £8 on the Chilean exchanges.[51] This would bring all but one of the five leading tin companies, which together produce roughly two-thirds of Bolivia's tin, under some measure of North American control.

Next in importance in Bolivian tin mining is the Caracoles Tin Company of Bolivia—a position it has reached in two short years of production. This company, organized in 1922 by the Guggenheim Brothers, was incorporated in Bolivia in that year with an authorized capital of $40,000,000, of which $16,000,000, the price of the properties, had in 1924 been paid up. The properties cover 5,800 hectares (14,326 acres) in the Quimsa Cruz district, about midway between La Paz and Oruro and some seventy miles from the railway.[52] In addition, the company has water rights and power sites on about six streams in the vicinity of the mines. Development has been costly owing to the long distance from the railroad and the extreme height of the mines, one of which is at an elevation of 18,000 feet. An aerial tramway connects the sorting station (altitude 15,300 ft.) with the concentrating mill (12,500 ft.), which every hour can carry from 13½ to 15 tons of ore from the mines to the mill, thus eliminating mule transport over twelve miles of rough mountain trail.[53] The two and a half day mule or llama caravan journey from the railway to the mill has been shortened to a few hours by means of an automobile road said to have cost the company anywhere from one to seven million dollars.[54] A highly efficient 200 ton mill, actually capable of handling twice that tonnage per day, has established a recovery record for Bolivia:[55] 86 percent on extremely low grade ore.[56] A general recovery in the other tin mining districts of Bolivia of little more than 50 percent establishes the efficiency of the Guggenheim plant. Moreover, a high grade concentrate is produced, running well over the 60 percent called for in the smelting contract with the Williams-Harvey Corporation. A new step in Bolivian tin mining is being taken by the Guggenheims, furthermore, in their development of some alluvial deposits near Potosí. The Aroifilla mines, bought from an Australian company, are the first placer tin mines to be worked in Bolivia, and the electrically driven dredges just completed are the first of their kind in the country.[57] Although the Caracoles Tin Company is already second only to Patiño Mines and Enterprises in the amount of tin it turns out, it is still in the development stage of recovering on its original investment, as its 1925 balance sheet showing no profits but losses of over a million bolivianos testifies.[58] Its stock is held entirely by the Guggenheim Brothers.

Other tin companies either owned outright by North Americans or in which American capital is interested are the Fabulosa Mines Consolidated,[59] the Bolivia Tin Corporation,[60] the International Mining Company, organized by W. R. Grace and Company during the war and at that time a large producer of wolfram, but now inactive,[61] the Andes Tin Corporation, a Boston concern owning the Concordia tin mines near Caracoles which were at one time described as "the most systematically worked tin mines in Bolivia" but which seem not to be producing at present,[62] the Berenguela Tin Mines, Ltd., a British company, which was optioned to United States' interests in 1924 at a price of £130,000,[63] and the Compañía General de Minas en Bolivia with 603 hectares in the Department of La Paz, 3,000,000 bolivianos capital, and an annual production of under 500 tons.[64]

Bolivian gold has had its fascination, even for American capitalists, and the traveler climbing up out of the La Paz valley on the Yungas Railway can look down on the abandoned gold placers of the Bolivian Goldfields Company, a North American concern which in 1915 was reported as having about 3,000 acres of gold washing claims just outside La Paz.[65] Some seventy miles north and east, along the Tipuani River, several days journey by mule from the altiplano, are the placers of the Bolivian Gold Exploration Company, owned by Americans, covering 120 hectares of land, capitalized at 3,000,000 bolivianos and producing about 350 ounces of gold a year.[66] But gold has become quite insignificant as a Bolivian product.[67] Silver, for which Bolivia was once so famous, is also overshadowed by the homelier metals, tin and lead, and except in a very few cases, wherever it is produced now in Bolivia, it is secondary to some other metal found in combination with it.[68] One of the oldest and most famous silver mines in Bolivia, the Huanchaca mine near Uyuni, has recently been purchased by North American interests. Its record production towards the end of the nineteenth century of about eight million ounces a year has probably never been equalled by any other individual mine,[69] but its output now is only some 140,000 ounces monthly.[70] The company is capitalized at Bs. 20,000,000 and has holdings of 8,314 hectares.[71] A short railway spur, owned and operated by the company, connects the mines with the Antofagasta and Bolivia Railway at Uyuni.[72]

Copper, for years Bolivia's third mineral of importance, has become so unprofitable to produce there that one of the two large copper companies, a Chilean concern, has closed its plant, and the British United Copper Mines at Corocoro was said in the spring of 1926 to be about to suspend operations.[73] The war created an artificial demand for certain minerals found in Bolivia, such as wolfram or tungsten, antimony and bismuth;

prices soared fantastically; and in wolfram and antimony, in particular, fortunes were made, largely by Bolivians,[74] although W. R. Grace and Company, through the International Mining Company, was very active in producing wolfram. In 1918 over seventy-five percent of the wolfram exports came to the United States.[75] Of bismuth, for which Bolivia is almost the only source, British interests control both the main supply and the price.[76]

This dull rehearsal of the facts regarding Bolivia's minerals and their development will serve to show the extent to which North American capital shares in the country's sole industry of importance. In the technical and administrative branches of Bolivian mining Americans are becoming increasingly prominent. In fact, the Director-General of Mines in Bolivia, Mr. C. Leonard Ball, whose business it is to stimulate the growth of the industry and a more intensive and efficient exploitation of the country's mineral resources, is an American. In the handling of the mineral output, American concerns like W. R. Grace and the American Smelting and Refining Company compete with the German and British metal-buyers.[77] And with a growing practical interest in Bolivia's natural wealth comes inevitably an increasing concern as to the course of political events in that country. This political interest and activity is very much harder to measure, however. It becomes prominent, of course, when a political crisis, like that of July, 1920, arises, or when tax reforms such as those instituted in 1923, are proposed. In the former case concessions granted by the old regime may be jeopardized, and the devil one knows is on the whole considered a safer bet. It is reputed that the American minister to Bolivia at the time of the 1920 revolution supported the Liberals, the worsted faction, so ardently that the Saavedra Government soon requested his recall. What connection, if any, his behavior might have had with the generous oil concession which the government of Gutierrez Guerra had just granted to an American company can be but a surmise. Less of a conjecture is the story of the resistance of some of the mining interests to the new tax program of the Saavedra Government. A temporary political group known as the Patiñistas appeared, opposing the Government's belated attempts to secure for the public treasury some of the profits reaped by the mining companies.[78] Failing to prevent the passage of the new tax decrees, they have employed the familiar tactics of evasion.[79] The profits tax of November 30, 1923, establishing a graduated levy on mining profits ranging from 4 percent on profits of 5 percent or less to 50 percent on profits of 150 percent or over,[80] superseded the absurd law of February 19, 1920 which, in the three years that it was in operation, yielded the national treasury only Bs. 1,786,613.[81] On the other hand, the returns from the new law, in the single year 1925, amounted to Bs 5,971,720.[82] The new export duties on tin, provided for by decree of January 16, 1924, are based upon the metal content of the concentrate and upon the tin quotations in London. In this way not only is the working of otherwise discarded dumps from the old silver mines made commercially possible,[83] but the national revenues increase in proportion as the price of tin rises. Since Bolivia derives more than one-third of her public revenue from her tin industry, the necessity for a careful revision of the taxes on the production and export of minerals can readily be seen.

Indeed, the tax reforms were badly needed. With

tin selling at £300 a ton, even under the new tax laws the tin companies stand to make profits of approximately 200 percent,[84] once their initial investment is recovered and they are on an earning basis. From this, in spite of the too loud protest of Patiño Mines and Enterprises to the contrary,[85] Bolivia benefits far too little. Almost eighty million bolivianos worth of tin was exported in 1925, on which the Bolivian Government succeeded in collecting in profits and export taxes over thirteen million bolivianos.[86] But with so big a share of the industry in foreign hands the enormous profits leave the country in the shape of dividends, most of them never to return. Her large export trade is almost entirely in minerals,[87] two-thirds of which were produced by foreign enterprise, with the result that the favorable trade balance unfailingly referred to in Bolivian bond circulars and by brokers dealing in Bolivian securities has very little meaning in terms of national prosperity. It matters little that in the thirty years from 1895-1924 Bolivia exported twice as much as she imported[88] if shareholders all over the world except in Bolivia reap the corresponding profits and spend and reinvest them elsewhere. An impractical though interesting gesture to check this flight of mining profits from the country is seen in a bill presented to the Bolivian Congress in 1926 providing for the investment in State bonds of forty percent of all dividends or profits derived from the operations of foreign-owned mining properties,[89] the proceeds to be used for railway construction. The irony of the proposal lies in the fact that by its very terms the richest mine-owner in Bolivia, a native Bolivian but in this practice of bleeding the country of its only tangible resources the greatest culprit of all, might escape.

The present demand for tin exceeds the supply by some 10,000 tons per year.[90] While this condition continues and until a substitute for tin is found,[91] the price of tin will in all probability remain high, which means relative prosperity for Bolivia. But the prosperity that comes to Bolivia from an advantageous tin market can only be termed such in comparison with the depression and threatened bankruptcy which descends upon the country when tin quotations are low.[92] An extractive industry, owned and operated largely by foreigners, yields Bolivia an income out of all proportion to the riches that are taken from her mountains every year. Like the ragged cholo who was treading on gold, Bolivia is figuratively barefoot among the nations of the world.

OIL

In the national economy of Bolivia tin so overshadows the country's other minerals, even the much coveted petroleum, and in South America the producing oilfields of Peru, Colombia and Venezuela have within recent years acquired such prominence, that Bolivia's potential oil resources sink into insignificance, with the result that, in considering the history of that trouble-breeding commodity, Bolivia and oil are as yet rarely associated. Production, of course, has not begun, and reconnaissance is an unspectacular and little noised process. The Bolivian oil country is, moreover, very remote, and development there is so costly as to give even the Croesus-rich Standard Oil pause. Yet the eastern Andes country is rich in oil. The chief Bolivian oilfields are an extension of the Argentine deposits around Salta and Jujuy, as the following sketch map shows.[93] From the Argentine frontier, along the base of the Cordillera Real, the narrow oil belt extends diagonally northward

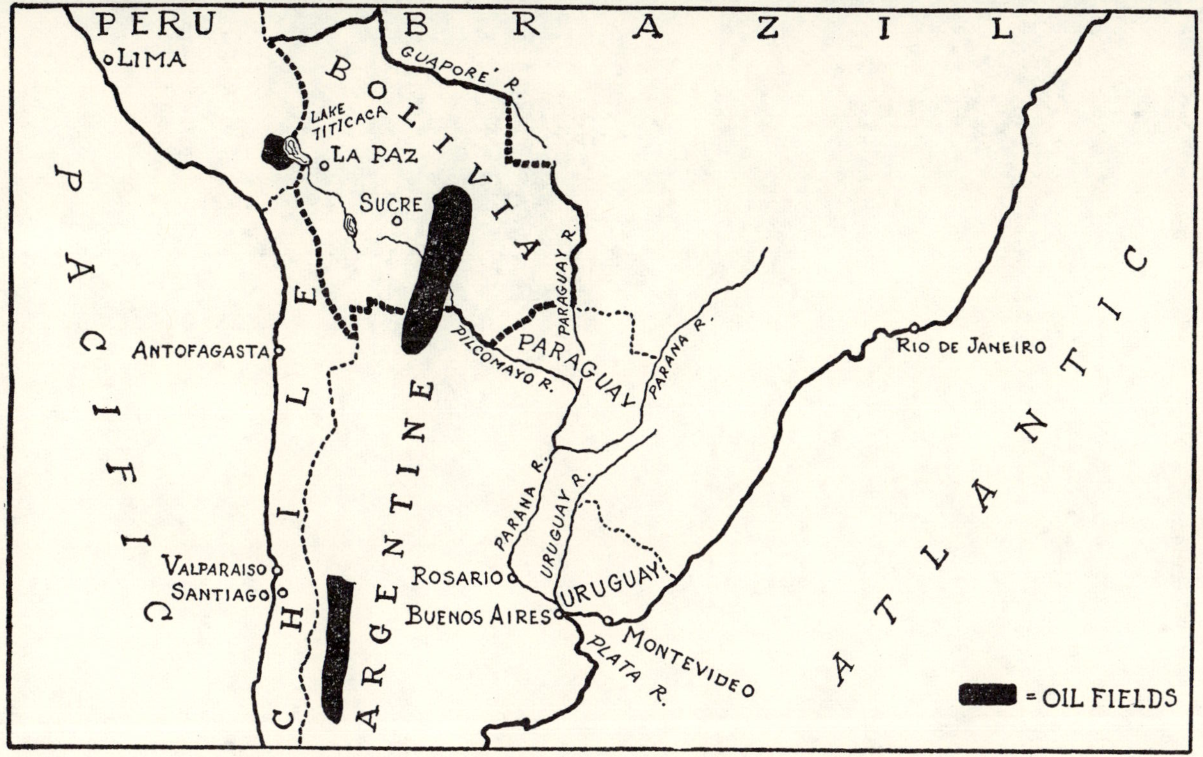

SKETCH MAP SHOWING BOLIVIA'S OIL FIELDS

(Reproduced from *Day, Handbook of the Petroleum Industry*, Vol. I, p. 147.)

for some three hundred miles. The best seepages are found in the departments of Tarija, Sucre and Santa Cruz. There are, in addition, two less important oil zones: one to the northwest in the Beni country, the other on the altiplano around Lake Titicaca. Such high grade oil has seeped through in some of these regions that the oil found in Santa Cruz can be used as kerosene, it is said, without any preliminary refining.[94] Systematic exploration of this remote region is so recent, however, that very little of a positive character is known of Bolivia's oil resources.

In providing for the exploitation of her oil, Bolivia, like many of the countries of South America,[95] has taken warning from Mexico's experience in attempting an eleventh-hour protection of her national interests, and on June 16, 1921, passed an oil law limiting to 100,000 hectares the amount of petroleum lands any one company or individual could exploit, restricting oil concessions to fifty-five years, and providing for a minimum royalty to the Government of eleven percent of the oil produced.[96] As far back as 1916, after more than three million hectares had been conceded outright, the Bolivian oil deposits were nationalized and the further granting of oil lands in perpetuity prohibited. This cautious, though belated policy of locking the stable was abandoned early in 1920 when not only was the tax on oil lands reduced,[97] but sixty-six year concessions to some two million hectares were awarded in less than ten days.[98] The 1920 oil legislation did, however, raise the State's royalty from ten to twelve and a half and even fifteen[99] percent, and provided that twenty-five percent of the net profits derived from exploiting the oil deposits on public lands should be paid into the local treasury of the department in which they were located.[100] The law of 1921, which regulates the oil industry in Bolivia today, compromised on the State's share in the output, putting the minimum royalty at eleven percent. Recognizing the industry as a public utility, the law permits concessionaires to utilize such public lands as they may need and to expropriate private lands, with compensation. It exempts them from customs duties during the life of their concessions, but levies a maximum land tax of fifty centavos per hectare after exploitation has begun, with a super tax of thirty percent on private holdings of over 100,000 hectares.[101] The concessionaires may build and operate railways and establish telephone and telegraph communications. On the other hand, they must comply with the law's specific requirements regarding development of their concessions and the percentage of Bolivian labor to be employed,[102] and must accept the Calvo clause requiring foreign concessionaires to waive the right of appeal to their home governments and to submit disputes with regard to their interests to the Supreme Court of Bolivia. Under penalty of cancellation the holders of concessions are forbidden to alienate, transfer or hypothecate their rights to foreign governments or their representatives, or to admit them as partners or associates, and for the transfer of an oil concession to any foreign company or individual special permission from the Government is required.

The 1921 law was not retroactive. Hence its restriction of the size of oil holdings did not apply to the large concessions which had been granted in 1920 and earlier, nor did it affect the titles in perpetuity that had been secured under former laws. Two types of oil concessions are found, therefore, in Bolivia: the large private holdings in fee, and the leased properties which are developed in partnership with the State (*en sociedad con el Estado*). In the Standard Oil Company's extensive holdings in Bolivia both types are represented. These comprise in all over seven million acres: one-third leased under a partnership concession, the balance owned in fee through the purchase of old Bolivian and Chilean titles.[103]

The largest single oil concession granted by the Gutierrez Guerra Government in 1920 was one of a million hectares to the Richmond Levering Company of New York, which was transferred to the Standard Oil Company of New Jersey on July 25, 1922 for about $2,500,000.[104] Modified to fit the new oil law, which in turn may have altered previous legislation in order to adapt the Government's royalty to the Standard Oil's idea of a profitable basis for exploitation, the concession runs for fifty-five years, the land and all development on it to revert to the State without indemnity at the end of that time; at least eleven percent of the oil produced is to be turned over to the State; and rights to the exploitation of the subsoil only are granted.[105] Over a period of two years the company was privileged to explore an area of four million hectares in the Departments of Santa Cruz, Chuquisaca and Tarija; at the end of that time it had to choose its million and start drilling in accordance with the petroleum law. The contract grants the usual privileges regarding use of public lands, expropriation of private lands, installation of all necessary equipment, construction and operation of railways, roads, canals, and telegraph, telephone and wireless communication, exemption from customs duties and limited taxation up to the time production should begin. Exclusive right to produce, refine and sell oil in the concession area is assured. On the other hand, not only does the concession prohibit recourse to any foreign government in the case of disputes over the company's rights, but includes two additional clauses designed to safeguard the independence of the country and to prevent foreign oil interests from encroaching on Bolivia's sovereignty. One of these forbids the concessionaires from alienating or hypothecating the concession to any foreign government; the other makes the company promise not to interfere in the internal politics of Bolivia nor "to place the capital, income, employees or laborers of the company at the electoral or political service of either party" in Bolivia. In this last might be traced signs of an uneasiness on the part of the Saavedra Government lest certain Liberal leaders who had been influential in securing the original Levering concession might look for their reward in terms of political support now, the Liberal Government of Gutierrez Guerra having been overthrown in the revolution of July, 1920.[106] In fact, with the Levering concession the Standard Oil acquired an obligation to an ex-Minister of Finance under the Liberal regime which cost the company a troublesome lawsuit, and as a feature of the settlement a possible competitor in the very heart of its own concession, a thorn in the side of the company whose policy it is to brook no rivals. The amusing spectacle of a Bolivian-American enterprise growing up some day, like an enclave, in the midst of the Standard Oil Company's territory is not without its irony.

The terms of the Levering-Standard Oil concession tried specifically to limit the holdings of the concessionaires in Bolivia to one million hectares, whether acquired through partnership concessions or by fee title, while the oil law of June, 1921, recorded another futile attempt to restrict the size of petroleum concessions in Bolivia.

The convenient subsidiary is, however, the legal answer to such restrictions, and by this means the Standard Oil Company of New Jersey has acquired rights to a vast acreage which it owns outright in perpetuity. In 1921, a group of American and Bolivian capitalists, headed by William Braden, the founder of the Braden Copper Mines in Chile, and his son, Spruille Braden, purchased, for 15,000,000 bolivianos, worth at the time between $2,000,000 and $2,500,000, more than five million acres of oil lands in the same departments in which the Levering concession is located.[107] The 2,114,-850 hectares included in the deal were Bolivian and Chilean properties to which title had been granted before 1916,[108] when the law nationalizing petroleum was passed. These properties have since been acquired by the Standard Oil Company of New Jersey. In addition, the Richmond Levering Company acquired by private purchase about 700,000 hectares in the Santa Cruz-Chuquisaca-Tarija region, east and south and between the Braden properties,[109] all of which have been absorbed since by the Standard Oil Company. The Government's gesture in refusing to allow the transfer to the Standard Oil of 85,000 hectares granted to a Bolivian in Cochabamba,[110] though indicating a natural fear of the monopoly of the Bolivian oil industry by this one powerful company, is the exception that reduces the national precautions against monopoly to an absurdity.

For the Standard Oil Company of New Jersey does possess a virtual monopoly in Bolivia. British oil interests competed keenly but unsuccessfully for the extensive oil lands purchased by the Braden interests. In 1920, when the Levering concession was granted, a similar one was awarded to Jacob Backus, the general manager of the Bolivia Railway,[111] providing the right to exploit a million hectares of oil-bearing lands in the department of La Paz and in the Beni oil region, on the basis of a fifteen percent royalty to the Bolivian Government. Backus did not have sufficient capital to develop the concession, but looked either to the Bolivian Railway Company or to the Dutch-Shell interests to take it over.[112] This did not happen, and in March, 1924, the concession lapsed,[113] as had practically all the other concessions that were granted in the wholesale allotment of oil lands, to the amount of five and a half million hectares,[114] that took place in 1920 or earlier.[115] In 1923 and 1924, exploration and exploitation concessions totaling almost a million hectares each were granted in the Beni and La Paz districts, in Cochabamba and in the Gran Chaco or Tarija region,[116] but if the development of these is being undertaken at all it is not significant. An entirely new American oil venture, in the northern field of Bolivia, the Bolivian Petroleum Company, has just offered to the public 200,000 of its shares as a speculation.[117] The Atlantic Refining Company is associated with the enterprise; it will conduct the exploration of the Bolivian Petroleum Corporation's concessions on approximately 3,125,000 acres in the Lake Titicaca district, and may, if it chooses, exploit the concession jointly with the Bolivian Petroleum Company, maintaining entire control of the management. Since the Atlantic Refining Company is one of the former Standard Oil companies,[118] which, though no longer financially combined, still maintain close cooperation in the refining and marketing of oil, this cannot be considered altogether an independent venture. Since 1916 Chileans have been interested in Bolivia's oil resources, and have secured a number of concessions and organized innumerable companies to develop them, but in actual exploitation they have done practically nothing.[119] From as early as 1906, when the first serious interest in Bolivian oil was manifested, Bolivians have at various times secured concessions and even attempted to work them, but the natural obstacles to be overcome are so enormous that the exploitation of petroleum in Bolivia calls for more capital than Bolivians are in a position to command.

The only development of any significance at present is, therefore, that of the Standard Oil in southeastern Bolivia. The Standard Oil Company of Bolivia was organized in 1921 to take over the Braden properties, and this with the Standard Oil Company of New Jersey, of which it is a subsidiary, in 1923 started exploration of the little-known oil country. This was followed soon after by drilling, under the utmost difficulties, as the oil region is traversed by bad mule and ox trails only, over which all the heavy machinery and supplies must be hauled from the railway head at Embarcación in the Argentine, whither they have been shipped by boat and train from the United States.[120] At times even the trails are not passable, and new roads or spurs of roads and trails have had to be built at great cost, one little stretch of eleven kilometers in length, for example, costing Bs. 250,000. The authorized capital of the Standard Oil Company of Bolivia is $5,000,000.[121] The money paid for its various concessions and expended in exploration and drilling represents an investment by the Standard Oil Company of several millions in the Bolivian oil industry, with at present seventeen abandoned wells and at most only five successful ones to show for it.[122] The Standard's operations in Bolivia have been well described as one of the greatest "wildcatting"[123] adventures ever undertaken in any oil field. Production is, of course, a thing of the future. It will be five years at least before it can be expected, and it may even be indefinitely postponed, the productive wells being capped and held for a future supply. When production does begin, the big problem of getting the oil out will have to be faced. The Andes create a transportation difficulty which makes an outlet to the Bolivian plateau and the Pacific impossible. Since it is impracticable to pipe Bolivia's oil over the mountains, the only alternative is to construct a pipe line hundreds of miles long and at a cost of several million dollars to the Paraguay River, where the oil could be loaded into barges and taken to the Atlantic.[124]

In view of these difficulties it is little wonder that smaller companies, poorly equipped with capital, do not enter the Bolivian oil industry—if indeed the country can be said to have one as yet—as competitors of the Standard Oil. For the same reason the proposals of Lopez[125] and others that the Bolivian Government should itself engage in petroleum development so as to prevent foreigners from getting control of the country's oil resources and exploiting them to their own benefit chiefly, are vain. Bolivia has not the capital nor the technical experience. Moreover, she sorely needs the revenue this hidden asset might supply. The oil industry in Bolivia must be a foreign enterprise, and foreigners will, in the last analysis, develop the resources of poor and backward countries only on their own terms. This is the dilemma which Mexico is facing and which, on a lesser scale, confronts Bolivia. Already the Standard Oil Company has succeeded in getting the State's royalties reduced from twelve and a half and fifteen percent to eleven, on the ground that at the higher rate it cannot make the production of oil in Bolivia commercially successful. So long as production is postponed, the oil law of 1921 and Bolivia's other mining laws applying to petroleum are not disputed, but let the oil companies once begin to feel the pinch of increased taxation that will accompany production—profits taxes, higher land taxes, Government royalties and the like—and the opposition is likely to start. Such questioning and even denial of a nation's laws, when it occurs, is, needless to say, a challenge to the nation's sovereignty and an unwarranted intervention in its internal affairs.

In one of the Aymará legends of Bolivia a friar, by a clever operation, removes the stomach of a poor Indian while the latter sleeps. On waking, the Indian can find no scar but, feeling a sharp pain, he knows what fate has befallen him in the night, and through exhaustion and fear he sickens and dies.[126] Bolivia, in fact any country whose economic life depends upon extractive industries which foreigners own and control, is much like the ill-fated Indian. Mining is indispensable to Bolivia as a source of national revenue, and to a far lesser degree, as a means of livelihood for a portion of her population. It is an advantage, moreover, to have foreign concerns introducing efficient mining methods, thereby to some extent eliminating waste in the development of the country's resources. But a purely extractive industry, primarily in foreign hands, is an uncertain basis upon which to build a nation's credit. In the first place, mineral deposits are necessarily limited, and although there is no evidence of an approaching exhaustion of Bolivia's mineral resources, the possibility does exist. Secondly, a national treasury which derives almost forty percent of its revenue from a commodity whose value fluctuates to such extremes as has the price of tin in the past, is in a precarious position. Lastly, where no manufacturing or other industries grow up alongside the mining industry, the benefits to the country are only temporary. Employment is provided for a time, some roads are built, in some instances well-equipped plants are erected and efficient mining and milling methods introduced, steps are taken to introduce new standards of living, and in the more paternalistic enterprises schools and hospitals are conducted. The nation's slow assets are, moreover, liquified and the national revenues increased. But once the deposits are worked out, the enterprises move on and leave not only the mines themselves but the communities that have grown around them, empty shells. As Bryce pointed out in writing a quarter of a century ago of the Bolivian plateau, "Great as is the mineral wealth of the Bolivian highlands, it is less on them than on the development of the agricultural and pastoral resources of the eastern part of the republic that future prosperity must in the long run depend. Mines are a transitory source of wealth; they do not help to build up an intelligent and settled body of responsible citizens."[127]

Bolivia, so far as the great mass of her people goes, is a sleeping country; while she sleeps the riches of her vast mountain ranges are being drained; nor is the development of her mineral resources helping her population to wake up. Most of the inhabitants are hardly aware that it is going on; those who take part in it do so, figuratively speaking, in their sleep. In spite of the mining activity which means so much to the Government in terms of revenue, if Manco Capac, like a Bolivian Rip Van Winkle, should return after a sleep of some five hundred years, he would find the Indians of the plateau tilling the soil in the same primitive way (with even some of the finer art of terracing and irrigating of the Inca days lost), herding their flocks, weaving and knitting the same woolen garments, satisfying, though often less completely than under the well-organized Inca Empire, their primitive essential wants, but no farther advanced in culture and education, with hardly any further conception of the world beyond the Andean plateau, and with very little more equipment for facing its complexities. The social foundation of sound credit, an alert and progressive people, is not emerging from the country's chief industry, and the natural wealth of Bolivia is doing little to set her on the road to progress. The rich minerals of this highland republic require more than the alchemy of foreign exploitation to transmute them into an agency for the advancement of Bolivian prosperity and culture.

CHAPTER V

LLAMA OR LOCOMOTIVE

"*Falta caminos! falta ferrocarriles!*" (We need roads! we need railways!) No other cry persists in Bolivian politics like this one. The need of railways is twofold; politically, to join the eastern departments, cut off by the Cordillera Real from the center of life in the republic, to the plateau and the valleys adjoining the altiplano; and economically, to make Bolivia's natural wealth accessible not only to the world at large but throughout the country itself, so that the east and west may supplement each other as nature provided but also hindered. Dr. Isaiah Bowman in 1910, in writing of the completion of the railway connecting La Paz and Oruro, said: "The junction of the capital with Oruro brings about a political solidarity, itself as important for Bolivia's economic development as the railroads are important in their industrial effects. Four large cities, centers of as many great population groups, have developed in distinctly separate parts of Bolivia, viz., La Paz, Oruro, Cochabamba, and Sucre. Revolutions have in the past gained dangerous headway in consequence and have been difficult to stamp out because of the distances to be overcome through the barren tracts that separate the various population groups. Quick transportation between Oruro and La Paz now gives these cities and the high plateau groups of people a balance of power

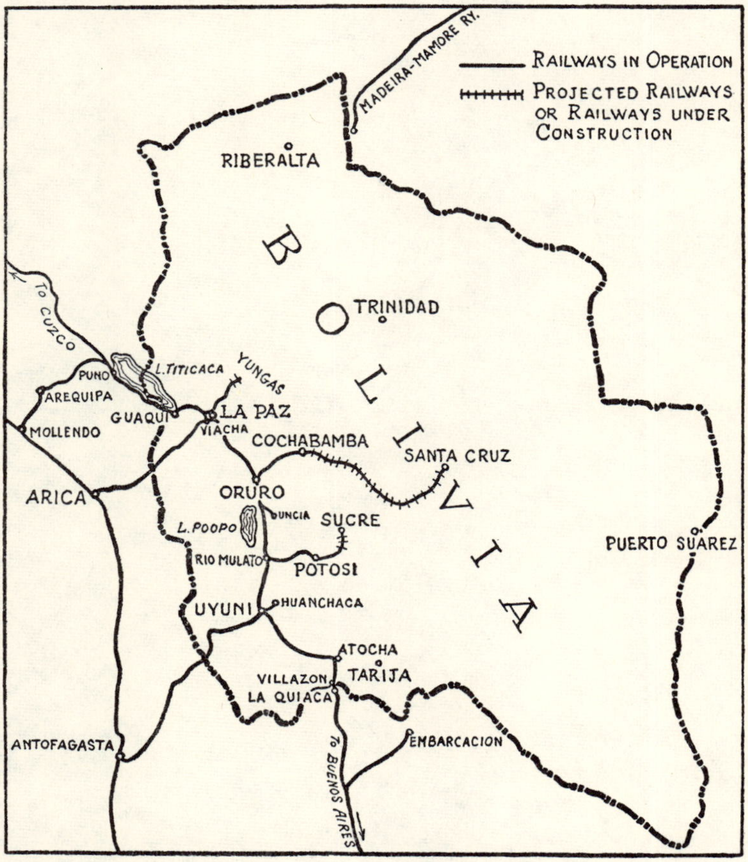

Sketch Railway Map of
Bolivia

over Sucre or Cochabamba acting individually. The extension of the railway to Cochabamba would effect still further consolidation politically; and, by offering cheaper communication, would lead to better acquaintance and greater friendliness than has heretofore been possible."[1] Cochabamba has since been linked to the plateau cities, and has become such an integral part of the political life of the country that the Cochabambino looks upon the Paceño with the intense jealousy that only well-matched rivals can feel. Sucre, though the legal capital of Bolivia, is sufficiently isolated through the absence of any rail connection with the rest of the country to make its role in Bolivian affairs quite insignificant. As for Santa Cruz, its isolation is so complete that talk of secession is rife and, moreover, furnishes a potent argument for the extension of the railway from Cochabamba for which Bolivia has just secured a new American loan.

Since Bolivia is essentially a West Coast country because of its former Pacific littoral and the comparative proximity of its mineral resources to the Pacific Ocean, it was but natural that its first railway, inaugurated in Oruro, the heart of the mining country, in 1892, should have its terminus in a Pacific port, the city of Antofagasta. This road was the beginning of the longitudinal railway system in Bolivia which, running diagonally across the altiplano in a southeasterly direction for some five hundred and forty-eight miles, links Peru with the Argentine, and forms the Bolivian section of the much discussed Pan-American Railway. The sections of this system, part built by the British Antofagasta and Bolivia Railway Company, part contracted for in 1906 with the North American banking houses, Speyer and Company and the National City

Bank, the rest constructed by the Ulen Contracting Corporation of New York and only finished in 1925, will be discussed later. Other links of this landlocked country with the ocean were provided in 1908 when the railroad from La Paz to Guaqui on Lake Titicaca was completed, connecting Bolivia with the Southern Railway of Peru terminating at the Peruvian port of Mollendo, and in 1913 with the construction of the Arica-La Paz Railway by Chile under the terms of the Bolivian-Chilean Treaty of 1904.

The mining regions of the plateau were thus put within practical reach of the sea. But the two other essential features of Bolivia's railway policy were still unsatisfied: the joining of the fertile agricultural region of the east with the plateau so that an extensive interchange of products might be set up; and the establishing of ready communication between the distant eastern departments and the capital in order that the secessionist sentiment centering in Santa Cruz might be checked. The long-repeated clamor of the Yungeño landowners for a more adequate means of transporting their coca, sugar cane and fruit than the *fletero,* the human beast of burden of Bolivia, or the slow-moving pack train, led to the initiation of the La Paz-Yungas Railway in 1915, which was to connect the capital with some port on the Beni River about two hundred miles away. The line was carried over the Eastern Cordillera and by most skilful engineering down the eastern slopes of the Andes for some fifty-six kilometers to an altitude of 10,000 feet. There, for lack of capital to continue the construction, it now stops. Terminating abruptly and quite informally in a practically uninhabited region, it is practically useless for the transportation of goods, and offers no serious competition to the Indians, mules and burros that stream daily over the steep trails into the Yungas valleys.

The second eastern route was more satisfactorily begun, though at an absurd cost, when the line from Oruro to Cochabamba was opened to traffic in 1917. This is the first link in an east-west Pan American railway which, starting at either Arica or Antofagasta, would put the railways of Brazil and Paraguay in touch with the systems of Bolivia, Chile and Peru and connect the Atlantic and Pacific Oceans latitudinally.[2] Such a line, which for long must remain an ambitious dream,[3] would run from Cochabamba to Santa Cruz and then branch, a northerly extension to connect with a navigable point on one of the Amazon tributaries, the other to continue in a more easterly direction to Puerto Suarez on the Paraguay River. A careful survey of the projected Cochabamba-Santa Cruz Railway has been made, and a loan of $14,000,000 has just been placed in New York, half of which is to be applied to commencing construction. With the cost estimated at between $30,000,000 and $50,000,000, the undertaking obviously is far from financed. Like the Potosí-Sucre Railway which, though begun in 1916 and involving a distance of only one hundred and two miles, is still unfinished, the Cochabamba-Santa Cruz line is likely to be an object of concern to Bolivian politicians and statesmen alike for many years to come. While this line is, and has been for some time, a political demand of the first order in Bolivia, the people of Santa Cruz are many of them looking to a railway south either to Yacuiba on the Argentine frontier or to Embarcación, feeling that their interests are more closely allied to those of northern

Argentina.[4] Such a road would run through the rich oil country now being explored and developed by the Standard Oil Company of New Jersey.

This then, in brief, is the railway situation in Bolivia.[5] Except on the level plateau, where the gradient is rarely over one percent and the average construction costs have been £5000 per kilometer,[6] or more than $40,000 per mile, railway building in Bolivia is extremely costly. The east-west railways, where the mountainous character of the country makes grading extremely difficult, average £11,000 a kilometer (approximately $89,000 per mile), the Oruro-Cochabamba line over £19,000 ($154,218 a mile.) The need of importing heavy construction materials over bad trails is an added reason, and one which accumulates in force with the remoteness of the country in which the construction is going on.[7] But a very powerful factor in running the costs of construction up so high is the need of borrowing foreign capital at a big discount in order to build them at all.

The following table[8] will show the amount of capital that has been required to construct the 2,100 kilometers (1,260 miles) of railways now in operation in Bolivia.[9]

Line	*Length*	*Total cost*	*Cost per kilometer*	*Maximum grade*
Antofagasta & Bolivia Ry., Bolivian section:				
Ollague-Uyuni	175 km.	£462,000	£2,750	1.10%
Uyuni-Oruro	314 "	1,221,000	3,880	1
Viacha-La Paz	30 "	400,000	13,333	2.42
Bolivia Railway Co.:				
Uyuni-Atocha	90 "	621,630	6,907	3
Rio Mulato-Potosí	174 "	1,761,702	10,120	3
Oruro-Cochabamba	205 "	3,898,080	19,000	2.6
Viacha-Oruro	202 "	1,241,093	6,143	1
Peruvian Corp., Ltd.:				
Guaqui-La Paz	96 "	400,000	4,150	1.5 (except for 6% into La Paz)

Line	*Length*	*Total cost*	*Cost per kilometer*	*Maximum grade*	
Arica-La Paz Ry.	233 km.	1,105,000	4,742	2	
La Paz-Yungas Ry.	53 "	530,000	10,000	6	
Potosí-Sucre Ry.	100 "	1,150,000	11,500	3	(74 km. not yet built)
Atocha-Villazón Ry.	128 "	2,000,000	10,100	3	(approx. cost)
Machacamarca-Uncia Ry.	96 "	991,667	10,320	2.5	
Cochabamba-Arani	60 "	150,000	2,500	1.5	
Cochabamba-Vinto	18 "	60,000	3,800	1.5	
Corocoro-Tarejra	8 "	41,600	5,200	1.9	
Uyuni-Huanchaca	38 "	228,000	6,000	3.5	(approx. cost)

The Bolivian tin magnate, Simón I. Patiño, built the Machacamarca-Uncia line, connecting his mines with the railway system, and is the principal stockholder in the local company that constructed the short lines running from Cochabamba to Arani and to Vinto.[10] The Arica-La Paz Railway, as has been stated, was the work of the Chilean Government. The Bolivian Government built the short spur that runs from the Corocoro copper mines to the Arica-La Paz line, and from the proceeds of special taxes started the Yungas Railway and the railroad from Potosí to Sucre. The funds derived from the national and departmental revenues set aside for these purposes were quite inadequate, however. In the case of the proposed Cochabamba-Santa Cruz railway, to which the Government started in 1916 to devote certain sources of income, the yield for two years provided less than enough to construct three miles.[11] This illustration, though extreme, serves, nevertheless, as an example of the absurdity of the Government's attempting to finance railway construction in Bolivia. Approximately $80,000,000 has been spent already on the building of Bolivia's railways. Needless to say, most of this capital came from abroad, either in the form of railway loans to the Bolivian Government, or as investment in private railway enterprise initiated and carried out by foreigners.

Although British interests control the Bolivian railway situation at the present time, the initiative for building the main system and some of the capital used in its construction was American. The ill-fated project for the Madeira-Mamoré Railway, which in 1872 seriously threatened Bolivia's credit reputation abroad,[12] was launched by a citizen of New Bedford, Col. George E. Church. As a highly speculative venture, the story of this undertaking has some interest. If plantation rubber had not caused the wild rubber of the Amazon basin to sink into comparative insignificance, the revival of the scheme to overcome the obstacles to river navigation and to a practicable outlet to the Atlantic which the rapids of the Madeira River present, might have had considerable importance for Bolivia. A railway from the Brazilian town of Sao Antonio on the Madeira, to Guajara-Mirim, situated on the Rio Mamoré in Bolivia, a distance of some one hundred and seventy miles, was completed in 1912, built by Brazil in accordance with the Treaty of Petropolis, signed in 1903, to compensate Bolivia in part for the loss of the Territory of the Acre. That same year the Bolivian Government granted a concession to the Madeira and Mamoré Railway Company, a British concern which had been registered in Maine in 1907 with a share capital of $11,000,000,[13] to construct a Bolivian branch, sixty-four miles long, from Guajara-Mirim to Riberalta on the Beni, but with the collapse of the wild rubber industry this company, which belonged to the Farquhar Trust, most of whose vast undertakings went to pieces around this time, went bankrupt[14] and the project for extending the Madeira-Mamoré Railway was abandoned.[15] The elimination of the dangerous rapids of the Madeira would doubtless increase enormously the effectiveness of the Beni, Mamoré and Guaporé Rivers, which drain two-thirds of Bolivia,[16] as means of communication for eastern Bolivia, but the most urgent economic necessity vanished with the sudden turn in the rubber industry,[17] and the Government for political reasons has lacked any great interest in the project.[18] The Madeira-Mamoré Railway, therefore, plays a very inconspicuous part in the life of Bolivia.

The contrary is true of the railway system of the altiplano. The sections from Viacha, a point on the plateau near La Paz, to Oruro, from Oruro to Cochabamba, from Rio Mulato to Potosí, and from Uyuni to Atocha, 416 miles in all, and known as the Bolivia Railway, were built under what is commonly called the Speyer Contract, negotiated in May, 1906, with the North American banking houses, Speyer and Company and the National City Bank. Brazil's payment to Bolivia of £2,000,000 under the Treaty of Petropolis as indemnity for the latter's lost rubber territory in the northeast proved the occasion for at least two railway bids, one from the French firm, Schneider & Company del Creusot, and this from the United States. The former proposal[19] provided for the construction of 1,200 kilometers or 720 miles of railways at an estimated cost of 110,000,000 francs, which at par would be equivalent to about $22,000,000, or slightly over $30,000 a mile. Of the capital required the Bolivian Government was to subscribe fifty million francs, Schneider and Company the balance, with the Government's guarantee of three percent on the capital used in building and equipping the system. After seventy years all the lines, with all rolling stock and equipment, were to become the exclusive property of the nation. Schneider and Company were to provide all materials used in construction, to secure in perpetuity one square league of land in colonizable territory for each kilometer constructed, and for the seventy years life of the company a preferential option on any new railway construction in Bolivia and on the development of navigation on the River Beni. The usual terms regarding free use of such public lands and forests as were needed, exemption of construction materials from taxes, and freedom from competition for twenty-five years in a fifty kilometer zone on each side of the tracks of the proposed lines, were included in the contract. In five years' time the lines were to be completed, as well as a highway from Cochabamba to Santa Cruz.

This European proposal, made in 1904, was allowed to lapse. The following year an extensive survey of the country and a scheme for a railway system a thousand miles in length, to cost on an average of $38,752 per mile and to be built entirely by American capital, was embodied in an elaborate reconnaissance report[20], which was the basis of the Speyer contract of the following year. This contract, the subject of much criticism within the last year or two as the first mortgage bonds issued under it have approached maturity, leaves Bolivia at the present moment with a railway system of unquestionable importance in getting her minerals to the coast. The cost to Bolivia, however, has been some $22,000,000, including her obligatory investment in the second mortgage bonds of the company and her guaranteed interest on the first mortgage bonds;[21] nor has Bolivia any chance, short of expropriation, of ever owning the roads, as the concession was granted in perpetuity. The country is, moreover, confronted with a weakened credit reputation abroad because of the threatening bankruptcy of the Bolivia Railway Company.[22]

Further bids on the building of the proposed lines had been rendered impossible by the Government's pledge not to begin other railway negotiations until a decision had been reached with the Speyer syndicate that organized the reconnaissance studies.[23] The proposals advanced by Speyer and Company and the National City Bank were finally accepted in May, 1906. These have been described as utterly fantastic,[24] and a comparison of the mileage completed with the ambitious system that was projected would seem to bear out the criticism. Of the thousand miles of railroad planned only four hundred and sixteen, or less than half, were actually built, and the picture drawn by the Director General of Public Works, in approving the plan, of connecting the railways of the Argentine with the large rivers of Brazil, is yet far from realized.[25]

The terms of the Speyer contract[26] provided for the transfer of the concession to a company which it should organize, with power to issue £3,750,000 in first mortgage bonds, to be sold at 80,[27] and £2,500,000 in second mortgage income bonds, to be taken by the Bolivian Government at par, the former to mature in twenty years (January 1, 1927), the latter in twenty-five (1932). In addition, this new company was empowered to issue as much stock as it liked. Thus the bankers transferred all their rights and obligations to a corporation of limited liability, and, after seeing that the bonds were distributed and after promoting the enterprise to the extent of bringing the Bolivia Railway Company into existence, withdrew from all responsibility. W. R. Grace and Company of New York, the well-known Latin American exporting and importing house, as purchasing agents of the Speyer syndicate, saw to it that in the early stages at least, American materials were used in the construction of the roads.[28]

In accordance with the contract the Bolivia Railway Company was organized in Connecticut in 1907 with an authorized capital of $10,000,000,[29] of which the National City Bank and Speyer and Company received shares to the amount of $9,996,500 in payment for the concession.[30] Actually only $3,500 of the share capital was paid up, the balance of the money for the enterprise being derived from the purchasers of the first mortgage bonds, chiefly Europeans, and from the Bolivian Government which, by the contract, was obliged to take the company's second mortgage bonds. The Bolivia Railway Company was to have the right to construct, own and operate the new system of railways, to import construction materials and railway equipment free of customs duties for thirty years, to be exempt from all taxes or imposts of any sort during the same period, and to acquire up to 1,000 square leagues (1 league equals 1,785 hectares) of public lands in any part of Bolivia at the minimum legal price of ten centavos per hectare if suited to agriculture and cattle-breeding, or one boliviano if the land contained rubber trees.[31] The building of the roads was begun by the South American Construction Company[32] on a basis of cost plus 10 percent, but so wastefully, it is alleged,[33] that it was turned over to the Antofagasta and Bolivia Railway Company, a British concern, which completed the mileage now comprising the Bolivia Railway and in 1908 leased the system for 99 years. The total cost of the Bolivia Railway Company's lines was £6,673,232, or at par, $32,475,284. The difference between this total and the issue of first mortgage guaranteed bonds and second mortgage bonds, a little over five and a half million dollars, was met by an additional issue of 6 percent first mortgage bonds without Government guaranty.[34] At present the Antofagasta and Bolivia Railway owns a majority of the first mortgage bonds and the greater part of the stock of the Bolivia Railway Company, although about $1,000,000 worth of the bonds are in the hands of American citizens.[35]

So far as Bolivia was concerned, the leasing of the new system to the "Antofagasta" changed the character of the enterprise altogether. The frank expectation that the Bolivia Railway Company would compete with the British company, by connecting with the Peruvian railway to the north and with the Argentine system at La Quiaca, was doomed by this merger.[36] From this time dates the monopoly which the Antofagasta and Bolivia Railway Company exercises over Bolivia's railways, a control so complete that it reduces materially the effectiveness of Arica as an outlet for Bolivia. By means of excessive freight rates on goods exported by way of Arica,[37] which must travel from Oruro to Viacha over a line operated by the Antofagasta and Bolivia Railway, the big mineral output of the Oruro district is deflected to the longer route via Antofagasta.[38] Through this manipulation of the traffic handled by the Bolivia Railway Company the earnings of the company have been so reduced,[39] that the Bolivian Government for the entire twenty years since the bonds were issued has had to cover the biggest part of the five percent interest which it guaranteed on the first mortgage bonds,[40] while, needless to say, Bolivia has received nothing on the second mortgage income bonds she holds. The former fell due January 1, 1927, and since the interest only and not the principal was guaranteed, the company has had to admit its inability to pay them.[41] If the threatened foreclosure should be carried out, Bolivia stands to lose not only the full amount she invested in second mortgage bonds, $12,150,000, which she has hoped to recover in 1932, but also the guaranteed interest payments for which, according to the Speyer contract, she was to be reimbursed in thirty years. Furthermore, with new railroad irons constantly in the fire, Bolivia can hardly afford to stand discredited in the New York and London money markets, as a possible field for railway investment, by the noise of such a failure. A reissue of bonds at the face value of the old ones, expropriation of the lines, with compensation, as a public utility and government ownership in the future, and a revaluation of the railroads with a new bond issue based on the new valuation are among the various forms of liquidation which have been suggested.[42] In June, 1927, the Bolivian Government issued a decree expropriating the lines, but whether this is more than a gesture remains to be seen. The Minister of Public Works has declared since, that the Government does not intend to act "coercively".[43] To date no steps have been taken to execute the decree, and the railroad is operating under the same management as heretofore. As this goes to press, a commission representing the bondholders, lessee and stockholders, is in La Paz to negotiate with the Bolivian Government for the reorganization of the financial affairs of the Bolivia Railway Company. How much the holders of the first mortgage bonds, which have been selling recently at 50 or thereabouts, can collect on them is a question. The Antofagasta and Bolivia Railway Company is, of course, the majority bondholder, and can rely on the large profits it derives from its railway monopoly in Bolivia to offset this loss. It seems fairly certain that Bolivia will need to write off the capital sunk in second mortgage bonds as loss, except for the fact of the railways themselves, which are an unquestionable asset to the nation. She will, moreover, be relieved of the large monthly interest payments which have been a constant drain on the public treasury. Such is the inglorious end of the Speyer contract, a transaction which cost the National City Bank and Speyer and Company practically nothing, netted them several millions of dollars on the sale of their share of the Bolivia Railway Company's stock, and won for this latter British company the key to the control of Bolivia's entire railway system.

The next time North American capital figures in the history of Bolivian railroad finance is in 1917 when the Bolivian Government secured a loan of $2,400,000 at six percent from Chandler and Company, which enabled it to continue the construction of the La Paz-Yungas Railway. In the placing of this loan, issued at 90,[44] the Equitable Trust Company was associated with Chandler, which in the same year was made financial agent of Bolivia in the United States for three years with an option on Bolivia's borrowings in the New York market during that period.[45] An attempt to secure an additional loan in the United States was checked by the revolution in 1920, which overturned the Liberal party and set the Republicans under Saavedra in power. Construction has been carried on by Bolivians, and quite economically, in view of the precipitous character of the country through which it passes and in comparison with the very high cost of the Bolivia Railway Company lines.[46] The capital to continue is not available, however, with the result that the owners of the fertile valleys of North and South Yungas, restive at the delay which continues their isolation, are discussing the merits of automobile roads as cheaper and more easily built.[47] In fact, this solution of the problem of communications for the remote east country, frequently and forcibly presented,[48] has at last been adopted. The Yungas Railway as originally planned was not only to supply an outlet for the Yungas valleys but to open up the Beni country, by carrying the line some two hundred and eighteen miles from La Paz to the head of steam navigation on the Beni River, but with less than thirty-four miles completed and with the work at a practical standstill,[49] the realization of this project is likely to be long postponed. Meanwhile the one train per week run over the Yungas line and its present abrupt terminus bear mournful testimony to the frequently losing struggle of the railway to replace the Indian and the pack animal.

The most recent and the most notorious part played by North Americans in Bolivian railway building is that of the Ulen Contracting Corporation of New York in connection with the Atocha-Villazón Railway. The southernmost stretch of the Bolivia Railway Company's lines, running from Uyuni, where the Antofagasta trains turn west to the Pacific, to the little Indian village of Atocha, left a gap of one hundred and twenty-eight miles in the longitudinal system that was to connect Buenos Aires by rail with La Paz, southern Peru and the Pacific. This line follows the old mule track from the Argentine into Bolivia, one of the most famous of the early South American roads, and much used in the colonial days when the trading monopoly granted to Panama caused much of the goods destined for Argentina to travel this long overland route.[50] As early as 1912 a loan was negotiated in France for £1,000,000, at five percent, to finance a portion of this missing link, and with the proceeds[51] construction was begun by a French company. First, disagreement with the contractors, and then, in 1920, the Saavedra revolution caused suspension of the work. In the spring of 1921 a new contract was signed for the construction, for the account of the Bolivian Government, of a line to bridge the gap. The new contractors were the Ulen Contracting Corporation, a subsidiary of Stone and Webster, in turn affiliated with the American International Corporation and the National City Bank.[52] The road was to be finished in approximately five years. The estimated cost was $10,000,000.[53] American track equipment and motive power was to be installed.[54] Construction was to be financed by a $7,000,000 bond issue,[55] with the understanding that the Bolivian Government would furnish later any additional sums up to $10,000,000 that might be needed. These 20 year 8 percent Government bonds, redeemable at any time at par, were to be taken by the contractors at 87½,[56] and disposed of by them at whatever price they could get for them. In addition, the contract provided for a flat fee of $1,000,000 to the construction company when the road was completed.[57] The negotiation of the refunding loan of 1922 led to the conversion of these bonds into bonds of the new issue. Before the road was completed, bonds to the amount of $10,000,000 were issued; for $8,000,000 worth of them the Bolivian Government received 87½, according to its original contract with the Ulen Company, which had been modified on June 9, 1922, to make the conversion possible;[58] for the balance 91½. In the New York market they brought a price of 101. On this transaction the Ulen Contracting Corporation reaped $1,270,000, though doubtless bearing its share of the bankers' fairly heavy expenses in advertising the bonds, to which must be added its ten percent fee of $1,000,000—a total of over two and a quarter million dollars for building one hundred and twenty-eight miles of railroad. Nor was the job really finished when the line was turned over to traffic in time for Bolivia's centenary in the summer of 1925. A fine piece of grading was done and under difficult conditions, for the road drops from the Andean plateau at Atocha to the level of the Argentine pampa, never so abrupt a descent as farther north in the Yungas country, but steep enough to put engineering skill and ingenuity to a fair test. But, apart from this, there is much cause for criticism of the job. Carelessness in laying the track and in protecting the road against the heavy seasonal rains of that region, and inadequate and inferior equipment and rolling stock make it necessary for Bolivia to spend a part of its latest loan, another million dollars at least,[59] in putting the Atocha-Villazón Railway into efficient running condition. Yet this railway has already cost the country $10,000,000 or $78,125 per mile.[60] Some justification for the poor workmanship may lie in the rush to finish the road in time for the centennial celebration, which meant completion almost a year before the date originally contracted for, but the Bolivian Government, which provided the Ulen Company financial compensation for this change in the contract,[61] should not have been doubly penalized for hastening the work.

Competition for control of the Atocha-Villazón Railway has been strong between the Antofagasta and Bolivia Railway and certain Argentine railway interests. Aware of the value of a free outlet to the Argentine as a means of checking the "Antofagasta's" monopoly, many Bolivians have been anxious to keep the new line out of the hands of the powerful British company. This sentiment has evidently prevailed, for the lease has at last been awarded to the Argentine firm of Dates and Hunt. But with the Antofagasta and Bolivia Railway in control of the connecting strip of road from Uyuni to Atocha there seems to be no reason why it cannot paralyze the Atocha-Villazón Railway in the same way that it has the Arica route, with this important exception, that lead, which is growing in importance as a Bolivian export, is mined principally in that part of Bolivia that lies south of Atocha and near the Argentine border. For Argentine manufactured goods and for other Argentine products destined for La Paz or any other parts of Bolivia north of Atocha, the "Antofagasta" is still in a position to make trouble. Furthermore, the long haul overland and the frequent handlings caused by the different gauges encountered on the journey from Buenos Aires will make the Argentine route an expensive one. The line is so new, however, that its future is purely conjecture.

The two remaining railway projects of any importance in Bolivia, the Potosí-Sucre Railway and the Cochabamba-Santa Cruz Railway, have very recently been brought under one financing plan through Bolivia's latest external loan, the $14,000,000 issue taken by Dillon, Read and Company of New York in January, 1927. Foreign capital has been sought at various times for the former, which was started in 1916 with the proceeds of special taxes and internal loans.[62] Though the entire distance is only one hundred and two miles, the funds have not been available to carry the road beyond the one hundred and seventh kilometer, or sixty-four miles.[63] From the refunding loan of 1922 something less than a million dollars ($916,731) was secured for this purpose; in addition, the loan contract provided for an additional issue of $4,000,000, the estimated amount required to complete the line, when certain requirements regarding the national revenues could be met. But, although the Equitable Trust Company and the other American bankers associated with it in that loan have repeated their willingness to advance this amount, the Bolivian Government has refrained from taking it, possibly through a natural hesitation at issuing any more bonds under this much-criticized contract, and probably with the intention, just realized, of combining this railway with the Cochabamba-Santa Cruz line as one banking project. The immediate needs in 1925 were met by a loan of £600,000 secured by Sr. Patiño in London at par and 8 percent,[64] a negotiation which the North American bankers considered a violation of the contract with them, involving as it did some of the revenue from tin exports pledged as security for the refunding loan. The following year the Antofagasta and Bolivia Railway, which is constructing the Potosí-Sucre Railway, offered Bolivia £1,200,000 at 92 and 7½ percent interest[65] to finish it, but on condition that Bolivia lease it the Atocha-Villazón Railway.[66] This proviso proved a stumbling block to the transaction. From the proceeds of the last American loan $5,000,000 is to be devoted to the completion of this line to the nation's legal capital. It is of so little importance commercially or industrially, however, that the reasons that prompt the outlay of capital needed to complete it would seem to be more sentimental and political than practical. Whether there will be sufficient traffic for many years to warrant the investment seems doubtful.[67]

American contractors have been favored by the North American bankers, notably the Ulen Contracting Corporation and the Foundation Company. The syndicate that made the refunding loan of 1922 even went so far as to try to stipulate construction by the Ulen Company as one of the terms of the loan.[68] This failing, they are reported to have favored the Foundation Company,[69] an American concern which is practically remaking Peru but has had little share in Bolivia's development beyond the organization of a cement company with certain privileges that are likely to secure for it a cement monopoly in Bolivia.[70] Nothing ever came of either of these attempts to exert pressure in behalf of American construction companies. The award for the Potosí-Sucre Railway has since been made to the Bolivia Railway Company, controlled by the Antofagasta and Bolivia Railway, the latest contract calling for completion by the middle of 1929.

Bids for the Cochabamba-Santa Cruz Railway were called for simultaneously in New York, London, Paris, Berlin, and Buenos Aires. The time for presenting bids expired October 20, 1927. Messrs. Dates and Hunt, the same Argentine contractors to whom the Atocha-Villazón Railway has been leased, have submitted proposals but whether they stand a chance, in view of the source of the loan secured for this road, is a question. It remains to be seen whether Dillon, Read and Company advance any favorites among North American contractors and with what success.[71] Leonard Kennedy and Company, Inc., and the Foundation Company are the only American construction firms whose names have been associated with this project so far, both having submitted bids for the construction of the first section of the railway.[72] Access to further credits will probably be an important factor in determining to whom the contract shall be awarded. The money available for beginning the line to Santa Cruz, less than $7,000,000, is not sufficient for a quarter of the work, even taking the lowest estimate into consideration.[73] The political and economic arguments advanced for this road have much validity, but the same question arises here as in the case of the Yungas: whether an automobile road had not better precede the railway.[74] The initial cost would be infinitely less, communication between the tropical east country and the plateau would be much sooner established, and an automobile road would be quite adequate, probably, for the traffic of the near future. The two trains weekly that go over the expensive road from Oruro to Cochabamba, and the freight statistics for that line do not hold out great hope for the projected railway to Santa Cruz. Yet the Government, for political reasons, does not dare to disregard the unanimous opposition of the people of Cochabamba and of Santa Cruz to the substitution of motor roads for their cherished railway.

Numerous other railway projects for Bolivia have been discussed, most of them with Santa Cruz either as their center or their objective, but none of them have enough substance at present to call for consideration here. The railways described above are the only ones of significance in Bolivia. For these, Bolivia has assumed three-fifths of her foreign debt and expended, in addition, some $22,000,000 of her far too slender capital. The question naturally arises whether the burden is worth it in terms of national growth, of which the proper index is not a country's trade balance but the rate of cultural and social progress of its people. A practical measure of the efficacy of the railways themselves is the freight they carry, for it is in freight, not passengers, that a railway's importance and hope of profitable operation rest. It is interesting to check Bolivia's railways against these two tests.

In the life of the Bolivian Indian and cholo the railway has made very little appreciable difference. Both seem to love to travel, and the third-class carriages, for which fares are very low, are usually full to overflowing. A more picturesque sight can hardly be imagined than a Bolivian railway station, where the Indian women squat on the ground selling their native stew and highly spiced *empanadas* (meat pies) and where men and women in costumes of riotous color throng to and fro. But apart from this greater ease in getting from one village to another, the railway has not altered their manner of living nor thinking. It has not brought the Indian sophistication any more than it has subjected him to the drab clothes of "civilization." The same primitive conditions exist that were to be found thirty-five years ago when the first railway in Bolivia was inaugurated; the same illiteracy and poverty prevail. Nor has the railway become for the Indian in any sense a necessity. The railroads are used, of course, by the mining interests to transport machinery and to ship their output, and have without question brought about a good deal of exploitation that was hitherto not practicable. But the mining industry, as has been pointed out in the last chapter, lies, on the whole, outside the general current of Bolivian life, and is largely a foreign enterprise, enriching foreign or at least non-resident stockholders—in the heart of Bolivia and yet not in any sense essentially Bolivian. It cannot, moreover, provide sufficient freight to keep the railways busy to capacity. In the movement of their native products the Indians, and the mestizos too, to a large extent, continue to rely on their animals. The llama, which subsists on the sparse vegetation of the plateau without cost to its owner—on the contrary, a source of wealth not only as a beast of burden but as a provider of wool, fuel and food—is to the Indian a much more satisfactory carrier than a railway train with its enormous freight rates and its unnecessary speed. Driving his llama caravan provides an occupation and a break in the monotony of life, too. It is little wonder, as a Bolivian writer has pointed out, that the llama is looked upon as a sacred animal, and included in the Indian ceremonies as the symbol of wealth and prosperity.[75] Burros and mules must be fed, but even at that they are cheap compared to freight charges. Besides, they can go anywhere, whereas a railway is confined to its tracks. As for the bigger and more sophisticated importers and traders, there is nothing in their *mores* to make them shun the railway for the pack animal, but the Indian is so self-sufficient and his tastes so simple that his consumption of goods that might be carried by rail is practically nil. Internal commerce is hence comparatively slight and freight shipments correspondingly infrequent and slender. The mestizo consumes much more than the Indian but less than the whites, who are, it must always be remembered, only fifteen percent of the population. "The consumption of these three social categories of the population", says Gonzalez, "might be summarized thus: if a white man consumes annually on an average 700 bolivianos' worth, the mestizo would consume 300 and the Indian 120; and as these last two include 85 percent of the total population, we have a country with a population satisfying its needs with one-third what a homogeneous white race would need."[76] It is primarily this condition that makes the outlook doubtful for anything like an adequate return on the large capital investment that railway construction in Bolivia demands.

Railroad policy in such an undeveloped and undercapitalized country should, therefore, be a matter of very careful deliberation. It is an economic fallacy to assert that railways necessarily bring prosperity. To make railway investment a reasonably safe proposition—to remove it from the realm of mere speculation—it must be possible to foresee a high degree of development of the country through which the roads are to run. Especially must this be true where construction and operating costs are high, as they are in Bolivia. It is on freight that railways profit, and unless a road can count on handling considerable freight it is doomed to failure. These are considerations which, when applied to Bolivia, make the prospect gloomy. The need of arterial railways to export her minerals and to make her widely separated and diversified regions serve each other is unquestionable. The real issue is to what extent the country can afford to burden itself borrowing money abroad in order to build railways on its own account or to guarantee private railway investment.

CHAPTER VI

BOLIVIA'S BLANK CHECK TO THE BANKERS

BOLIVIAN 8'S OF 1947 AND THE BOLIVIAN PUBLIC DEBT.

IN 1908 Bolivia had the distinction of being a country without a foreign debt;[1] by February, 1927, her external obligations had mounted to well over forty million dollars,[2] all of which, except for a small loan of £600,000 obtained in London in 1925,[3] was borrowed in the United States. The inverse ratio which seems to exist between the extent of a nation's material development and the amount of its per capita indebtedness[4] would assign Bolivia a place in the rearguard of the nations of South America and indeed of the world. Compared with the public debts of the "A B C" powers and of the small but progressive state of Uruguay, Bolivia's $14 per capita debt, in size less than one-twenty-fourth of her per capita wealth, seems very small, and puts Bolivia alongside of Peru and Colombia as practically virgin fields for investment.[5] The attractiveness of public investment there as elsewhere, however, depends both upon security and yield. The foregoing chapters have dealt with aspects of the Bolivian situation affecting the former: the nature of the population and the conditions influencing immigration and colonization; the character of the national resources and the chances of their development; the nation's industrial life and its transportation system. But security depends, too, upon the conditions under and upon which loans are negotiated and the purposes to which they are to be applied; and both security and yield are inseparable from the terms of the loan contracts themselves. It is essential, therefore, to know the uses to which the forty odd million dollars borrowed in the New York market have been put, the prices paid for the money, and the terms on which it was loaned.

Apart from short term loans and revolving credits which have been repaid,[6] Bolivia has successfully turned to New York four times within the last ten years for capital. Little is known about the latest loan, that of $14,000,000 made early in 1927 by Dillon, Read and Company of New York, beyond the fact that the price paid for the bonds was 90½, and that they were sold to the public at 98½. These are 31 year bonds, and carry 7 percent interest.[7]

The first bit of North American long-term financing of Bolivia, except for the Morgan loan of 1908 which will be considered later, was the Yungas Railway loan of $2,400,000 at 6 percent[8] made in 1917 by Chandler and Company, at that time fiscal agents of Bolivia in the United States,[9] and the Equitable Trust Company of New York. Taken by the bankers at 90,[10] the bonds were sold to the public at 96.[11] They were specifically secured by a first mortgage on the electric railway to be built with the proceeds of the loan from La Paz to Coripata in the Yungas, a first lien on the Government-owned branch of the Arica-La Paz Railway to the copper mining town of Corocoro, and a first charge on the general revenues of the Department of La Paz as well as on certain revenues of the department specially pledged to the service of the bonds. The loan contract

PERMANENT FISCAL COMMISSION

Statement of the Public Debt of Bolivia, June 30, 1926

EXTERNAL DEBT

Date of Law Authorizing the Loan		*Interest*	*Amortization*	*Price*	*Bankers*	*Amount Issued*	*Amortized*	*Balance in Circulation*	*Balance in Bs. 3 to $1*
Nov. 17, 1914	Yungas Ry. Loan	6%	2%	90%	Chandler & Co.....	$2,400,000.00	$611,500.00	$1,788,500.00	5,365,500.00
Feb. 25, 1920	Sanitation Loan (La Paz & Cochabamba)	6%	4%	90%	Ulen Contracting Corporation	2,253,000.00	852,000.00	1,401,000.00	4,203,000.00
May 24, 1922	American Loan of 1922	8%	2%	....	Stifel, Nicolaus & Co., Spencer Trask & Co., Equitable Trust Co.	29,000,000.00	2,706,000.00	26,294,000.00	78,882,000.00
Dec. 1, 1924	Loan for the Potosí - Sucre Ry. (£600,000 at $4.86)	8%	5 yrs.	100%	Anglo-South American Bank & Glyn Mills & Co.	2,916,000.00	758,548.80	2,157,451.20	6,472,353.60
						$36,569,000.00	$4,928,048.80	$31,640,951.20	94,922,853.60 Bs.

INTERNAL DEBT

		Interest	Amortization	Total Issue	Amortized	In Circulation	To Be Issued	Total Indebtedness
Jan. 17, 1907	Internal Bonds	3%	1%	Bs. 5,060,050	3,589,350	1,470,700	1,049,476.48	2,520,176.48
Jan. 15, 1909	Acre & Pacific Bonds	8%	2%	2,435,800	664,600	1,771,200	2,606	1,773,806
May 2, 1911	(Supreme Decree) Acre Indemnity Bonds	3%	3%	352,300	122,700	229,600	86,968.50	316,568.50
Jan. 22, 1914	Bonds of the State, 1914	8%	1%	10,000,000	1,893,000	8,107,000	....	8,107,000
Jan. 12, 1924	Bonds of the State, 1924 (Bs. 10,000,000 Authorized)	8%	1%	8,251,500	212,400	8,039,100	....	8,039,100
Dec. 12, 1923	Special Bonds of the State, 1924, for Antofagasta & Bolivia Railway Co.	3%	2%	500,000	20,500	479,500	....	479,500
				Bs. 26,599,650	6,502,550	20,097,100	1,139,050.98	21,236,150.98

FLOATING DEBT

Banks—Ordinary Account	Bs. 8,373,311.17
Banks—Different Accounts	3,118,694.77
Sight Obligations	3,017,743.25
Mortgage Banks	323,630.53
	Bs. 14,833,379.72

SUMMARY

External Debt	Bs. 94,922,853.60
Internal Debt	21,236,150.98
Floating Debt (to the Banks)	14,833,379.72
	Bs. 130,992,384.30

La Paz, July 6, 1926

provided for the purchase in the United States of materials used in building the railway and of rolling stock and equipment.[12] As in all railway investment, it was hoped that the initial drag of interest and amortization charges would be counteracted later by sufficient earnings to make the road self-supporting, but the forced suspension of building, leaving the portion of the road that is constructed practically useless, as has been described in the chapter on railways, has left this loan a dead weight on the Bolivian Government. The bonds, when handled at all in the New York market, now sell for around 82.[13] A balance of $1,788,500 was outstanding on June 30, 1926.[14]

Bolivia's second piece of financing in the United States was in 1920, just prior to the political revolution of that year, when the Government issued $2,253,000 in 6 percent bonds, the so-called Sanitation Bonds of 1920, to mature in 1934, which the Ulen Contracting Corporation took in payment for the construction of the sewer systems of La Paz and Cochabamba. The contract called for the use of American materials in construction.[15] These bonds were secured by a first lien on fifteen different customs duties and internal revenues, largely departmental.[16] The rate paid the Bolivian Government was 90 percent.[17] The prices at which the bonds were offered to the public, ranging from 82.24 to 97.74, provided a yield of from 8.25 to 8.50 percent.[18] There is now no active market for them. As sanitation is a form of public works that provides no revenue, the full weight of serving and retiring these bonds falls on the Bolivian Government. The amount outstanding on June 30, 1926 was $1,401,000, the 4 percent amortization rate having accounted for the balance.[19] Both the Yungas Railway and the Sanitation loans were served by local revenues and constituted only contingent liabilities on the national treasury.[20]

In the history of Bolivian public finance these were, however, comparatively insignificant operations. The loan which overshadows all previous public borrowings and, owing to certain peculiar stipulations of the contract, even the political and administrative life of the country, was the $33,000,000 authorized bond issue negotiated in 1922 with the Stifel-Nicolaus Investment Company of St. Louis, the Equitable Trust Company and Spencer Trask and Company of New York. Apart from the two foreign loans just described, the Bolivian Government had on three previous occasions resorted to credit operations abroad:[21] in 1908, when £500,000 was secured from J. P. Morgan and Company[22] at 6 percent interest for the purpose of stabilizing Bolivian exchange, which had been upset by the financial crisis of 1907 in the United States,[23] and to assist in establishing the currency on a gold basis; again, in 1910, when £1,500,000 was obtained in Paris at 5 percent to establish the Banco de la Nación;[24] and lastly, in 1913, when the Credit Mobilier loaned the Bolivian Government £1,000,000, also at 5 percent, to build the Atocha-La Quiaca Railway.[25] These loans were taken by the bankers at 90, 87 and 90 percent respectively. The bonds of the Morgan loan were not publicly offered; instead, at the time of the first French loan, £425,000 were purchased by the Bolivian Government and paid into the Banco de la Nación to cover a part of the Government's subscription to the stock of the bank. A large share of the second French loan, nearly 13,000,000 francs,[26] was never drawn by the Bolivian Government but remained on deposit with the Credit Mobilier at 3 percent interest, owing to the decline in the value of the franc which would have made a transfer of funds at the time very costly to Bolivia. Positive advantage of the franc's depreciation was taken in 1920 when, by means of an internal short term 8 percent loan of Bs. 11,600,000 from the three principal banks of the country,[27] the 1920 revolution having caused the breaking off of negotiations with Imbrie and Company for a 6 percent loan for this purpose,[28] the entire French loans, which had not specified payment in gold, were liquidated. This transaction, which netted the Bolivian Government some ten million bolivianos,[29] would have resulted in a clear saving to Bolivia if the money advanced by the Bolivian banks had not been repaid the following year in 8 percent foreign gold bonds whereas the French bonds carried only 5 percent interest.[30] Thus the French loans were consolidated in the now famous "Nicolaus" loan of 1922. By the terms of this loan the outstanding Morgan bonds, carrying only 6 percent interest, were called in and paid, since their security conflicted with some of the liens pledged to the 1922 bonds. An authorized 8 percent bond issue of $10,000,000[31] to be delivered to the Ulen Contracting Corporation for the completion of the Atocha-Villazón Railway, of which, $5,000,000 had already been issued,[32] was for the same reason included in the new refunding loan. Thus Bolivia's entire foreign debt, except for the Yungas Railway and the Sanitation bonds, was consolidated in the new American loan, which refunded a share of the internal debt as well.

The year 1920 marked a crisis in Bolivian politics. The Liberals, who had been in power for the preceding ten years, were ousted in an almost bloodless revolution in July, 1920, by the Republicans under the leadership of Bautista Saavedra, who later became president. Foreign loan negotiations,[33] principally the $10,000,000 loan at 6 percent from Imbrie and Company for the cancellation of the French debt, were cut short by the political disturbance. The country was so far committed to this last transaction, however, that the local banks had to be called upon to tide over the emergency. But this, and other short-term borrowings of the new government, made to meet the annual deficits in the budget which are a chronic ailment of Bolivian finance,[34] had soon to be met. Since 1915 the policy of issuing customs notes had been a burdensome feature of internal financing because of the high rate of interest they bore. Three issues had been made, two by the old Liberal Government and one by the Republican regime, all carrying 9 percent. These badly needed refunding. Moreover, no government could hope to retain control of public affairs in Bolivia that did not attempt to promote railway development. The Saavedra Government soon needed money and so badly[35] that towards the end of 1921 it agreed to a six months loan of $1,000,000 at 6 percent[36] from the St. Louis firm of Stifel-Nicolaus, which contained, as alternative to an exorbitant commission of $90,000, an option on the blanket loan which the Government was considering and a preferential option for three years on any external loan the Government might make within that period.[37] The National City Bank, through the American International Corporation, had already outlined a plan for an 8 percent refunding dollar loan of $25,000,000, three-fifths to be issued at once, which, owing to favorable exchange rates, it was estimated could reduce the $17,000,000 of Government indebtedness, mostly internal, to $12,000,000,[38] and might as a consequence restore Bolivian exchange to par, thus eliminating the 40 percent or more premium Bolivia was paying in buying dollars to meet her foreign obligations.[39] In the apparent competition with the National City Bank which ensued,[40] the Stifel-Nicolaus Investment Company won out, and by virtue of the prior option embodied in the emergency loan contracted in December, 1921, which prevented Bolivia from seeking the best terms in the open market, the much-criticized refunding loan of 1922 was concluded in the spring of that year. As the most spectacular single act of the new administration the loan became the butt of the Opposition's attack on the Saavedra Government. As a result, more is publicly known of the loan negotiations and terms than is usually the case with government financing, and to anyone interested in the expansion of our foreign government credits and in the relations of North American bankers with a weak and undeveloped South American state, the facts are of singular interest.

"The Republic of Bolivia external 25 year secured refunding 8 percent sinking fund gold bonds", more easily described as Bolivian 8's of 1947 and in Bolivia known as the "Nicolaus Loan," were issued to the amount of $29,000,000 with an additional $4,000,000 authorized, making a total authorized issue of $33,000,000,[41] a sum far in excess of the amount originally contemplated by the Bolivian Government.[42] Associated with the original banking house, Stifel-Nicolaus, in the issue, were the Equitable Trust Company of New York, which acts as trustee, and Spencer Trask and Company. The bonds carry very specific and inclusive security, covering in 1922 almost half the total national revenue,[43] in 1920 considerably more than half,[44] in 1925, owing to the tax reforms instituted in 1923,[45] which enormously increased the tax on mining profits, almost two-thirds of the national income.[46] So remarkable is the extent of the security pledged that the provisions of the contract with reference to security are worth quoting in full:[47]

> ARTICLE IV, Section 2
>
> ". . . the Republic hereby affects and encumbers with a first lien or pledge and charge in favor of the Trustee the following shares of stock, funds, revenues and taxes as security for the full payment of the principal, premium and interest of the Bonds, and of all other expenses and amounts required for or incident to this Contract or to the service of the Loan, to wit:
>
> (a) All of the shares, not less than 114,000, of the Banco de la Nación Boliviana belonging to the Republic and which the Republic represents are sufficient at present to control said Bank. . . . In case the capital stock of the Banco de la Nación Boliviana should be increased at any time during the life of this Loan, the Republic shall acquire such proportion of the additional shares as may be necessary to maintain the said control; the shares so acquired shall immediately thereafter be pledged as security for this Loan; . . .
>
> (b) All revenues representing dividends payable upon said shares during the life of this Loan;
>
> (c) The tax upon mining claims or concessions;
>
> (d) The revenues received by the Republic from the alcohol monopoly;
>
> (e) 90 percent of revenues received by the Republic from the tobacco monopoly;

> (f) The tax on corporations other than mining and banking;
> (g) The tax upon the net income of banks;
> (h) The tax on interest on mortgage cedulas;
> (i) The tax on the net profits of mining companies;
> (j) All import duties;
> (k) Surcharge on import duties;
> (l) All export duties. . . .
>
> Section 4. "As further security hereunder, the Republic hereby constitutes first mortgages and liens upon all the properties and earnings of the railroads constructed and to be constructed from Villazón to Atocha and from Potosí to Sucre, including their franchises, concessions, equipment and other appurtenances, and upon the net income of said railroads after deducting the expenses of operation. . . .
>
> "In case the said railroads, or either of them, should be sold as a result of the foreclosure of the mortgage or the enforcement of said lien, the purchaser at such sale, and his heirs, personal representatives, successors and assigns, shall have, . . . the right to operate the said railroad for a period of 99 years from the date of such purchase. . . ."

Thus not only were the entire customs receipts, the source of 45 percent of the total revenue of Bolivia,[48] pledged, along with certain collateral and indirect taxes, but some direct taxes as well, such as those on the net profits of mining companies, on corporations, and on the net income of banks. This was in itself a departure from the customary practice regarding security for foreign indebtedness. Moreover, to insure the actual collection of these taxes, and so that a steady income to cover the service of the debt might be counted on, it was stipulated in the contract that a Permanent Fiscal Commission of three, two members of which should be nominated by the bankers, should have charge of the collection of taxes in the Republic during the quarter century life of the loan.[49] The law authorizing the commission gave it power to supervise the collection of taxes both of a national and departmental character, and to revise the nation's accounts. The Supreme Decree of June 13, 1923, fixed more specifically the tax collecting powers of the commission, and named the president of the commission Inspector General of Banks and Monopolies.[50] It was provided that one of the two commissioners recommended by the Bankers should serve as chairman or president of the commission and as a director of the Banco de la Nación Boliviana. The other North American member of the commission has been made Director-General of Customs, although this was not required by the contract.

The purpose of the loan was, as the title of the bonds in part implies, to refund a certain amount of the outstanding debt, and, in addition, to build highways and construct and equip railways. The most burdensome of the outstanding obligations were the *Vales de Aduana* or Customs Notes of 1915, 1920 and 1921, representing a total of $5,393,115 bearing interest at 9 percent.[51] In addition to the time obligation to the local banks for the money advanced to cancel the French debt, requiring $3,501,086 for its conversion, there were other floating and short-term obligations to the amount of $4,782,455 to be paid, including the $1,000,000 six months Nicolaus loan. Thus $14,175,570, or almost one-half of the total amount issued, was applied either

Proceeds of the Refunding Loan of 1922 and Their Distribution

(Compiled from *Segunda Memoria de la Comisión Fiscal Permanente*)

PROCEEDS			DISTRIBUTION		
Authorized		$33,000,000	(1) To completion of Atocha-Villazón Railway		$8,903,189.91
Issued					
(1) For conversion of Ulen Railway construction bonds of 1922 and for completion of Atocha-Villazón Railway	$10,000,000		To railway and highway construction		
			Potosí-Sucre	$916,730.72	
			Yungas	464,105.98	
			Cochabamba-Santa Cruz	102,378.75	
			Villazón-Tarija	155,007.87	
					$1,638,223.32
(2) For refunding debts, payment of maturing obligations and construction of railways and highways	19,000,000		(2) To conversion of debt		
			Loan *re* French bonds	$3,501,085.95	
			Customs Notes (3 issues)	5,789,172.93	
			Morgan Bonds	102,855.91	
		$29,000,000			$9,393,114.79

Authorized for Potosí-Sucre Railway but not issued			$ 4,000,000
Sale of bonds			
(1) $8,000,000 at 87½	=	$7,000,000	
2,000,000 at 91½	=	1,830,000	
			$8,830,000.00
Miscellaneous credits (interest paid by Ulen, uninvested balances, etc.)			73,189.91
			$ 8,903,189.91
(2) $19,000,000 at 92	=		$17,480,000.00
Miscellaneous credits (interest on certain bonds, difference in exchange, etc.)			453,749.96
Total			$17,933,749.96
Grand total			$26,836,939.87

(3) To fund part of floating debt and meet administrative expenses (includes repayment of preliminary 6 months loan of $1,000,000)	$4,782,454.87
To service of loan	1,674,485.29
(4) To commissions *in re*negotiating loans..	441,666.00
To miscellaneous (balances outstanding and difference in exchange)...................	3,805.69
	$26,836,939.87

to the refunding or the consolidation of a good share of the country's indebtedness, external and internal. Except for the Customs Notes, the refunding bonds bore a higher rate of interest than the obligations refunded, involving an ultimate loss to Bolivia, and, with the exception of the French loans and Morgan bonds, covered short-term or floating obligations which had been issued to meet budget deficits or ordinary administrative expenses and should surely under the dictates of wise economy have been paid out of current revenues.[52]

The part of the proceeds to be set aside for railways included the conversion of the $5,000,000 of railway bonds of 1922 issued to the Ulen Contracting Corporation, an additional $5,000,000 to be set aside for the completion of the Atocha-Villazón Railway, and over a million and a half for other railways and highways.[53] When the state of the country's revenues would permit, that is, when the average annual income from the pledged revenues for the last five years equalled at least one and a half times the amount required for the annual service of $33,000,000 and when the country could show a balanced budget, an additional $4,000,000 might be issued for the completion of the Potosí-Sucre Railway.

The bonds are not redeemable before 1937, and then, like the Polish 8's of 1950 which, issued at 95, are callable at 105, they may be called as a whole but not in part and redeemed at 105 and accrued interest,[54] a price thirteen points higher than that at which they were issued. A recent writer on foreign investments says: "Such provisions place a heavy financial burden upon the borrowing country. In the first case it is unable to convert its obligations at lower rates, and in the second instance it must repay a sum far in excess of that actually received. These burdens are, however, the penalty which a state pays for a weak credit standing."[55] A 2 percent cumulative sinking fund provides for amortization of the bonds. The annual service of the loan calls, therefore, for $2,900,000 a year.

The disadvantages of the prior option possessed by the Stifel-Nicolaus Company became clear during the course of the loan negotiations when the Bolivian Government, in dire straits and bound to accept the terms offered, was helpless to better them through the ordinary course of competitive bidding.[56] A French offer of $15,000,000 in the spring of 1922 had to be rejected on a reminder from the Bankers of their prerogatives under the contract for the six months loan signed December 5, 1921. Not only this option but the preferential option on any loan which the Republic might wish to contract during the next three years,[57] a condition agreed to by the Bolivian Minister in Washington to the dismay of the Minister of Hacienda, tied the latter's hands when he came to New York to complete the negotiations, and made it impossible to consider the "flattering" proposals made to the Bolivian Consul General in New York by another financial house.[58] In the fall of 1922, Bolivia had to reject the offer of a loan of £3,000,000 at 5 percent, made in London, for the same reason.[59]

Not only did the option keep off competitors but it compelled Bolivia, in urgent need of money, to accept far severer terms than her past external debt record or the conditions of her earlier borrowings abroad could have possibly led her to anticipate. The first detailed proposal from the Bankers, dated March 17, 1922, included redemption after fifteen years at 110; all the guaranties listed above as well as the taxes on petroleum and consular receipts; a second mortgage on the railroad system controlled by the Bolivia Railway Company; a specific stipulation that the Potosí-Sucre Railway should be constructed by the Ulen Contracting Corporation; a Permanent Fiscal Commission of three to consist of the Minister of Hacienda, one member nominated by our State Department, and a banker residing in New York who should be final arbiter in all questions; and a net price of 87½ and expenses.[60] These terms the Bolivian Government considered onerous and out of keeping with Bolivia's position as an independent nation, whose credit reputation up to this time had been impeccable. With reference to the Permanent Fiscal Commission, Ramón Rivero, Minister of Hacienda at the time, said: "This was considered deplorable; we indicated at once that the organization of such a 'High Commission' would not only affect the economic life of the nation but Bolivia's political autonomy, creating an intervention which no sovereign people could accept; hence we requested that this condition be withdrawn, suggesting in its place a commission of control such as was approved in the law of March 27, 1922, to consist of three expert accountants, dependent on the Ministro de Hacienda, two of whom might be North Americans, nominated by the Bolivian Government on suggestion of the Bankers in conformity with our laws. This was quite different from the intervention proposed."[61]

The chief points to which objection was taken were the price, the redemption figure, and the additional security. The threat of maturity of the preliminary loan was alleviated by an arrangement with Mr. Eli Bernheim of the Columbia Bank, which provided for the advance of a sufficient sum to meet this obligation if the negotiations for the refunding loan should fall through.[62] On the recommendation of Mr. Samuel A. Maginnis, former United States Minister to Bolivia and counsel for Bolivia in these negotiations, Mr. Bernheim was made technical adviser on a commission basis, which was to net him one-third of the increase in yield if the bonds sold for 90, one-half of the increase in yield if they sold above 90.[63] Rivero reports an immediate improvement in the attitude of the bankers after Bernheim's appointment. The final terms agreed upon were redemption at 105, the omission of the petroleum taxes and the other additional guaranties from the security pledged, a stipulation that the contract for the Potosí-Sucre Railway should be awarded to the firm offering the best terms, a Permanent Fiscal Commission as authorized by law, and a price of 92 on the first $24,000,000, of 93 on the balance, on which the bankers maintained a simple option.[64] The contract was signed May 31, 1922. On June 2nd, the bonds were offered to the public at 101 and accrued interest; the ready response led to the closing of the books at 10:30 A. M. the same day.[65] The strong political opposition of the fall and winter following, causing apprehension of a possible default,[66] made them fall to as low as 83⅛, but the futility of the attempt to secure any belated modification of the terms once recognized, the opposition to the loan practically ceased, and the quotations of the bonds on the New York Stock Exchange, where they are listed, rose steadily until in January, 1927, they hit a high level of 105½.[67]

As a weapon of attack in the domestic political situation, criticism of the 1922 loan was directed at the Saavedra Government rather than at the bankers, and even at the present time, the "Nicolaus Loan" is singled out as one of the worst manifestations of "saavedrismo," whereas the Permanent Fiscal Commissioners in La Paz, representing the New York bankers, are in general welcomed and accepted as a beneficial force in the financial administration of the country. Undue haste in concluding the negotiations[68] led to misunderstandings, to the acceptance of terms which upon more careful deliberation might have been rejected outright or greatly modified, and to a carelessness with regard to some of the security pledged that caused much controversy and some necessary modification later.[69] The clumsiness of the negotiations and the significance of the contract soon became apparent and, in September, 1922, President Saavedra instructed the Consul General in New York to try to secure modifications in the contract on a number of points as a necessary preliminary to acceptance of the loan in Bolivia. The Government was so bombarded with criticism of the loan, which in turn was jeopardizing Bolivia's credit abroad, that Saavedra appointed a commission "free from political affiliations"[70] to study and report on it. The commission's report of March 14, 1923, examines minutely the objectionable features of the transaction and is, in effect, a severe censure of the Bolivian Government for accepting such extensive credits on such stringent and allegedly illegal terms.[71]

Apart from the price and the interest rate which, though considered exorbitant,[72] were accepted as inalterable after the contract had been signed and the bonds issued and sold, the chief points of attack were the redemption feature of the bonds, and the pledging of doubtful security such as the mortgage on the still unbuilt Potosí-Sucre Railway, the Morgan Bonds, which were not the property of the nation, and the Government's shares of the Banco de la Nación, which, though indubitably a proprietary interest of the Republic, gave the bankers a throttle hold on the affairs of Bolivia's most important bank. Criticism was directed, also, at the refunding operation which was considered of doubtful advantage to Bolivia, at the form of amortization of the bonds, the 90-day deposit period prior to redemption, the inclusion of the Bankers' counsel fees in the expenses of the Trustee, the required monthly remittances for service of the loan, the provision for the sale of the pledged Bank shares in case of default, and at the restrictions on the issues of new bonds for the Potosí-Sucre and Atocha-Villazón Railways. All of these points, except that regarding debt consolidation, which was an economic and purely internal question, were carefully answered by the Bankers' counsel, Curtis, Mallet-Prevost and Colt, in a memorandum dated July 30, 1923.[73] Finally, the report of the Bolivian commissioners condemned the Permanent Fiscal Commission as a slur on Bolivia's sovereignty, and deplored the fact that in determining the basis for the election and powers of the Permanent Fiscal Commission the Government did not heed the "patriotic" warnings of the Bolivian Minister in Washington to the effect that Bolivian control should prevail in the Commission, since otherwise the Government was consenting to the creation of an organ superior to the state. This position seems to have been a theoretical one, however, so much so that one of the leaders of the opposition, and secretary of the special commission, several years later was found expressing criticism of the Permanent Fiscal Commission on the ground that it was not sufficiently active in reorganizing Bolivia's financial system.

The loan contract, as has been stated, provides for redemption of the bonds, as a whole but not in part, after May, 1937, at 105 and accrued interest;[74] at maturity they are payable at par. The opposition charged that not only was this provision illegal, and hence not binding on Bolivia, since the laws authorizing the loan stipulated the right of conversion upon six month's notice, but that Bolivia's inability to redeem the bonds for fifteen years was an enormous disadvantage to the country, in making it impossible for the nation to convert the bonds on more economical terms when the country's credit improved and interest rates in the world markets dropped, or to get further credits on better terms while these well-secured and high interest-bearing bonds were on the market. As an instance of the latter handicap, the Morgan 6's of 1908 were cited which were retired through purchase by the Banco de la Nación at the time the first French 5's were issued. It was requested, therefore, that redemption at 105 on any interest payment date be substituted for the fifteen-year non-callable period. The Bolivian charge of illegality was based on a so-called "secret law," passed at the same time as the public law of May 24, 1922, authorizing the loan, which repeated the proviso of the earlier law of February 10 for redemption on six months notice. No mention of this provision was made in the final public law, however, and the Bankers contended, and it would seem justly, that they could not be bound by the terms of a law which had never been promulgated and was hence unknown to them. The non-callability of the bonds had, moreover, been insisted on from the start and the Bolivian Government was fully informed of this provision when it signed the contract. As for the Bolivian contention that all countries "in the defense of their legitimate interest" reserve the right to convert their loans at any time, the Bankers pointed out that the contrary was the case and cited a great number of Government bond issues in which redemption is prohibited either during the entire life of the loan or for a stated number of years. The disadvantage to Bolivia of this restriction, which for a long period prevents conversion at a lower rate, is undeniable, but such restrictions are common practice in government financing and are fairly essential to the attractiveness of any bond issue. They do not, moreover, prevent a nation from obtaining new credits on better terms later, provided its economic condition and its credit reputation have improved, even while higher rate bonds of the same country are available, for the less speculative bond will appeal to a new class of investor. Instances abound in the history of public finance of the adjustment to its credit reputation of the terms on which a country can borrow abroad. As a matter of fact Bolivia has herself just secured a new seven percent loan. To cite but one other case, Chile five times within the last thirty-three years secured pound sterling loans at four and a half percent while her five and six percent bonds were still on the market, and only this last fall she obtained a six percent loan in New York while bonds of her eight percent dollar loans of 1921 and of the seven percent loan of 1922 still had an active sale.[75]

A more serious criticism was that regarding the Banco de la Nación Boliviana. Organized in 1910 with the proceeds of the first French loan, the Bolivian Government purchased a majority of its shares,[76] but in order to keep the administration of the bank in private hands it was provided that the private shareholders should have a majority representation on the board of directors. One of the early acts of the Saavedra rule was to gain control of the bank by decreasing the directorate from seven to five members, three of whom should represent the Government. The constitutionality of this act is to be tested in Bolivia's Supreme Court as a result of suit brought against the Government by the private shareholders.[77] But even if the decision should be favorable to the latter, they will not be satisfied, as they are anxious to have the bank thoroughly reorganized on the lines of our own Federal Reserve Bank and are fearful that the transfer of the Government's shares in the Banco de la Nación to the New York bankers may stand in the way of any such achievement. It is reasonable to suppose that the North American bankers would approve of a change in Bolivia's banking system that would tend to increase the prosperity of the country and the soundness and efficiency of the Banco de la Nación. Nevertheless, exercising as they do the power to vote a majority of the Banco's shares, outsiders are in a position to control a clearly internal and vital financial situation. As yet the bankers have never withheld their proxy, but no important question has so far arisen to test their use of this undoubtedly dangerous power.

The Trust Contract calls for all of the Government shares in the Banco de la Nación as collateral, it being understood that the shares pledged would always be enough to control the bank, and, in case of default, for their public sale in New York without judicial procedure. The Bolivian commissioners contended that the shares had been pledged illegally. They objected, too, to this unprecedented contingent increase in security as the loan was amortized, and to the public sale in New York of an entirely unknown Bolivian company, not listed on the Stock Exchange, which they considered would be ruinous. They therefore requested that, since there had been no authority to pledge them and since, "by reason of the objects and nature of the Banco de la Nación Boliviana, the control of this institution cannot be assigned nor transferred nor mortgaged in favor of any other person, company or entity, and especially not to a foreign person, company or entity" the shares belonging to the Republic be returned.[78] That the Government's shares were not inalienable the Bankers' counsel proved from a number of Bolivian laws according to which their sale or transfer was contemplated; as public assets the Bankers contended that they fell under the blanket pledge of "resources" necessary to secure the new loan provided for in the law of May 24, 1922. As for the public sale of the shares in case of default in payment, although contrary to Bolivian law, this procedure is wholly in keeping with the laws of the State of New York under which the contract was drawn up. Furthermore, in spite of the commissioners' contention to the contrary, the cables and messages transmitted to La Paz during the negotiations prove that the Bolivian Government was fully aware of the Bankers' insistence on the shares as part security and should have realized in advance the significance of pledging away the control of a semi-public and vital institution such as the Banco de la Nación.

The other guaranties over which difficulties arose were the Morgan Bonds, which were the property of the Banco de la Nación and hence not available security, the alcohol monopoly which had been abolished the year before, the tobacco monopoly or tax which, in the former case, was already pledged to railway construction and, in the latter, had been abolished years ago, and the mortgage on the Potosí-Sucre Railway which the Government considered was not available as security until the $4,000,000 authorized under the contract for the construction of that road was issued. The Bankers seem to have a clear legal claim to the last of these, although a questionable one from the point of view of justice. At any rate, the Government, whether because of price or through a desire to combine this with a larger railway loan,[79] has been unwilling to issue the remaining $4,000,000 and was extremely anxious to release this security.

The questions arising over the Morgan Bonds and the alcohol and tobacco monopolies evinced either a deliberate misrepresentation on the part of the Bolivian Government or a carelessness both on Bolivia's part in supplying accurate information with regard to the security demanded and on the part of the Bankers in not investigating these pledges more fully. Bonds of the Morgan Loan of 1908 to the amount of £292,000, which were represented by Ramón Rivero, Minister of Finance and financial agent of Bolivia at the time, as the property of the Republic, in reality belonged to the Banco de la Nación. As the contract called for their cancellation[80] so that the valuable security back of them might be released, there was nothing for the Government to do but reimburse the Banco, which was done in internal bonds of the Republic,[81] now unfortunately quoted at thirty points below par.[82]

The difficulty with regard to the abolished alcohol monopoly was remedied by the substitution for it of the income from the taxes on the manufacture of national alcohols and brandies in the departments of La Paz, Oruro and Tarija; the collections from these taxes for the years 1922 and 1923 averaged about Bs. 860,000, whereas the gross receipts from the alcohol monopoly during the last two years of its regular operation, 1920 and 1921, averaged approximately Bs. 1,190,000.[83] The inferior value of the alcohol taxes as security is of little actual significance, however, since the tax reforms of 1923 and the improved fiscalization of the Government revenues under the Permanent Fiscal Commission[84] have more than doubled the income from the total revenues pledged.

The naiveté of the Bolivian Government in trying to secure a modification of the contract for the refunding loan resulted only in the discouraging rejoinder that since the contract was a trust contract, no changes were possible without the consent of the eight thousand odd holders of the bonds, a thing next to impossible to secure. The Republic was told that it was at liberty to address itself to the bondholders direct but that the attempt would be long, costly, and probably fruitless, and would have as its sole outcome a depreciation of Bolivia's credit.[85] The appeal, therefore, came to naught. Possibly it was not as naive as on the surface it appears. When the details of the transaction became known in Bolivia, particularly to the opposition party, the Government was confronted with a critical situation and thought to save its face by trying to get rid of some of the most objectionable features of the contract, even refusing for several months to authorize the signature of the permanent bonds unless the modifications were agreed to, a position President Saavedra adhered to until "strong representations" made to the Bolivian Government by our Department of State forced him to give in. Bolivia must have realized that the legal position of the Bankers was unassailable, that the correspondence would show the Government in full cognizance of all the conditions before the contract was signed and hence by that signature agreeing to them. To the purchasers of the bonds the assurance that their investment would yield eight percent for fifteen years at least, provided all went well with Bolivia, was a strong inducement for taking a chance on them; sold to the public on this condition, the Bankers could hardly in good faith now ask the bondholders to relinquish this privilege. As for releasing the Bank shares, which the Bankers had demanded by way of protecting their lien on the dividends payable on them, neither the Bolivian Government nor the underwriters of the loan nor the purchasing public could have foreseen that the revenues which in 1922 yielded slightly over Bs. 12,000,000, just about enough to cover the contract requirement, would by 1925 be producing more than Bs. 27,000,000, hence making the dividends on the Bank shares of comparatively little importance as security. Sentiment might prescribe the relinquishing of a lien under such circumstances, particularly of an asset so inextricably bound up with the financial life of the country as the Government's shares in a semi-public institution like the Banco de la Nación, but the Bolivian Government must have known that in such transactions sentiment is not likely to operate. Besides, the Bankers are always confronted with the possibility of a time when tin will drop in value and cannot be counted on so heavily to produce the revenue to serve and secure this loan, a contingency which makes for caution in the matter of releasing security. The initial mistake had been the prior option, which cut off from the start all possibility of competition.[86] This and the Government's urgent need of money forced the acceptance of an unquestionably shrewd and hard bargain, in which the negotiations were perfectly open and above board but the whip handle always in the hands of the bankers. When it came to a showdown at home Saavedra was not prepared to face the music.

One valid criticism of the loan, and one which can be laid at the doors of the bankers to the extent that they urged a large refunding loan at this time,[87] was the assumption of so heavy a load of indebtedness at a high interest rate with so little of a productive nature to show for it. The purposes of the loan as set forth in the contract have been faithfully carried out, as the report of the Permanent Fiscal Commission for 1925 shows, but in the way of constructive achievement these leave much to be desired. The table on pages 102-103 shows the proceeds from the sale of the bonds and the ends to which they were applied. These fall into four classes: (1) railways and highways; (2) refunding or consolidation; (3) maturing obligations and administrative expenses; (4) and commissions in connection with the loan. The only one of these that may be considered productive in the sense of having a potential earning capacity is the ten and a half million dollars that went into railways and highways, little more than one-third of the total issue. The last two, which consumed $9,588,606.16 of the total,[88] are clearly unproductive except in so far as the consolidation of floating obligations systematizes a nation's finances and raises its credit abroad. Apart from the amount expended on commissions, which may have been necessary to secure more favorable terms, but constructively was a dead loss to Bolivia, this portion of the loan was clearly a resort to the doubtful and costly practice of long-term borrowing at high interest to meet current expenses and deficits in the budget, proof that the nation was living beyond its income.

The refunding operations, to which roughly nine and a half million dollars, or about one-third of the total issue, was applied, could be considered a constructive measure to the extent to which they reduced the interest rates on the obligations converted thereby or actually lowered the principal of the internal loans refunded. The Government was severely criticized both for converting old external bonds to new ones bearing a higher rate of interest and for exchanging internal for external obligations when the rate of exchange made Bolivia the loser on interest payments abroad. The Morgan 6 percent bonds, amounting to something over a million and a half dollars,[89] were converted at 8 percent, involving an ultimate loss to Bolivia although effecting an immediate saving in service and amortization charges.[90] The internal 8 percent loan of Bs. 11,600,000 to redeem the French bonds, although on conversion calling for a slightly larger annual service and amortization charge, had to be converted, as the credit from the Bolivian banks would carry 10 percent interest if extended beyond the two year period for which the loan had been made.[91] The 9 percent Customs Notes, which the Government had hoped to retire in five years through a 20 percent sinking fund, were converted into 8 percent 25 year bonds calling for the payment in gold dollars annually of $578,916, their duration and the loss in dollar payments when the exchange was bad offsetting somewhat the advantage of a lower interest rate.[92] The Ulen railway bonds of 1922 bore a fixed price to the Bolivian Government of 87½, were redeemable at any time at par, and carried 8 percent interest and 2½ percent amortization charges. In consideration of a premium of $150,000 the Ulen Contracting Corporation agreed to accept bonds of the new issue in their place, the first $8,000,000 at the same price and the remaining $2,000,000 at 91½. Considering the less favorable redemption clause, the loss to

Bolivia in being forced to accept a lower price for these bonds than she was getting for the other bonds of the refunding issue,[93] the compensation to the Ulen Company for the change in contract, the expense of issuing two sets of bonds and certain interest losses involved, the special commission appointed to secure modification of the Nicolaus contract charged that the Bolivian Government lost upward of $1,000,000 on this conversion.[94] Even if this charge is correct the fact that so much of the nation's acceptable security was pledged to these bonds, and to the Morgan Bonds and Customs Notes,[95] makes complaint with regard to their conversion academic or, as was the case, political. To relieve the exchange situation and to improve Bolivia's credit abroad some consolidation of her public debt was probably necessary. Above all, and this was the most impelling factor, the Government was hard up, the country had about reached the saturation point on the absorption of internal loans,[96] and new foreign credits were essential. To obtain them the pledged securities had to be released.

Bad financial habits such as recurrent deficits made up by short term internal borrowings at an average of 9 percent interest[97] and, even worse, by the highly questionable issue of customs notes, had created an impasse which only a drastic financial operation like the 1922 refunding loan could meet.[98] The prior option, moreover, gave the Bankers power to dictate the terms. System was temporarily introduced into the nation's finances at the cost of eight percent for twenty-five years, a discount of eight points per bond, not to mention the half a million dollars in special fees spent in securing that favorable a rate, and the exercise of the tax-collecting function by a North American commission. And yet by 1925 the nation was not cured of its chronic deficit, and its floating obligations, reduced to a reasonable figure by the refunding operation, had climbed once more to over sixteen million bolivianos.[99]

Bolivian 8's of 1947 sell at present around 105; the country's credit at the moment is good. As against this must be set the fact that the debt capacity of the country is reached, if indeed not passed, while the need of foreign capital for important public improvements is far from satisfied.[100] The chairman of the Permanent Fiscal Commission in his 1926 report to the Minister of Hacienda says, and quite justly, that when a nation's debt calls for more than forty-six percent of the annual revenue, the point of prudence has been overstepped.[101] His advice to the country is a program of economy and an increase in taxation as alternatives to further borrowings to make up the annual deficits—sage advice, indeed, when it is remembered that of the Bs. 65,743,291 increase in the public debt from the years 1921-1925, more than Bs. 26,000,000 had to be applied to making up the deficits for 1921, 1922 and 1923.[102] The biggest loan transaction in the history of Bolivia, although putting the public debt on a fairly systematic basis, left the country with a large and expensive burden to carry but without the funds necessary to carry forward public works essential to the nation's development. The hypothecation of the country's principal sources of revenue leaves only a second lien available for further loans,[103] which would for this reason be at a disadvantage in the money market.[104] The drastic tax reforms of 1923 caused so much criticism that the immediate future holds little if any promise of new or higher taxes. Forty-eight percent of the population, moreover, contributes less than two percent of the taxes to the national treasury,[105] and the nation is dependent for its revenues largely upon one commodity of a fluctuating and externally fixed value. The nature of the population and the geographical obstacles to development of the country's abundant resources act as a check on any easy optimism as regards an immediate and sustained increase in national prosperity. One wonders, then, how further loans to Bolivia, whether for railways and highways or for the purchase of Tacna-Arica, can be considered in anything but the light of a risk. In fact, in spite of the high price which Bolivian 8's of 1947 commanded,[106] the refunding loan of 1922 would seem to have been a highly speculative enterprise.[107]

CHAPTER VII

A POTENTIAL PROBLEM IN AMERICAN IMPERIALISM

"THE quintessence of all ethics", says Count Keyserling in his *Travel Diary of a Philosopher*, "is contained in the warning of Sri Krishna's: Rather fulfil thy own Dharma, no matter how low it may be, than the most illustrious Dharma of someone else." This is as sound international ethics as individual, and might well be addressed as a *laissez-faire* injunction to those modern imperialists who, with specious reasoning, point to the fine roads and recent sanitation in Haiti or to the educational system of the Philippines developed under American administration of the islands, as justification for our occupation of these territories. The white man's burden should be to see to it that the other races of the world are permitted to work out their own destinies, no matter how different and, in some respects, inferior to our own they may appear, rather than to try to transplant a ready-made civilization upon a soil and people neither ready nor anxious for it. Young India under Mahatma Gandhi, and the intensely nationalistic student movement of China have voiced this yearning of the Oriental to fulfil his own Dharma, lowly as it may seem to Western eyes. Other racial groups have not been so fortunate in expressing their desire for a development free from foreign dictation, or have not so consciously or powerfully articulated their will to be themselves, but the resentment against foreign domination is present, as the persistent plea of the Filipino nationalist group for independence and the anti-foreign sentiment in Mexico reflected in her 1917 Constitution testify.

An absolute policy of *laissez-faire* for the "backward" peoples and areas of the world is not, however, as simple as it would seem to the non-cooperationist group in India, intent on remedying what had become for them an intolerable situation. The interdependence of all quarters of the globe in this specialized industrial age makes the raw materials of one section essential to the highly organized manufacturing industries of another; and the former are practically without value except for the demands of the latter. The revival of hand spinning and weaving in India was, perhaps, sound enough as a protest against the effects of British capital domination on the Indian population, but as part of a program to make India economically independent of the rest of the world Swadeshi contained a fundamental fallacy for international life in the twentieth century. Many nations, most nations in fact, are not equipped by nature to be self-sufficient. Non-cooperation with outside nations, whether by means of home-spun khaddar or of high-tariff walls is not possible for the world of today—as, in the latter case, the recent tariff manifesto of international bankers demonstrates.[1]

The policy of hands-off would be simpler if a complex society did not, in its very complexity, create motives for foreign penetration. The need of raw materials, markets, and an outlet for surplus capital on the one hand, on the other the need of foreign capital to develop latent resources, make inevitable some form of relationship between the highly industrialized and over-capitalized states with the potentially rich but undeveloped areas of the world. The desire of the peoples within these areas for development of their resources varies. Sometimes, as in India and in China, foreign capital has been attracted by the opportunities for the exploitation of some important commodity or for the development of trade relations and, as a result, without invitation or persuasion of the local inhabitants, large sums have been invested. At other times, more ambitious nations, with abundant natural resources but few liquid assets, have deliberately sought capital abroad. In the former cases the responsibility of the foreign capitalist and his government to abstain from interfering in the internal life of the country which he has sought out for investment is especially great—though history proves that the contrary has been the case and that either direct conquest or the establishment of a protectorate, veiled at times, at others unabashedly naked, has frequently resulted. Hypocritical mouthings about the white man's burden, the *mission civilitracise*, or the spread of Kultur should not be allowed to obscure the real reasons for penetration. If conditions exist or develop which make the safety of the investment uncertain, the uncertainty should be reckoned as but a part of the price to be paid —usually repaid, too, in higher interest rates or bigger dividends[2]— for investing in outlandish and unstable regions.

In the cases where foreign capital has been deliberately sought, the situation is somewhat different. A country that makes a bid for foreign capital investments or seeks government credits abroad, accepts them on certain fixed terms, and assumes a responsibility towards its share of the fulfilment of those terms. The investor needs in these latter instances just as scrupulously to avoid attempts to mend the ways or make over the sovereign people in whose fortunes he has acquired a stake, but if the sovereignty of the borrowing country is limited as a result of stipulated conditions which the borrower was in advance free to accept or reject, the lender cannot to the same extent be charged with usurping authority and undermining the nation's independence, although he may be thought a driver of hard bargains.

Bolivia falls within this latter category, and herein lies such justification as there may be for the Permanent Fiscal Commission which for twenty-five years was authorized to collect Bolivia's taxes—an undeniable limitation of the country's sovereignty, and yet one that was quite frankly made part of the price Bolivia must pay for the capital she was trying to obtain. It is as beside the point as the self-laudatory claims of imperialism to the material and social betterment of the states brought under its sway, to enumerate the advantages to Bolivia of such a commission, to describe the increased revenues, the more systematic, honest and effective fiscalization of the national income since the Fiscal Commission began to function. The Commission was clearly established to see that the service of the 1922 refunding loan was regularly maintained, and to collect and preserve intact from other conflicting liens or claims the revenues pledged as security. Such advantages as accrue to Bolivia from the work of the Commission are incidental. But the amount of sovereignty relinquished in accepting such a body was yielded knowingly, albeit under the compulsion of extreme need, and the present lack of animus in Bolivia against the Permanent Fiscal Commission testifies not only to the fairness of its work but to this distinction between an interference whose measure and nature was known and accepted in advance and a usurpation of internal powers against the will of the victim state. A hard bargain the New York bankers unquestionably struck with Bolivia, and one of its shrewdest features was the insistence upon a foreign surveillance of Bolivian finances during the life of the loan. The potential danger to Bolivian independence of such a body has been well described in a recent work on dollar diplomacy: "The Permanent Fiscal Commission holds the economic key to the life of the Republic and the Bankers control the Commission. As yet there has been no default, and no political issues have been raised, but this loan contract ties the representatives of the loaning Bankers into the heart of Bolivian political life by placing in their hands the control of Bolivia's public revenues. Should a default take place, the members of the Commission automatically become the central figures in the Bolivian political world, and the Loan of 1922 takes precedence over all other public considerations. There is, in this relation, an international issue of the first magnitude between the Government of the United States and the Government of Bolivia. While the issue may never arise, the fact remains that representatives of an American banking syndicate are administering the finances of a sister Republic."[3] But at the present stage of the game the Permanent Fiscal Commission in Bolivia cannot in any fairness be pointed out as a demonstration of North American imperialist domination in South America, partly because of Bolivia's voluntary acceptance of such a body, inevitable as the exigencies of the case may have made it, but more particularly, because the tax-collecting function in Bolivia is being exercised by North

American bankers as individuals, without official participation by the United States Government. In this the situation differs from that in Nicaragua, Salvador and other Caribbean countries.

Imperialism involves more than foreign investment alone, for, if the contrary were true, Great Britain could be charged with imperialist control of the United States for much of the nineteenth century, and the United States with imperialist intent in Canada at the present time. Monopolistic possession of the credits of a borrowing country or of corporate investments in that country may lead dangerously near to unwarranted control of its internal life—and, in case of any emergency affecting foreign investments there, may involve the threat if not the actuality of action by the home government to protect those investments. But this element of governmental interference in the debtor country's affairs is a necessary feature of genuine imperialism, and an imperialist situation cannot fairly be said to have developed before this factor of domination or interference by an outside government enters in. The period of foreign expansion of the United States which began with the Spanish-American War, has brought certain areas directly under the control of this country, either as actual possessions, as in the case of Porto Rico, the Philippines, the Virgin Islands and Hawaii, or as protectorates or quasi-protectorates, such as Cuba, Haiti, Santo Domingo, Nicaragua, and the Republic of Panama. In some other countries of the Caribbean, as in Salvador, the United States Government has either already participated in the administration of a loan contract or has engaged itself to do so in certain eventualities.[4] In South America the United States has never taken any positive or official action to protect the growing investments of its citizens,[5] although the Monroe Doctrine and an undifferentiated fear of "*Yanqui imperialismo*" have developed in many countries of the Southern continent a dread of North American domination.

Bolivia, still in the early stages of inducing capital from the United States to invest in its mineral resources and its bonds,[6] with the exception of an almost negligible radical element,[7] has not yet arrived at this anxious state. As has already been pointed out, the opposition to the refunding loan of 1922, Bolivia's biggest single piece of financing in North America, was directed against the political group within the country that saddled the country with it rather than against the New York bankers. Except for petroleum, in the exploitation of Bolivia's natural resources Chilean and European concessions and capital actively rival American, while British and German metal buyers are severe competitors of American in handling the mineral output. Bolivia's principal railway system, though built by Americans, is operated and largely owned by a British company. In Bolivia's export trade the United States occupies a very inferior position to Great Britain, although in supplying Bolivia's import needs this country is in the lead.[8] Neither can Bolivia, psychologically, be considered as lying under the shadow of the United States but rather, like most of South America, has her eyes turned to Europe for intellectual stimulation and social standards. North American investments in Bolivia exceed those of any other foreign country, but they have not monopolized the field by any means,[9] nor does the preponderance of American capital, at present at any rate, represent the domination of Bolivian life by North Americans. With the United States in the position of leading creditor nation of the world, Bolivia, like many other borrowing countries, has had to turn to this country when she needed capital, but with the removal of the British embargo on foreign loans there is no reason to suppose that London will not share in the future bidding, as the Patiño loan of £600,000 secured in London in 1925 when unissued credits were already available in New York illustrates.

American imperialism in Bolivia is not, therefore, a thing of the present, and the future is always a matter of conjecture, a preeminently dangerous procedure. It may be of interest, however, on the strength of this survey of the Bolivian situation and in view of the analogy suggested by the similar ethnic and geographic conditions in Mexico and Bolivia and a political and historical tradition common to most South American countries, to inquire whether we may at any time expect the United States Government to be confronted with a situation in Bolivia calling for the protection of American interests abroad, such as has made Mexico for years a recurrent problem in United States diplomacy and the American press. In Mexico proximity creates a fear of annexation which makes for intense bitterness against the United States, while the magnitude of the total investment stimulates a strong demand for intervention from the North American holders of Mexican shares and bonds. Both of these factors are, of course, absent in the Bolivian situation. But all foreign investment presents the same general dilemma: the absence of any legal claims on a foreign state to meet its obligations or to protect foreign capital within its borders, combined with the demand of foreign investors that their stakes abroad be protected and, in the case of public loans, that the promised return on their investment be assured. In the case of a great deal of foreign investment, such as in Canada or in a well-established and prosperous South American state like Argentina, this constitutes no real problem. The same is not true, however, in weak and unstable countries, where the public revenues are likely to be mismanaged and a shift in government to mean a repudiation of the nation's obligations; in countries like Russia and Mexico where the social and political organization has undergone vast changes and the commitments of the old regime have been either rejected outright or are under fire; or in potentially rich but undeveloped countries where the exploitation of the natural resources outstrips social development and a steady and consistent growth of national prosperity, upon which the security of investment in such large measure depends, is not to be expected. It is investment ventures in such countries that have led to "dollar diplomacy", once an outright policy of the United States, now a vigorous undertone of American foreign relations.

In March, 1922, the United States State Department requested American bankers to keep it informed of all negotiations for foreign loans and to submit loan contracts to it for its information before they were signed.[10] In view of the fact that certain loans have been forestalled because of the Department's disapproval,[11] it has been asserted that all loans negotiated have, therefore, the State Department's approval.[12] Whether active approval is involved, or merely an absence of disapproval, only the carefully guarded files of the Department could prove. The request specifically declared that no judgment as to the merits of the loans from a business standpoint was involved in the Government's attitude, favorable or adverse. Since the loans that have been disapproved have concerned, principally, countries whose War indebtedness to the United States Government had not been refunded, or have involved the financing of monopolies, like the Brazilian coffee valorization scheme, which were considered harmful to citizens of the United States, there is not sufficient evidence available to justify any generalization as to the Government's attitude towards speculative money-lending in backward countries, although it has been asserted on fairly good authority that at times the State Department has suggested that a prospective loan might not be "productive", or has pointed out existing debts with prior liens on the prospective borrower's resources, or the possible difficulty of the borrower in obtaining the foreign exchange or dollars necessary to pay the interest on the projected loan.[13] In view of the international disputes to which such investments frequently lead, such loans might well be considered to involve questions of national policy, and a distinct service might be rendered both to creditor and borrower, not to mention to the American people who, in case of open conflict over foreign investments, must bear the brunt of their defense, if the State Department should set up standards of security and fairness, and should discourage proposals which failed to meet them.[14] Such a policy, however, might as a corollary imply protection of those investments which the Government had approved, and hence accomplish, in the case of its mistaken estimates, that very Government backing of private investments abroad which the opponents of modern economic imperialism are anxious to prevent. The desire of North American banking interests, moreover, for a reduced rather than intensified Government interference in their affairs would probably militate against the adoption of any such policy.[15]

Be that as it may, much of our Government's foreign policy revolves about the security of private investments. Most striking and powerful proof of this is to be found in the present joint Nicaraguan-Mexican muddle. Investors whose foreign securities seem in danger promptly run to cover under the wing of the State Department, as the history of Mexican-American relations so amply demonstrates—a situation which will not be altered until either speculative investing in foreign countries is discouraged to the vanishing point, an altogether unlikely procedure so long as surplus capital is abundant and high rates of interest go hand-in-hand with risk, or until the investor in shaky foreign securities is made to understand that in sinking his capital in them he himself must assume the risks involved and may seek no redress through his Government in case of loss. The new Mexican constitution specifically stipulates that foreign enterprises in Mexico will be entertained only on condition that their owners renounce the right to appeal to their governments in the case of disputes arising over their property interests.[16] A universal application of this principle, known as the Calvo clause, would greatly lessen the dangers of international conflict involved in the phenomenal expansion of American foreign credits within the last decade, and would incidentally remove an enormous burden from the shoulders of our Department of State. Such is, however, by no means the current theory underlying foreign investments among the leading countries of the world. As Mr. J. A. Hobson, in his classic study of imperialism, put it: "Investors who have put their money in foreign lands, upon terms which take full account of the risks connected with the political conditions of the country, desire to use the resources of their Government to minimize these risks, and so to enhance the capital value and the interest of their private investments."[17] There is sufficient evidence in our military and naval excursions to certain of the Caribbean islands and states in the interests of collecting debts and of establishing political conditions conducive to the safety of foreign investment, to show that what is known as economic nationalism[18] has become a guiding principle of American foreign policy.

It is in confronting this reality that one finds the potentiality of trouble in American investment in Bolivia, as well as in any other undeveloped and comparatively unstable country. Whether the reader accepts the judgment of Bolivian bonds and securities as speculative will depend upon the force of the preceding chapters. An external debt which commands considerably more than half the nation's revenue as security and the service of which constitutes by far the largest item in the national budget; the sterility of much of this debt so far as essential public improvements are concerned and the great need of further borrowing abroad though the debt limit has been more than reached; almost overwhelming geographical drawbacks to offset the great natural wealth of the country; and the mentally vigorous and alert element in the population in such a minority that either great political stability or material development within the near future seem extremely dubious—these are adduced as proof that Bolivian bonds, even though the 8's of 1947 are selling at high prices, are a risky investment.

The American empire has been conceived by one

writer on imperialism as including not only the obvious and unquestionable possessions of the United States, but certain "nominally independent dependencies" as well, which latter, thanks largely to Cuba and the trade of that island with the United States, outstrip the former in commercial value to the United States.[19] In the latter group are included Cuba, Haiti, the Dominican Republic, Panama, Nicaragua and Liberia. To add Bolivia to this list now would be overstepping the bounds of truth and judicious statement. True, North American investment in Bolivia exceeds that of any other country by some forty or fifty millions of dollars; a North American oil company has a practical monopoly of petroleum exploitation there; North American bankers and citizens have, except for the small loan placed in London last year, an exclusive interest in Bolivia's external debt, and by reason of this interest, not only collect Bolivia's taxes and customs but, through their power to vote the Government's shares in the Banco de la Nación Boliviana, are in a position to control the Bank's future development. One representative of the bankers is director-general of customs; the other is chairman of the Permanent Fiscal Commission and a director of the national bank. North American construction companies, using only American materials, are building Bolivia's railways, sewers and pavements with the proceeds of Bolivian bonds. These conditions, which have a familiar sound in the annals of modern economic imperialism, exist, moreover, in a country where a creole minority of only fifteen percent of the population, under the guise of democracy, rules over a primitive, physically undernourished and psychologically crushed Indian population; where the average density of population is only 2.5 inhabitants per square mile, while the barrenness of one-third of the country and the inaccessible character of the other two-thirds makes a refreshing of the population stock through immigration unlikely for some time to come; and where the chief source of national wealth is a mineral of fluctuating value and an extractive industry so conducted that a lion's share of the profits is exported, never to return to the country, a fact in itself giving the apparent favorable trade balance no reality.

The setting is there, the characters are already on the stage, the dominant motive, a desire for security, is present. Whether the curtain shall be rung up and the signal given to act another scene in the drama, and too often tragedy of modern imperialism, depends upon a set of circumstances which no man can with certainty predict. Battleships and marines can do little by way of persuasion or threat to a nation situated hundreds of miles from the coast and at an elevation of 12,000 feet or more above sea-level—a situation cynically offered as explanation of Mr. Kellogg's interest in providing Bolivia with the port of Arica. Blustering boasts like that made by the former United States minister to Bolivia at the time of the 1920 revolution that a "bluff at the use of force was the only way to deal with these people," though not conducive to friendly relations, are not likely to have very serious consequences. But that subtler kind of imperialism, which has been described in the following words as our variation of the familiar theme, might easily develop from the Bolivian situation: "Lending money to unstable governments, or investing money in unruly countries, has been one of the most widespread features of imperialism, and has usually led to annexations, in European practice, whereas in American practice 'dollar diplomacy' leads to financial receiverships, that is, to the collection of the customs duties of a Haiti or a Santo Domingo by American officials, or to other methods of financial supervision. It may be pointed out in this connection that the American method is more subtle, achieving as it does the desired financial and economic domination, without political annexation and often, as in the case of Cuba, without much impairing political self-government."[20] At the far end of the southern continent another writer has expressed the same idea not so differently: "In olden times imperialism was satisfied with no less than a general levy of the inhabitants of a conquered territory to make them serve as slaves; later on, it took possession of the land, leaving the people a certain autonomy; today it contents itself with taking hold of the sources of wealth, leaving the land and the inhabitants to themselves."[21] To which he might have added, so long as it it quite safe to do so.

APPENDIX

Republic of Bolivia and The Equitable Trust Company of New York

Trust Contract—New York, May 31, 1922

Contract made at the City of New York this 31st day of May, one thousand nine hundred and twenty-two, between the Republic of Bolivia (hereinafter called the "Republic"), party of the first part, and The Equitable Trust Company of New York, a corporation organized under the laws of the State of New York (hereinafter called the "Trustee"), party of the second part;

Witnesseth:

Whereas, the Republic desires to obtain a loan for the purpose of refunding a part of its outstanding indebtedness, of meeting certain maturing obligations, of constructing and equipping certain railways and of constructing highways; and

Whereas, in order to carry out the above purposes, the Republic proposes to create and issue its Bonds to the aggregate principal amount of Thirty-three Million Dollars ($33,000,000) United States gold, to be secured under this contract and as hereinafter stated; and

Whereas, the Republic desires The Equitable Trust Company of New York to act as Trustee under this contract and as Transfer Agent of such Bonds, with the powers and duties hereinafter prescribed.

Now, therefore, in consideration of the premises and of the mutual covenants and undertakings hereinafter contained, the parties hereto covenant and agree to and with each other as follows:

Article First

REPRESENTATIONS BY THE REPUBLIC

The Republic declares and represents:

Section 1. That by virtue of the law of the Congress of the Republic number   of May 24, 1922, the Executive Power of the Republic is duly authorized to conclude the present contract, to issue bonds of the Republic as hereinafter provided, and to secure the same in the manner hereinafter set forth.

Section 2. That all legal and other acts, conditions and things which should have been done or should have happened or existed prior to the issue of the Bonds hereinafter mentioned, have existed, happened or been done as required by the Constitution and laws of Bolivia and strictly in accordance therewith.

Section 3. That all of the properties and revenues mentioned under Article Fourth below belong to the Republic in absolute ownership, and that the same are free and clear of all liens and encumbrances, except as specifically mentioned in said Article, and that the liens and encumbrances thus specifically mentioned will be discharged in the manner hereinafter provided immediately following the execution of this Contract.

Section 4. That it has outstanding the following internal obligations, none of which is secured by any of the funds, revenues and taxes pledged hereunder, namely:

(*a*)	Bank's various accounts	500,000	Bolivianos
(*b*)	Time obligations	5,836,321	"
(*c*)	Foreign bankers	49,125	"
(*d*)	Special railroad guarantees	2,741,479	"
(*e*)	Bank's current accounts	7,318,163	"

Section 5. That the statements, representations and statistics contained in the document annexed hereto entitled "Statistical Information" and made a part hereof as "Schedule A" are true and correct in every particular.

Section 6. That the Republic has never defaulted on any of its external loans.

Article Second

THE BONDS

Section 1. The Bonds shall be known as "Republic of Bolivia External 25-Year Secured Refunding 8% Sinking Fund Gold Bonds". The total amount of Bonds to be issued shall not exceed $33,000,000.

Section 2. The Bonds shall be dated May 1, 1922, and mature May 1, 1947. The definitive bonds shall be of denominations of One thousand Dollars ($1,000) and Five hundred Dollars ($500) each, in such proportions as the Bankers hereinafter mentioned shall determine.

Section 3. The Bonds shall bear interest represented by coupons at the rate of eight percent. (8%) per annum, payable semi-annually on May first and November first of each year. When and as paid the coupons shall be cancelled by the Trustee and delivered to or upon the order of the Minister of Finance.

Section 4. The Bonds, as to principal, premium and interest, shall be payable at the principal office of the Trustee in the City of New York in gold coin of the United States of America of or equal to the present standard of weight and fineness.

Section 5. The Bonds and coupons shall be in the English language and shall be substantially in the forms of the annexed "Schedule B" and "Schedule C" respectively.

The definitive Bonds shall bear the engraved facsimile signatures of the President of the Republic and also of its Minister of Finance, and shall be signed in the City of New York by a special delegate or delegates of the Republic appointed for that purpose. They shall also have affixed thereto or engraved thereupon the seal of the Ministry of Finance of the Republic. The coupons shall bear the facsimile signature of the Minister of Finance of the Republic.

Section 6. The Bonds shall be payable to bearer or, if registered, to the registered holder thereof, with the privilege on the part of the holder, under such regulations as the Trustee may prescribe, to have Bonds registered as to principal and premium. The Republic shall keep with the Trustee in the

City of New York books for such registration and transfer of bonds; and the Trustee is hereby authorized so to register and transfer Bonds therein. After such registration, the principal and premium shall be payable only to the registered owner, but the Bonds may be transferred to another registered owner or may be discharged from registry by being transferred to bearer. The coupons shall, in all cases, be payable to bearer.

SECTION 7. The bearer of any coupon or of any bearer bond, or, if registered, the registered owner of such registered bond, may be deemed and treated by the Republic and the Trustee, and each of them, as absolute owner of such coupon or bond for the purpose of receiving payment thereof, and for all other purposes; and no notice to the contrary shall affect the Republic or the Trustee.

SECTION 8. Each Bond shall bear endorsed thereon a certificate in the English language substantially in the form annexed hereto marked "Schedule D". No Bond shall be valid until such certificate shall have been signed by the Trustee, and such certificate so signed shall be conclusive evidence and the only evidence that the Bond so certified has been duly issued in pursuance of this Contract and that the holder is entitled to the benefits thereof.

SECTION 9. The Loan represented by the Bonds shall constitute and is hereby declared to be a direct liability and obligation of the Republic and a part of the external public debt, irrespective of any security provided hereunder; and the Republic hereby pledges its faith and credit to the due and punctual payment of the principal, premium and interest of the Loan and of all amounts required for or incident to the service of the Loan and for the performance of all undertakings herein contained on its part to be performed.

SECTION 10. In case any Bond, with its coupons, shall become mutilated or be destroyed or lost, the Republic may execute and deliver to the Trustee and thereupon the Trustee, at the request of the Minister of Finance of the Republic, shall authenticate and deliver a new Bond of like amount, tenor and date, bearing the same number and designation, in exchange or substitution for and upon surrender and cancellation of the mutilated Bond and its coupons, or in lieu of and substitution for the Bond and its coupons so destroyed or lost; but in case of a destroyed or lost Bond, such new Bond shall be issued only in the discretion of the Republic and of the Trustee, upon receipt by the Republic and by the Trustee of evidence satisfactory to them of the destruction or loss of such Bond and its coupons, and upon receipt also of indemnity satisfactory to said Republic and Trustee.

SECTION 11. As and when from time to time requested by Stifel-Nicolaus Investment Company, Spencer Trask & Co. and The Equitable Trust Company of New York (hereinafter called the Bankers) the Republic shall make or authorize to be made application for official listing of the Bonds upon the New York Stock Exchange and upon any other Exchange, and shall prepare and sign the necessary prospectuses and other documents, and otherwise comply with the requirements of such Exchanges. The Republic shall do such acts and execute such agreements as may be necessary to obtain the official listing of the Bonds on such Exchanges.

SECTION 12. Pending the engraving and execution of definitive bonds, the Republic shall execute and deliver to the Trustee one or more temporary printed or typewritten Bonds substantially of the tenor of the definitive bonds, except that not more than one coupon shall be attached thereto and except that said temporary bonds need not bear the engraved fac-simile signature of the President of the Republic or of its Minister of Finance but shall bear the seal of the Ministry of Finance of the Republic or of the Consul General of Bolivia in New York affixed or printed thereon and shall be signed by the Consul General of Bolivia in the City of New York who has been duly authorized for that purpose. Temporary bonds may be issued in such form and in such denomination or denominations as the Bankers may determine. Each temporary bond shall have printed upon its face "Temporary Bond Exchangeable for Engraved Bonds" and shall be duly authenticated and delivered by the Trustee in the same manner and with like effect as the definitive bonds. Temporary bonds shall be exchangeable for other temporary bonds of equal denomination, or of different denominations if approved by the Bankers, and for definitive bonds when engraved and executed; and upon such exchange the temporary bonds shall forthwith be cancelled by the Trustee and, having been so cancelled, shall be physically destroyed in the presence of representatives of the Trustee and of the Republic. Said representatives shall execute duplicate certificates attesting the destruction, and shall deliver one counterpart thereof to the Republic and one counterpart to the Trustee. Until so exchanged, such temporary bond or bonds shall in all respects be secured under this Contract, and when and as payable interest shall be paid to the bearer of the coupon, if represented by a coupon; if not represented by a coupon such interest shall be payable to the bearer of the bond or bonds on presentation thereof and such payment shall be noted on the Bond or Bonds. Without unreasonable delay, the Republic shall cause definitive bonds in engraved form to be duly executed and delivered to the Trustee, to be exchanged for such temporary bonds upon surrender thereof to the Trustee.

SECTION 13. The Bonds shall always be exempt as to principal, premium and interest from any and all imposts, contributions or other taxes now or hereafter levied or collected by or within the Republic, whether national, departmental, municipal or of any other nature, and whether they be on the Bonds or the income derived therefrom or on the holder thereof by reason of his ownership or possession of such Bonds, and whether the latter be a citizen of a state friendly or hostile to the Republic of Bolivia. This Contract and all other documents, whether public or private, and whether executed in the Republic of Bolivia or elsewhere under the terms of this Contract or in execution thereof, shall also be exempt from the payment of all stamp or other duties and taxes imposed by the Republic to which this contract or such documents would otherwise be subject.

SECTION 14. Any Bonds not presented for payment on the date of their maturity or not presented for redemption when called for that purpose shall, after the lapse of thirty years from and after the date of such maturity or the date fixed in the call for redemption, as the case may be, cease to be an obligation of the Republic; and, upon presentation to the Republic after the expiration of such period shall be cancelled and destroyed and the holder thereof shall have no rights whatever under this instrument or by reason of such Bonds. Any coupons not presented for payment on the date of their maturity shall, after the lapse of ten years from and after the date of such maturity, cease to be an obligation of the Republic, and no holder thereof shall have any rights whatsoever under this instrument or by reason of such coupons; and, upon presentation to the Republic after the expiration of such period, such coupons shall be cancelled and destroyed.

For the purposes aforesaid, the Republic grants to the holders of the Bonds and coupons the periods of thirty years and ten years respectively from the dates of their respective maturities or redemption; and hereby renounces any law which authorizes the Republic to refuse recognition of such additional periods; but after such respective periods shall have elapsed, the Bonds and coupons respectively shall be of no avail whatever as an indebtedness of the Republic. The Trustee accepts the above concession and renunciation on behalf of the bondholders.

Article Third

INTEREST AND PAYMENT AND REDEMPTION OF BONDS

Section 1. The Bonds shall be payable at maturity at par. They shall not be redeemable prior to May 1, 1937: on and after that date they shall be redeemable at the option of the Republic at 105% of their par value and accrued interest as a whole, but not in part (except through the operation of the sinking fund) on any interest payment date.

Section 2. Until the principal, premium and interest on said Bonds shall have been fully paid or provided for as hereinafter stipulated, the Republic shall pay or cause to be paid to the Trustee in each half year in New York in the manner hereinafter in Article Sixth and Section 3 of Article Eighth provided on or before the first days of April and October of each year, beginning with October, 1922, a sum equal to five percent (5%) of the par value of all Bonds which may theretofore have been authenticated and delivered hereunder; and in addition to said sum such further sum as may be required to cover the compensation of the Trustee in connection with the service of the Loan. The first mentioned sum thus to be provided, *i. e.*, the 5% of the par value of bonds authenticated and delivered, shall be applied by the Trustee: first, to set aside for the payment of such interest an amount equal to the interest due on all outstanding Bonds on the next interest-payment date; and second, the balance, at any time after amounts in excess of said interest requirements shall have been received by the Trustee, as follows:

(*a*) To the purchase for the sinking fund in the open market or by tender, either at one time or from time to time (but not before September 1, 1922) as the Trustee in its absolute discretion may deem best, of Bonds of this issue at prices not exceeding 105% of their par value and accrued interest, exclusive of necessary brokerage charges which shall be considered as expenses of the Trustee;

(*b*) If, in the course of any semester of any Bond year (that is to say, from May 1st to October 31st of the same year, or from November 1st to April 30th of the succeeding year), the Trustee should be unable to purchase Bonds as aforesaid in the open market or by tender at not exceeding 105% and accrued interest, then and in that case the unexpended balance in the hands of the Trustee at the end of such semester shall be retained by the Trustee to be later applied in the same manner to such purchases whenever market conditions shall permit. Whenever such unexpended balance, together with future additions thereto of similar unexpended semester balances, including interest earned on such balances, shall amount to $500,000, that sum shall continue to be held by the Trustee for the purposes aforesaid, that is to say, for the purchase of Bonds as and when the market shall permit at not exceeding 105% and accrued interest. Whenever and as often as such fund shall be reduced below $500,000 by reason of purchases made as aforesaid (not, however, after May 1, 1937), it shall again be increased up to $500,000 by the addition thereto of subsequent unexpended semester balances.

(*c*) After said reserve fund of $500,000 shall have been accumulated, all future unexpended semester balances up to and including the semester ending April 30, 1937, except in so far as the same may be required to reinstate said $500,000 fund as above provided, shall, at the end of each semester, be returned to the Republic by the Trustee by the placing of such amount to the credit of the Minister of Finance of the Republic in the Banking Department of The Equitable Trust Company of New York.

(*d*) From and after May 1, 1937, said fund of $500,000 shall continue to be used for the purchase of bonds as aforesaid whenever market conditions shall permit, provided, however, that said fund shall not be so expended at any time when the Trustee shall have on hand available for the purchase of bonds, at least $5,000 out of amounts received by it in respect of subsequent semesters in excess of the interest requirements of such semesters. Said $500,000 fund, if depleted in this manner after May 1, 1937, shall not thereafter be again accumulated.

Any portion of said fund remaining unexpended at maturity shall be applied to the *pro rata* payment of bonds at par or in the event the bonds should be declared due as provided in Section 12 of this Article, to their payment *pro rata* at 105% of their par value and accrued interest.

SECTION 3. Any balances, other than the reserve fund above mentioned, which may remain in the hands of the Trustee on April 1, 1938, or on April 1st of each succeeding year to and including the year 1946, after setting aside as above provided the amount required for the payment of the next semi-annual interest instalment, shall be applied by the Trustee on the first day of May next succeeding to the redemption at 105% of Bonds then outstanding.

SECTION 4. The particular Bonds to be redeemed on each occasion as aforesaid shall be determined by lot, drawings to be made at the office of the Trustee in the Borough of Manhattan, City of New York. Such drawings shall be held under the direction of a representative of the Trustee and, at the option of the Minister of Finance of the Republic, in the presence of such representative of the Republic appointed for that purpose as may appear at the drawing. Drawings for Bonds to be redeemed as aforesaid shall be held not later than twenty-five days prior to the date of redemption as set forth in Section 3 of this Article.

SECTION 5. Forthwith after every drawing to determine the particular Bonds to be redeemed as aforesaid, the Trustee shall give notice in writing to the Republic of the Bonds which have been drawn for redemption and shall also give to the holders of the Bonds so drawn like notice in the manner hereinafter specified. Said notice to the holders of Bonds shall be given by an advertisement to be published not less than once a week for three successive calendar weeks in a newspaper of general circulation in the City of New York to be selected by the Trustee, in each instance, upon any day of the week and in any such newspaper. The first publication shall be made not less than twenty-two days prior to the date fixed for the redemption of said Bonds. If the holder of any registered Bond so drawn shall have filed with the Trustee a written request that notice of the result of any such drawing be mailed to him at an address given in such request, notice shall be so mailed to him by the Trustee on or before the date of the first publication of notice as aforesaid. The aforesaid notice to holders of Bonds shall state the number of the Bond or Bonds drawn and the date and place for surrender and payment.

SECTION 6. On the date so specified for redemption the holder of the Bond or Bonds to be redeemed shall surrender the same to the Trustee, with all coupons maturing after the date on which they are to be so redeemed; and upon such surrender the Trustee shall cause to be paid to the holder of such Bonds out of the funds available for that purpose the amount payable to him in respect of such redemption. Any Bonds not so surrendered shall cease to bear interest after said redemption date and all coupons for interest subsequent to said date shall be null and void.

SECTION 7. All Bonds purchased as provided in this Article and all Bonds redeemed as aforesaid, together with all coupons attached thereto, shall forthwith be cancelled by the Trustee, and having been so cancelled shall be physically destroyed in the presence of representatives of the Trustee and of the Republic. Said representatives shall execute duplicate certificates attesting such destruction, and shall deliver one counterpart thereof to the Republic and one counterpart to the Trustee.

SECTION 8. The Republic shall have the right to redeem all, but not a part (except as hereinbefore provided), of the Bonds outstanding on any interest-payment date on or after May 1, 1937 at 105% and accrued interest upon not less than 90 days notice to the holders of Bonds given in the manner provided in Section 5 of this Article for twelve consecutive weeks and upon the deposit with the Trustee, prior to date of the first publication of said notice, of the funds required for such redemption. All Bonds outstanding on May 1, 1947, shall be paid at par and accrued interest.

SECTION 9. Upon the payment in full of all bonds as provided in this Article, or upon the deposit with the Trustee of a sum sufficient under this Article to redeem all such Bonds, or sufficient to cover the payment of all such Bonds at maturity and the interest thereon up to such maturity, and upon payment of all other sums required by this Contract to be paid by the Republic, this Contract shall cease and determine, except that the Trustee shall hold said sum paid as aforesaid and use the same either (1) for the redemption of all outstanding Bonds in the manner provided in this Article for redemption of Bonds; or (2) for the payment at maturity of all outstanding Bonds, and the interest on such Bonds from time to time as the coupons representing such interest shall mature, and for the payment of all other sums required by this Contract to be paid by the Republic; and any securities or cash then held by the Trustee not required for the payment or redemption of said Bonds or the other payments required to be made hereunder, shall be delivered to or upon the order of the Minister of Finance of the Republic.

SECTION 10. All the usual expenses incurred in good faith by the Trustee in connection with the drawing or purchase of the Bonds under this Article or for the payment of the principal, premium or interest of the Bonds, or otherwise in the service of the loan, including counsel fees, the cost of cabling and the publication of notices et cetera, shall be paid by the Republic as herein provided.

SECTION 11. The mortgages, pledges, liens and other charges in favor of the Bonds shall be cancelled upon the petition of the Republic after the Republic shall have placed in the hands of the Trustee at such times and on such conditions as it may do so, in compliance with this Contract, the necessary funds for the total redemption or payment at maturity of all the Bonds and the payment of the interest thereon.

All shares of stock then held by the Trustee under the provisions of Section 2 of Article Fourth below shall thereupon be delivered by the Trustee to or upon the order of the Minister of Finance of the Republic.

SECTION 12. In case default shall be made in any of the payments called for by this Contract, or in case default shall be made in the due performance of any of the covenants of the Republic hereunder, and such last mentioned default shall continue for a period of thirty days, after written notice thereof and demand of performance by the Trustee, the Trustee may, and if thereunto requested by the holders of not less than 10% in amount of the Bonds issued and outstanding hereunder at the time of such default, shall declare due and payable immediately all Bonds then outstanding, and the Republic shall thereupon pay said Bonds at 105% of their par value, plus interest accrued thereon.

ARTICLE FOURTH

SECURITY

SECTION 1. In order that the Loan represented by the Bonds to be issued as aforesaid shall be secured by a first lien or pledge and charge upon all of the funds, revenues and taxes hereinafter mentioned, the Republic shall immediately

(*a*) Retire and cancel all "External Bonds of the Republic of Bolivia of 1922" at present outstanding by exchanging therefor Bonds of this issue and also cause to be cancelled and physically destroyed $4,000,000 par value of said Bonds heretofore issued but not delivered and at present deposited with the Guaranty Trust Company of New York, thereby releasing from lien the funds, revenues and taxes which at present secure those Bonds;

(*b*) Purchase and/or call for redemption all outstanding Bonds of the Republic (hereinafter called "Bonds of the Morgan Loan") issued under contract dated December 30, 1908 between the Republic and J. P. Morgan & Company of New York, and cancel all Bonds of that loan, thereby releasing from lien the funds, revenues and taxes which at present secure the same. To assure the retirement of said Bonds of the Morgan Loan, the Republic shall deposit with the Trustee at the time of the authentication and delivery of the Bonds mentioned in subdivision (*a*) of Section 1 of Article Eighth hereof £284,600 par value of said Morgan Bonds which are to be surrendered to J. P. Morgan & Company, as hereinafter in Section 4 of Article Eighth provided, and pending such surrender are to be held by the Trustee as part of the security hereunder.

(*c*) Purchase and/or call for redemption all outstanding Import Customs Notes of 1915, Export Customs Notes of 1920 and Customs Notes of 1921, thereby terminating the right of the holders of those notes to tender the same in payment of customs duties and releasing from lien the funds, revenues and taxes which at present secure those Notes.

(*d*) Pay all obligations owing by the Republic to local banks at La Paz which are secured by the Republic's shares of stock of Banco de la Nación Boliviana, thereby releasing from lien the shares which at present secure such obligations.

SECTION 2. Subject to the liens and charges at present existing in favor of said "External Bonds of the Republic of Bolivia of 1922" and of said bonds of the Morgan Loan and of said Customs Notes and of said obligations to local banks at La Paz, (all of which liens and charges the Republic shall forthwith discharge as aforesaid) the Republic hereby affects and encumbers with a first lien or pledge and charge in favor of the Trustee the following shares of stock, funds, revenues and taxes as security for the full payment of the principal, premium and interest of the Bonds, and of all other expenses and amounts required for or incident to this Contract or to the service of the Loan, to wit:

(*a*) All of the shares, not less than 114,000, of the Banco de la Nación Boliviana belonging to the Republic and which the Republic represents are sufficient at present to control said Bank. For the purpose of constituting a pledge of said shares, the Republic shall deliver to the Trustee hereunder as hereinafter provided either bearer certificates or certificates of stock duly endorsed in blank representing all of the shares referred to and also the certificate representing said shares now in banks at La Paz as security for the bank loans above-mentioned. In case the capital stock of the Banco de la Nación Boliviana should be increased at any time during the life of this Loan, the Republic shall acquire such proportion of the additional shares as may be necessary to maintain the said control; the shares so acquired shall immediately thereafter be pledged as security for this Loan; and bearer certificates or certificates of stock, duly endorsed in blank, representing such additional shares, shall immediately thereafter be delivered to the Trustee hereunder;

(*b*) All revenues representing dividends payable upon said shares during the life of this Loan;

(*c*) The tax upon mining claims or concessions (patentes mineras);

(*d*) The revenues received by the Republic from alcohol monopoly (monopolio de alcohol);

(*e*) 90% of revenues received by the Republic from the tobacco monoply (monopolio de tabacos);

(*f*) The tax on corporations other than mining and banking (impuesto sobre dividendos de sociedades anónimas no mineras);

(*g*) The tax upon the net income of banks (impuesto sobre utilidades bancarias);

(*h*) The tax on interest on mortgage cedulas (impuesto sobre la renta de letras hipotecarias);

(*i*) The tax on the net profits of mining companies (impuesto sobre utilidad de empresas mineras);

(*j*) All import duties (derechos de importaciones);

(*k*) Surcharge on import duties (recargo derechos de importaciones);

(*l*) All export duties (derechos de exportaciones).

If and when the $4,000,000 of bonds referred to in paragraph (*b*) of section 2 of Article Eighth below, or any part thereof shall be authenticated and delivered, all funds, revenues and taxes now or hereafter allocated by special laws to the construction of the Potosí-Sucre Railroad, shall thereupon become pledged as further security for all of the bonds of the present issue, without the necessity of further instruments or of any action on the part of the Republic.

SECTION 3. The lien upon the dividends, funds, revenues and taxes referred to in the preceding section shall be considered as a pledge of said dividends, funds, revenues and taxes and any precept or provisions of law requiring that such pledge remain in the possession of the pledgee or of a third party are hereby expressly waived, it being agreed that such pledge shall attach to said dividends, funds, revenues and taxes from the moment that the same shall be collected by the Republic.

The shares of stock of the Banco de la Nación Boliviana deposited hereunder so long as there shall be no default hereunder, shall be voted by the Republic in such manner as the Executive may deem proper not inconsistent with the provisions of this contract. From time to time in case such shares shall have been transferred into the name of the Trustee or its nominee, the Trustee, upon the written or cabled request of the Minister of Finance of the Republic, shall execute and deliver, or cause to be executed and delivered, to said Minister, or to his nominee named in such request, appropriate powers of attorney or proxy to vote such stock or to execute a waiver or consent with respect to such stock for such purpose, or purposes, as may be specified in such request, except that every such power of attorney or proxy may be limited so as to provide in effect that the powers thereby conferred do not include any power to vote for or to authorize a consent to any act or thing inconsistent with the provisions of this contract. In case of default hereunder, they shall be voted by the Trustee and the Trustee, at its option, may, and if so requested by ten percent (10%) of the holders of Bonds then outstanding shall, cause such of said shares as may not be bearer shares to be transferred into its own name or into the name of its nominee or nominees.

The Trustee may receive delivery of certificates representing the above mentioned shares in Paris, or elsewhere, and may hold the same in Paris, or in the United States, or elsewhere, in any safe deposit or banking institution selected by it. All costs and charges in connection with the custody or shipment of said certificates shall be paid by the Republic. It may surrender the same for the purpose of having them exchanged for certificates of different denominations or certificates in the name of the Minister of Finance of the Republic, or of his nominee or in the name of the Trustee or its nominee. All certificates in the name of the Minister of Finance of the Republic, or his nominee, shall be forthwith deposited with the Trustee, endorsed in blank or accompanied by proper instruments of assignment and transfer in blank. The Trustee shall not, however, be required at any time to accept a certificate for any shares of said stock, or to cause or permit a transfer thereof to be made to it if, in the opinion of the Trustee, such action would subject it to the risk of any liability.

So long as there shall be no default hereunder, the Republic shall be entitled to receive and collect all dividends upon the pledged shares and the Trustee, from time to time, shall deliver, upon the written or cabled order of the Minister of Finance, current dividend warrants, if any, pertaining to the said shares, or suitable assignments and orders in favor of said Minister, for the payment of such dividends and shall likewise pay over any sums collected by the Trustee as such dividends.

If and so long as the Republic shall be in default hereunder, the Trustee shall revoke all such orders and collect and receive all dividends on the above mentioned shares and the Republic authorizes the Banco de la Nación Boliviana, in such case, to pay such dividends to the Trustee, and all dividends so received by the Trustee shall be applied to the service of the loan. Anything herein contained to the contrary notwithstanding, it is hereby expressly agreed that the Republic shall not be entitled to receive any dividend, other than a cash dividend paid out of earnings accrued after May 1, 1922, or any sum paid upon the liquidation or dissolution of the Banco de la Nación Boliviana upon any share of said stock at the time pledged under this contract.

The Trustee shall be entitled to assume that any cash dividend received by it is paid out of earnings accrued since May 1, 1922, unless and until notified in writing to the contrary by the Bankers and, in the absence of any such written notice, it shall be conclusively presumed, as between the Trustee and the bondholders, that the Trustee, in making any payments thereof to the Republic acted in good faith.

In case any dividends shall be paid on any share of said stock at the time deposited hereunder, other than a cash dividend paid out of earnings accrued since May 1. 1922, or, in case of the liquidation or dissolution of the Banco de la Nación Boliviana any sums shall be paid upon any such share of stock, then in every such case, any such sum shall be paid to the Trustee and, when received by the Trustee, shall be applied to the purchase and/or redemption of bonds, as provided in Article Third hereof.

SECTION 4. As further security hereunder, the Republic hereby constitutes first mortgages and liens upon all the properties and earnings of the railroads constructed and to be constructed from Villazón to Atocha and from Potosí to Sucre, including their franchises, concessions, equipment and other appurtenances, and upon the net income of said railroads after deducting the expenses of operation.

The Republic hereby declares that said mortgages and liens are constituted by virtue of the present Contract and that no record thereof is necessary and that no further mortgages or other instruments are required to be executed or recorded in connection therewith. The Republic furthermore declares that said mortgages include the railroads and all their lands, servitudes, buildings, rails, bridges, cars, locomotives, telegraph and telephone lines, equipment and all other things of every kind and description in any manner relating to the same, and all other properties and appurtenances belonging to said railroads or for use in connection therewith, whether constructed and/or acquired or to be constructed and/or acquired, and as the same shall be constructed and/or acquired without the necessity of the execution or recording of any other instruments.

In case said rolling stock, equipment or any other things belonging to or used in connection with said railroads, or either of them, should be held or considered to be personal property not subject to mortgage, there is hereby constituted thereon a special lien and any provisions of law in conflict therewith are hereby waived, and it is further agreed that in the enforcement and execution of such special lien there shall be observed the procedure laid down in the Code of Civil Procedure of the Republic of Bolivia with reference to the foreclosure of mortgages upon real estate.

In case the said railroads, or either of them, should be sold as a result of the foreclosure of the mortgage or the enforcement of said lien, the purchaser at such sale, and his heirs, personal representatives, successors and assigns, shall have, and the Republic hereby grants to him and them, the right to operate the said railroad for a period of 99 years from the date of such purchase, with all the rights and privileges accorded by and subject to the provisions of the General Law of Railroads of the Republic of Bolivia of October 3, 1910, and its Regulations, and any laws amendatory thereof, approved prior to the date of this contract. In that case, the purchaser or any company that may be organized by the purchaser for the operation of said railroads, or either of them, as also the entire business and properties thereof, shall, in respect to said railroads be free from taxes and imposts of all kinds.

SECTION 5. If, during any fiscal year, the proceeds derived from the pledged dividends, funds, taxes and revenues should be less than one and one-half times the amount required for the annual service of the Loan, the Republic shall immediately pledge as further security for said Loan such additional taxes or revenues other than all present or future taxes on petroleum and on petroleum claims and concessions as may be approved by the Bankers to an amount sufficient upon the basis of the collection of such additional taxes or revenues during said fiscal year to increase the proceeds of all pledged dividends, funds, taxes and revenues to the proportion stated. If, during any fiscal year subsequent to the pledging of such additional taxes and revenues, all of the pledged dividends, funds, taxes and revenues (including such additional taxes and revenues), should exceed three times the amount required for the annual service of the Loan, said additional taxes and revenues shall, at the request of the Republic, be released by the Trustee from said pledge. The sums required for the above purposes shall be calculated upon the basis of the average rate of exchange in La Paz on New York for dollar sight drafts for the twelve months immediately preceding, or the rate current at the time of such additional pledge or request for release, whichever shall be more favorable to the dollar.

SECTION 6. As further security hereunder, the Republic agrees that so long as any Bonds remain unpaid or unprovided for, the liens and charges herein created upon the revenues of the Republic shall have priority, whether as to capital, interest or redemption of said Bonds, over all future charges or liens created on the said revenues; and that no lien or charge shall be created upon such revenues which shall take precedence of or which shall be on a parity with the said Bonds, or which in any manner whatsoever shall decrease, alienate, affect, impair or prejudice the security hereunder; and the Government will not consent to any act which in any manner whatsoever shall diminish or impair the security provided for by this contract.

SECTION 7. To further secure the Loan and to protect the credit of the Republic, the Republic shall not, prior to December 5, 1924, contract any external loan without the previous approval of the Minister of Finance of the Republic and of the Bankers. After that date and so long as any Bonds of the present Loan shall remain outstanding, the Republic shall not contract any further external loan unless

(*a*) The taxes and revenues pledged for the service of the present Loan shall, for a period of two years immediately preceding such new Loan, have annually produced at least one and one-half times the amount required for the service of the present Loan; and

(*b*) During each of said two years, the Republic shall have raised sufficient revenues to meet all of its ordinary general expenses, exclusive of capital investment, without borrowing therefor or without selling capital assets.

The sums required for the purpose mentioned in (*a*) above shall be calculated upon the basis of the average rate of exchange at La Paz on New York for dollar sight drafts for the two years immediately preceding, or the current rate at the time, whichever shall be more favorable to the dollar.

A statement in writing addressed to the Bankers, signed by the Minister of Finance of the Republic and countersigned by the Permanent Fiscal Commission hereinafter mentioned shall be conclusive, and the sole evidence of compliance with the conditions set forth in subdivisions (*a*) and (*b*) above.

SECTION 8. The dividends, funds, revenues, taxes and property hereinbefore mentioned are mortgaged and pledged as security for the entire indebtedness and for all the Bonds secured hereby. The Trustee may, in its discretion, enforce any of its rights, remedies and powers against all such property and revenues simultaneously or against any of them successively, until all of said Bonds shall be paid in full. No remedy, right or power conferred upon or reserved to the Trustee is intended to be exclusive of any other remedy, right or power, but each and every such remedy, right or power shall be cumulative and shall be in addition to every other remedy, right, power or action now or hereafter conferred upon it by law. The delivery of the Bonds shall be conclusive upon the Republic as receipt of value therefor, and the Republic will not plead in any proceeding or action failure of consideration for their issuance and delivery.

Article Fifth

PERMANENT FISCAL COMMISSION

Section 1. So long as any Bonds remain outstanding, beginning not later than August 1, 1922, the collection of all taxes, revenues and income of the Nation shall be supervised and fiscalized by the Permanent Fiscal Commission, the creation of which has been authorized by law No. .... of March 27, 1922.

The President of the Republic shall appoint the three Commissioners; of these, two to be appointed upon recommendation of the Bankers. At any time, at the request of the Bankers or by agreement between the President and the Bankers, the President will remove either or both of the Commissioners recommended by them, and any vacancy or vacancies thus created or otherwise occurring, shall be filled in the same manner as in the case of the original appointments.

Section 2. The Permanent Fiscal Commission shall exercise all the other powers conferred upon it by the law of March 27, 1922, and by the Regulation of that law to be issued by the Executive. For that purpose it shall select such assistants and employees as it shall consider necessary, provided that the total annual expenses of the Commission, excluding the compensation of the Commissioners, their allowance for living expenses and their travelling expenses, shall not exceed one-half of one percent (½%) of the amounts collected, or such other reasonable limit as may from time to time be agreed upon by the Minister of Finance and the Bankers. The compensation of the Commissioners and their allowances for living expenses shall be agreed upon between the Republic and the Bankers and may be changed from time to time by agreement between the Minister of Finance and the Bankers. The total cost of the Commission shall constitute a part of the service of the loan and shall be included in the amounts to be deposited monthly with the Banco de la Nación Boliviana as provided in Section 2, Article Sixth of this Contract.

SECTION 3. The Commission shall make its own rules which shall be approved by the President; it shall act by majority vote; and shall elect as its Chairman and Chief Executive one of the two Commissioners who shall have been recommended by the Bankers.

SECTION 4. In addition to its other duties, the Commission shall make a thorough examination of and report upon the finances and resources of the Republic, and the methods of collecting and disposing of the national revenues. Such reports, with the recommendations of the Commission, shall be presented to the President of the Republic and to the Bankers.

SECTION 5. So long as any Bonds of this Loan remain outstanding, the Chairman of the Commission shall be elected a member of the Board of Directors of the Banco de la Nación Boliviana, and the Republic shall take such action as may be necessary to secure his election and continuance in office as such.

ARTICLE SIXTH

DEPOSIT OF AMOUNTS REQUIRED FOR SERVICE OF LOAN AND REMITTANCES TO TRUSTEE

SECTION 1. The Republic shall forthwith from the proceeds of sale of the bonds to be issued as hereinafter in Article Eighth, Section 1, paragraph (*a*) provided, pay to the Trustee the sum of $1,200,000 being 5% of the $24,000,000 of bonds to be presently authenticated and delivered hereunder and accordingly the sum required under Section 2 of Article Third above to be paid to the Trustee in respect to the first semester of the first Bond year.

SECTION 2. The Republic shall cause the collector or collectors or other officials charged with the collection of the dividends, funds, revenues and taxes given as security hereunder, to deposit the same as and when collected, beginning on September 1, 1922, in a special account with the Banco de la Nación Boliviana (hereinafter called the "Bank"). The deposit thus constituted shall be for the benefit of holders of bonds and of the Trustee and is hereby agreed upon as the method by which the liens, pledges and charges constituted hereunder shall be made effective. The moneys to be deposited as aforesaid shall be kept separate and apart from all other funds of the Republic and shall be dealt with in the manner hereinafter provided. The deposits referred to shall continue to be made during each month until the sums deposited during such month shall equal one-twelfth of the amount required for the annual service of the Loan, including Trustee's fees but not the Trustee's expenses which shall be paid as provided in Section 2 of Article Ninth: thereafter all further dividends, funds, revenues and taxes collected during such month shall be retained by the Republic, and shall be free from any lien hereunder. If the amounts collected from the pledged revenues and deposited as aforesaid during any month should be less than one-twelfth of the amount required for the annual service of the Loan, including the Trustee's compensation, the Republic shall, on the last day of such month, provide the deficit out of its general revenues by depositing the same with the Bank in the special account above mentioned.

SECTION 3. On or before the first day of October 1922, and monthly thereafter, the Bank shall remit to the Trustee in New York the sums deposited with it as aforesaid during the preceding month (excepting the compensation and expenses of the Commissioners referred to in Section 2 of Article Fifth which shall be paid in the manner agreed upon from time to time by the Republic and the Bankers), so that the entire amount required for the semi-annual service of the Loan, including the Trustee's compensation, shall be received by the Trustee in New York not less than one month before the semi-annual interest payment dates. The cost of remittance shall be paid by the Republic.

ARTICLE SEVENTH

DEFAULTS AND REMEDIES

SECTION 1. In case default shall be made in the payment of any sums payable hereunder or default shall be made in the due performance of any of the other covenants of the Republic hereunder, and such last mentioned default shall continue for a period of thirty days after written notice thereof and demand of performance, the Trustee may, and if thereunto requested by the holders of ten percent (10%) in amount of the Bonds issued and then outstanding, and if indemnified to its satisfaction for its liability, costs and expenses in so doing, shall proceed to enforce the security hereunder.

SECTION 2. In the event referred to in Section 1 above the Trustee if indemnified as aforesaid shall proceed to sell the shares of stock of the Banco de la Nación Boliviana pledged hereunder. Such sale shall be at public auction at such place in the City of New York and at such time and upon such terms as the Trustee may specify. Notice of any such sale shall state the time when and the place where the same is to be held, and shall contain a brief general description of the securities to be sold. It shall be published twice a week for two successive weeks prior to such sale in a daily newspaper published in the City of New York, and a copy of said notice shall, at least two weeks prior to the date of sale, be sent to the Republic as hereinafter provided.

The Trustee shall have power in its discretion to adjourn any such sale from time to time as to the whole or any part of the shares to be sold, and if so adjourned shall have power to make such sale upon the date to which the adjournment is had without further notice of the time or place to which the sale may be so adjourned.

Upon completion of any such sale or sales, the Trustee shall transfer and deliver to the purchaser or purchasers thereof such of the shares of stock as shall have been sold, and the same shall thereupon be freed and discharged from the pledge and lien hereby created. The Trustee and its successors are hereby appointed true and lawful attorney or attorneys irrevocable of the Republic, in its name to make, execute and deliver to such purchaser or purchasers such good and sufficient assignments, transfers or other instruments as may be necessary or proper to vest in such purchaser or purchasers full and complete title and ownership of and to the shares of stock so sold.

The receipt of the Trustee for the purchase money shall be sufficient discharge for the purchaser or purchasers of any of said shares for his or their purchase money.

SECTION 3. In the event referred to in Section 1 above

the Trustee if indemnified as aforesaid shall proceed in the manner and to the extent provided by the laws of the Republic to foreclose the mortgages referred to in Section 4 of Article Fourth above. Whenever the Trustee shall institute such foreclosure actions or any other suits or proceedings in any court or before any official of the Republic of Bolivia for the purpose of enforcing any of the rights, remedies or powers conferred upon the Trustee by this Contract, it shall not be obliged to present any of the Bonds issued hereunder, it being hereby agreed that the presentation of this Contract alone shall be sufficient.

For the purposes aforesaid the Trustee shall itself alone be considered the creditor, and the Republic hereby covenants that it will in no case, nor upon any pretext whatever, object to the right of the Trustee to appear or to act as such creditor.

SECTION 4. In case of any sale of shares of stock as provided in Section 2 above, and/or in case of any sale of said railroads, or of either of them, the Trustee, or any holder of Bonds hereunder, or any other person, may bid for and may purchase the property sold, or any part thereof, and the purchaser or purchasers shall have the right to make payment of the purchase price by delivery of Bonds and unpaid and unmatured interest coupons, except so far as such purchase price may be required to be paid in cash for the purpose of meeting the costs and expenses of such sale and of the proceedings resulting therein. Such Bonds and coupons, shall, except as aforesaid, be received in payment of said purchase price to an amount equal to the sum which would be received in respect thereof upon the distribution of the proceeds of sale. In case the amount so payable shall be less than the amount due thereon, said Bonds and coupons shall be returned after being stamped to show partial payments.

SECTION 5. The proceeds of any sale made as aforesaid shall be applied by the Trustee as follows:

First: To the payment of the costs and expenses of such sale and of all proceedings resulting therein or connected therewith, including a reasonable compensation to the Trustee, its agents, attorneys and counsel, and all expenses, liabilities and advances made or incurred by the

Trustee in the conduct and enforcement of the rights and duties hereby conferred upon it and of the trusts hereby created;

Second: To the payment of the whole amount of principal, premium and interest which shall then be due and unpaid upon Bonds then outstanding with interest at eight percent (8%) per annum on the overdue instalments of interest; and if such proceeds should be insufficient to pay the full amount so due and unpaid, then to the payment thereof ratably without preference of any bond or coupon over any other, and without preference of principal over interest or of interest over principal; and

Third: To the payment of the surplus, if any, to the Republic or to whosoever shall be lawfully entitled to receive the same.

If the proceeds of said sale or sales shall be sufficient to pay both the overdue interest and interest thereon and the principal and premium on all outstanding Bonds, then upon such payment of interest, principal and premium such Bonds shall be cancelled.

If the proceeds of said sale or sales shall be insufficient to meet all of the above payments, then upon partial payment thereof the same shall be noted upon each Bond by the Trustee, and thereafter the principal, premium and interest due and payable on each Bond shall be reduced by the amount of such partial payment, and proper notation shall also be made on all unmatured coupons, reducing the amount of interest in proportion to the amount of principal and premium of the Bonds to which such coupons appertain.

SECTION 6. The Trustee shall give notice in the manner provided in Section 8 of Article Third hereof of its intention to apply the proceeds of such sale or sales to the total or partial payment of the Bonds and of the premium and interest thereon, as the case may be and shall in said notice fix a date and place for such application of proceeds; such notice having been given, interest on said Bonds shall from and after the date fixed for such application, if a total payment, cease, or, if a partial payment, be calculated only on the reduced principal, anything in the tenor of such coupons to the contrary notwithstanding.

SECTION 7. In case application as aforesaid of the proceeds of any sale or sales hereunder shall result in a partial payment on account of the principal or of the principal, premium and interest of the Bonds, the Trustee shall be entitled to enforce payment of and to receive all amounts remaining due and unpaid upon any and all of the Bonds outstanding as and when the same mature for the benefit of the holders thereof against any or all of the other revenues given as security by the Republic under the terms of this Contract and to continue to apply such revenues until all of the expenses and compensation of the Trustee and its agents, representatives and counsel, and the principal, premium and interest of all such outstanding Bonds shall be fully paid.

ARTICLE EIGHTH

ISSUE OF BONDS

SECTION 1. The Republic shall forthwith execute $26,-000,000 par value of Bonds and deposit the same with the Trustee to be disposed of as follows:

(*a*) Upon the written or cabled order of the Minister of Finance of the Republic, the Trustee shall authenticate and deliver $18,460,000 par value of said Bonds to or upon the order of the Bankers, but only upon the deposit with the Trustee of the sum of $10,600,000 to be disposed of as hereinafter provided.

(*b*) Upon the delivery to the Trustee of a certificate of the Guaranty Trust Company of New York certifying that said Guaranty Trust Company of New York has cancelled $4,000,000 par value of "External Bonds of the Republic of Bolivia of 1922" which, prior thereto, were authenticated by it, and also certifying that the aggregate par value of said bonds theretofore authenticated by it and not cancelled does not exceed $3,000,000, and upon the delivery to the Trustee of $3,000,000 par value of "External Bonds of the Republic of Bolivia of 1922", the Trustee shall authenticate and deliver to or upon the order of the President, Vice-President or Treasurer of the Ulen Contracting Corporation $5,000,000 par value of Bonds of this issue. Said $3,000,000 of "External Bonds of the Republic of Bolivia of 1922" delivered to the Trustee as aforesaid shall immediately thereafter be presented by the Trustee for cancellation to the Guaranty Trust Company of New York, Trustee of said bonds, and the Republic shall cause the same to be cancelled and physically destroyed.

(*c*) The remaining $2,000,000 par value of Bonds shall be held by the Trustee until November 1, 1923, on or after which date they shall be authenticated and delivered to or upon the order of the President, Vice President or Treasurer of the Ulen Contracting Corporation.

(*d*) Immediately upon the execution and delivery of this Contract the Trustee shall authenticate $540,000 par value of said Bonds and deliver the same to or upon the written order of the Bankers.

SECTION 2. The remaining $7,000,000 par value of Bonds shall be executed by the Republic and shall be authenticated and delivered by the Trustee as herinafter provided:

(*a*) $3,000,000 par value of said Bonds shall be authenticated and delivered to or upon the order of the Minister of Finance of the Republic, but in no event before January 1, 1924, unless the authentication and delivery prior to said date shall be approved in writing or by cable by said Minister and the Bankers, and only upon the receipt by the Trustee of a certificate of the Minister of Finance, countersigned by the Permanent Fiscal Commission stating

(1) That the revenues from the pledged dividends, taxes and income collected during twelve successive calendar months within the thirteen calendar months immediately preceding the calendar month in which the application for authentication and delivery of Bonds may be made, have equalled a sum at least 1½ times the amount required for the annual service of the loan, including the service of the bonds proposed to be issued; or

(2) If such revenues shall not have equalled said amount, that there have been pledged as further security hereunder such additional taxes or revenues other than present and future taxes upon petroleum and petroleum claims and concessions as may have been approved by the

Bankers to an amount sufficient upon the basis of the collection of such additional taxes or revenues during said twelve months' period, to increase the proceeds of all pledged dividends, taxes and revenues, so that the same shall not be less than 1½ times the amount required for the service of the loan, including the service upon the additional bonds proposed to be issued. The above mentioned certificate shall state that in making the foregoing calculations the average rate of exchange in La Paz on New York for dollar sight drafts for the twelve calendar months covered by said certificate, or the current rate at the date of such certificate (whichever shall be more favorable to the dollar), has been taken as the basis.

The Republic covenants that said Bonds, or the proceeds thereof, shall be used only for the purposes for which $3,000,000 par value of "External Bonds of the Republic of Bolivia of 1922" were reserved under Article Thirty-three of the Contract of July 8, 1921, between the Republic and the Ulen Contracting Corporation and that if further security be required hereunder for the issue of said Bonds, it will pledge as such further security such additional taxes or revenues other than present and future taxes upon petroleum and petroleum claims and concessions as may be approved by the Bankers to an amount sufficient to meet the foregoing requirements.

(*b*) The remaining $4,000,000 par value of Bonds shall be authenticated and delivered to or upon the written or cabled order of the Minister of Finance of the Republic, provided, however, that $2,000,000 par value of said Bonds shall not be authenticated and delivered until after January 1, 1923, and the remaining $2,000,000 par value not until after January 1, 1924, unless the authentication and delivery prior to said dates shall be approved in writing or by cable by said Minister and the Bankers, but only upon receipt by the Trustee of a certificate of the Minister of Finance countersigned by the Permanent Fiscal Commission stating that

(1) The Republic for twelve successive calendar months within the thirteen calendar months immediately preceding the calendar month in which the application for authentication and delivery of bonds may be made, has

raised sufficient revenues to meet all of its ordinary general expenses, exclusive of capital investments, without borrowing therefor, or without selling capital assets; and

(2) The revenues from the pledged dividends, taxes and income, collected during said twelve months' period, as also the average annual revenues from the same sources, for the five years preceding, have equalled a sum at least one and one-half times the amount required for the annual service of the loan, including the service of the Bonds proposed to be issued.

The above mentioned certificate shall state that in making the foregoing calculations the average rate of exchange in La Paz on New York for dollar sight drafts for the five years immediately preceding such issue, or the current rate at the date of such certificate (whichever shall be more favorable to the dollar) has been taken as the basis.

The Republic covenants that all Bonds, or the proceeds of Bonds, authenticated and delivered under Subdivision (*b*) of this Section 2, will be used for the purpose of completing the Potosí-Sucre Railroad.

SECTION 3. Whenever from time to time any Bonds shall be authenticated and delivered under Subdivision (*c*) of Section 1 or under Section 2 of this Article Eighth, the Republic shall pay to the Trustee such portion of 5% of the par value of Bonds so authenticated and delivered as the portion of the current semester then elapsed is to the whole current semester, but in no event shall the sum so paid to the Trustee be less than the amount of the interest payable upon such Bonds upon the next interest payment date. Before authenticating and delivering any Bonds under this Contract, the Trustee shall detach and cancel all matured coupons appertaining thereto.

SECTION 4. The $10,600,000 mentioned in Section 1 above shall be disposed of as follows:

(*a*) $200,000 shall be set aside by the Trustee and shall be by it applied as directed by the Minister of Finance of the Republic to the purchase and/or redemption of £40,200 par value of Bonds of the Republic issued under contract dated December 30, 1908, between the Republic and Messrs. J. P. Morgan & Company of New York, which the Republic represents constitute the balance of the bonds of said issue outstanding. Any balance of this sum which may not be required for the purposes stated shall, after all of said Bonds shall have been purchased or redeemed as aforesaid, be disposed of as the Minister of Finance of the Republic may direct and shall be subject to his written or cabled order. As soon as all of said Bonds shall have been acquired as aforesaid the Trustee shall present the same together with the £284,600 of similar Bonds to be delivered to the Trustee coincidentally with the authentication and delivery of the Bonds mentioned in Section 1 subdivision (*a*) above, to Messrs. J. P. Morgan & Company, and the Republic shall thereupon cause the same to be cancelled and physically destroyed.

(*b*) The Trustee shall set aside the sum of $6,500,000 as a special fund for the purpose of enabling the Republic to acquire all its outstanding Import Customs Notes of 1915, Export Customs Notes of 1920 and Customs Notes of 1921 which the Republic represents aggregate an amount not exceeding Bs. 19,485,475 all of which the Republic represents are redeemable at par. Immediately following the execution of this Contract, the Republic shall cease to accept any of said notes in payment of Export or Import Customs duties and shall immediately proceed through the Banco de la Nación Boliviana, to retire the same from circulation either by purchase or redemption. As and when so purchased or redeemed the Banco de la Nación Boliviana shall draw upon the Trustee against the special fund above mentioned for the amounts expended in said purchases and redemptions, and exclusive of interest upon said notes, not, however, exceeding the face value of the notes so acquired. Each of said drafts shall have annexed thereto a certificate of the Banco de la Nación Boliviana stating, (1) that it has cancelled and physically destroyed notes of a specified aggregate face value in respect of which such draft has been drawn, setting forth the name of the issue and the denominations and numbers of the respective notes; (2) the amount in Bolivianos expended in the purchase or redemption of such notes, and (3) the dollar equivalent of Bolivianos based upon the rate of exchange in La Paz for dollar sight drafts on New York on the date borne by such draft, and each draft shall also be accompanied by a certificate signed by the Minister of Finance of the Republic stating that the notes referred to in said certificate of the Banco de la Nación Boliviana were outstanding at the date of this contract and are notes described in subdivision (*b*) of this Section. No draft against said fund shall be paid by the Trustee unless accompanied by such certificates. Said drafts shall be drawn at the rate of exchange current at the time at La Paz on New York for dollar sight drafts as set forth in said certificate, but in no event at a rate which shall represent the Boliviano as worth more than 33 1/3 cents United States gold. In case at the time of such drawing the Boliviano should be worth more than said 33 1/3 cents the Republic shall provide the difference out of its general funds. When all outstanding notes shall thus have been acquired and cancelled, the Minister of Finance of the Republic shall so certify to the Trustee, and thereupon any balance of said special fund which may remain shall be disposed of as the Minister of Finance of the Republic shall direct and shall be subject to his written or cabled order.

(*c*) The sum of $3,900,000 shall be set aside by the Trustee as a special fund to be applied by the Republic to the payment of time obligations owing by the Republic to local banks in La Paz which, the Republic represents, aggregate an amount not exceeding Bs. 11,600,000 and are secured by certificates representing the Republic's shares of stock in the Banco de la Nación Boliviano. The Minister of Finance of the Republic may draw a draft or drafts upon the Trustee against said funds upon the condition and understanding, however, that such draft or drafts shall be honored by the Trustee only upon the compliance by the Republic with the following terms and conditions, viz.:

(1) That prior to or simultaneously with the honoring of any such drafts there be deposited with The Equitable Trust Company of New York at its Paris office and/or at its principal office in New York the shares of stock of the Banco de la Nación Boliviana mentioned in subdivision (*a*) section 2 of Article Fourth above, and

(2) That prior to or simultaneously with the honoring of any such drafts, there be delivered to the Trustee at its office in New York the certificate stated to be now in the possession of local banks in La Paz representing the above mentioned shares, together with a written statement of the Minister of

Finance stating (*a*) the number of shares of the Banco de la Nación Boliviana belonging to the Republic, (*b*) that the certificate so delivered to the Trustee is the certificate deliverable to the Trustee under this Clause (2), and (*c*) that said certificate, together with the shares which have been delivered to the Trustee pursuant to the preceding Clause (1), constitute full and complete title to all of the shares of said bank belonging to the Republic and that there are no other certificates or instruments outstanding which represent or purport to represent said shares or any lien thereon or any interest therein. Said statement of the Minister of Finance shall be conclusive evidence of the statements therein contained and shall be full protection to the Trustee for action in accordance therewith.

The drawing of drafts as aforesaid by the Minister of Finance against said special fund shall be sufficient evidence to the Trustee of the application of the said fund to the extent of such drafts to the payment of the above mentioned obligations, and the Trustee shall be protected in honoring such drafts provided the above mentioned conditions with reference to the delivery of the shares of Banco de la Nación Boliviana and the certificate representing the same shall have been complied with.

Any balance of said special fund which may remain after all drafts drawn as aforesaid shall have been paid, shall be disposed of as the Minister of Finance may direct and shall be subject to his written or cabled order.

Article Ninth

regarding the trustee

Section 1. The Trustee shall allow interest to the Republic upon all moneys deposited with it except moneys held by the Trustee to pay bonds and/or coupons due but not presented at the rate of ....percent. below the New York Federal Reserve rediscount rate prevailing from time to time for ninety days' prime paper, but in no case at a rate less than..............................per annum.

Section 2. The Republic shall pay to the Trustee a commission of.......................................percent on all amounts disbursed in the payment of principal, premium and interest of the loan, as the reasonable and customary compensation of the Trustee for all services rendered by it under this Contract except as herein otherwise provided.

On November 1st, 1922, the Republic shall pay to the Trustee on the latter's written request the commission and compensation above mentioned covering the period from the date of this contract to November 1, 1922, and the expenses which the Trustee may have incurred in good faith during the same period in the service of the loan or in the performance of any duty imposed upon it under this Contract. On the same date, November 1, 1922, and semi-annually thereafter during the life of this Contract, on May first and November first of each year, the Republic shall deposit with the Trustee such amount as the Trustee shall estimate may be required by it to meet all expenses reasonably incident to the service of the loan during the six months next succeeding and at the termination of each semester the account for the six months immediately preceding shall be adjusted.

SECTION 3. The Equitable Trust Company of New York is hereby appointed general representative of the Bondholders, that is to say, Trustee, to deal with the Republic and to exercise all other powers herein set forth, and the Republic recognizes and accepts such appointment. As such general representative and Trustee for the Bondholders, The Equitable Trust Company of New York shall have ample power to appoint agents to represent it in everything relating to said Bonds. During the life of the Bonds, the Republic shall always recognize in the United States of America such representative and Trustee, and every successor of The Equitable Trust Company of New York shall always be a trust company designated by the Bankers and appointed by the Republic, carrying on business in the City of New York, and having a capital and surplus aggregating at least $2,000,000. Any successor shall execute an instrument accepting its appointment, and thereupon, without any further act or deed, shall become vested with all the rights and duties of its predecessor hereunder. The retiring Trustee shall execute and deliver all instruments in writing necessary for confirming said successor Trustee in all the rights, powers and duties to which it succeeds.

SECTION 4. The Trustee in the execution of the Trust and duties hereunder shall be under full legal liability, except as in this Contract provided. It may, instead of acting personally, employ and appoint such agents or attorneys as it may deem desirable whose reasonable fees and expenses shall be a charge prior to that of the Bondholders upon any funds coming into the hands of the Trustee hereunder.

In taking or omitting any action hereunder, the Trustee may rely upon the correctness of any statements of fact contained in any certificate signed by the Minister of Finance of the Republic and countersigned by the Permanent Fiscal Commission.

SECTION 5. The Trustee shall not be answerable to the holders of Bonds and coupons for the default or misconduct of any agent, attorney, bank, or banker appointed or selected by it in pursuance hereof, if such agent, attorney, bank or banker shall have been selected with reasonable care, or for anything whatever in connection with this Trust, except for its own willful misconduct.

SECTION 6. The Trustee may at any time take such steps as it may deem proper for the enforcement of the rights of the Bondholders hereunder; and for that purpose shall be deemed and treated by the Republic as the general representative and attorney in fact irrevocable of the Bondholders, duly appointed and authorized to act as such by the terms of this Contract; and in the execution of its trust and duties hereunder shall be entitled to exercise for all Bondholders all the rights and remedies afforded by the Laws of the Republic of Bolivia, in favor of such Bondholders.

SECTION 7. The Trustee shall have in addition to other rights, powers and duties conferred by law and by this Contract, the following:

(1) It shall receive all sums paid to it in accordance with this Contract, and shall use and apply such moneys as herein provided.

(2) It may, subject to the terms of this Contract, act in accordance with the written or cabled orders of the Minister of Finance of the Republic, and such orders shall be full protection to the Trustee for action in accordance therewith.

(3) The Trustee shall keep in the City of New York accounts of receipts and disbursements in connection with

the Loan; and statements of such accounts shall be rendered to the Minister of Finance of the Republic at the expiration of each Bond year, and at such other times as the Minister of Finance may request.

(4) The statements of account rendered by the Trustee shall be conclusive upon the Republic, save as specific objections in writing thereto may be received by the Trustee from the Minister of Finance of the Republic within three (3) months after delivery of such statements of account to the Minister of Finance.

(5) The Trustee shall be chargeable for only such moneys as may be actually received by it in New York. It shall not be chargeable for any moneys deposited with the Banco de la Nación Boliviana, as provided in Article Sixth of this Contract, nor for the remittance of such moneys to New York.

(6) The Trustee shall be under no obligation or liability with respect to the application of the proceeds of this Loan, except as to such payments as by the terms of this Contract shall be made by it directly.

(7) The Trustee may purchase or otherwise acquire and hold any of the said Bonds, with the same rights as if it were not the Trustee hereunder.

SECTION 8. The Trustee may withdraw and resign by giving notice to the Republic of such intention, specifying the date when it is desired that such withdrawal shall take effect, which shall not be less than four (4) months after notice to such Republic shall have been given, unless a shorter notice shall be accepted by the Republic. In case the Trustee shall resign, or shall for any cause become incapable of acting, a successor or successors to the Trustee shall be appointed by the Republic, by a duly executed instrument in writing.

SECTION 9. The Trustee shall not be chargeable or liable or responsible to holders of Bonds and coupons for acts or defaults of the Republic or of any of its officers or representatives, or for acts or failure to act as such Trustee, or for any error of judgment or mistake made by it in good faith, or for the acts or defaults of any agent or agents selected by it with due care, or otherwise, except for its own wilful misconduct. It shall be protected in acting upon any notice, request, consent, certificate, bond, note, cablegram, or other paper or document believed by it to be genuine and to be signed or sent by the person or persons purporting to sign or send the same. It may advise with legal counsel (whose reasonable fees and expenses shall be a charge prior to that of the Bondholders upon any funds coming into the hands of the Trustee hereunder), and shall incur no liability for any action taken or suffered by it in accordance with the opinion of such counsel. It shall incur no liability in respect of the validity of this Contract or of any of the Bonds or coupons, or of the statements herein or therein contained, or in respect of the shares of stock pledged hereunder or any other security for said Bonds. It shall not be required to take any action unless indemnified to its satisfaction, and it shall be protected in any action taken by it at the request of the holders of 10% in amount of the Bonds outstanding.

Any request or other instrument required by this Contract to be signed and executed by Bondholders may be in any number of concurrent writings of similar tenor and may be signed or executed by such Bondholders in person or by agent or agents duly appointed in writing. Proof of the execution of any such request or other instrument or of a writing appointing any such agent and of the holding by any person of Bonds transferable by delivery shall be sufficient for any purpose of this Contract and shall be conclusive in favor of the Trustee or of the Republic, if made in the manner provided in this Article. The fact and date of the execution by any person of any such request or other instrument or writing may be proved by the affidavit of a witness of such execution or by the certificate of any notary public or other officer of any jurisdiction, authorized by the laws thereof to take acknowledgments of deeds, certifying that the persons signing such request or other instrument acknowledged to him the execution thereof. The amount of Bonds transferable by delivery held by any person executing any such request or other instrument as a Bondholder, and the distinguishing numbers of the Bonds held by such person, and the date of his holding the same, may be proved by a certificate executed by any trust company, bank, bankers or other depositary (whereever situated), if such certificate shall be deemed by the Trustee to be satisfactory, showing that at the date therein mentioned such person had on deposit with such depositary, or exhibited to it, the Bonds therein described; or such facts may be proved by the certificate or affidavit of the person executing such request or other instrument as a Bondholder, if such certificate or affidavit shall be deemed by the Trustee to be satisfactory. The fact and date of execution of any request or other instrument and the amount and numbers of Bonds held by the person so executing such request or other instrument may also be proved in any other manner which the Trustee may deem sufficient. The ownership of coupon Bonds registered as to principal shall be proved by the registers of such Bonds. Any request or consent of the owner of any Bond shall bind all future owners of the same Bond and all Bonds issued in exchange therefor or in place thereof, in respect of anything done by the Trustee in pursuance of such request or consent.

SECTION 10. At any time or times in order to facilitate the execution and performance of any of the trusts or powers created by this Contract or to conform to any legal requirement, the Trustee and the Republic shall have power to appoint and to unite in the execution and delivery of all instruments and the performance of all acts necessary or proper to appoint another trust company or one or more persons designated by the Republic and approved by the Trustee, either to act as co-trustee or co-trustees jointly with the Trustee, or to act as separate trustee or trustees in respect of any matter herein provided for, and in any case with all such of the powers, rights and duties hereby conferred or imposed upon the Trustee, and for such term, if any limitation is placed thereon, as may be specified in the instrument of appointment, the same to be exercised either jointly with the Trustee or separately, according as such instrument or instruments may prescribe; and if the Republic shall be in default hereunder and such default shall not have been remedied, the Trustee shall have power, with the approval of the Bankers, without notice to or any action on the part of the Republic, and without the necessity of the execution of any such instrument of appointment by the Republic, to appoint such co-trustee or co-trustees or separate trustee or trustees as aforesaid, and to execute all instruments and to perform all acts necessary or proper for such purpose. The Trustee may receive the opinion of any counsel approved by it as to the necessity or propriety of appointing any such co-trustee or separate trustee and as to the force and effect of any such instrument to be executed or any act to be taken to effect such appointment, and as to any other matter arising under this Section 10, and such opinion shall be full protection to the Trustee for any action taken or omitted to be taken by it pursuant thereto.

SECTION 11. The Equitable Trust Company of New York hereby accepts this appointment as Trustee, as also the liens and other securities above mentioned.

ARTICLE TENTH

NOTICES

Any statement, notice, request or other communication under this Contract from the Trustee of the Republic shall be in writing addressed to "El Ministro de Hacienda de Bolivia", and shall be deemed to have been duly made or given if delivered at the Legation of the Republic in the City of Washington, or at the Consulate General of the Republic at the City of New York. Service of such notice or other communication shall be deemed complete as of the date of such delivery. Any notice or other communication from the Republic to the Trustee shall also be in writing and may be given directly or through the Bolivian Legation at Washington, or the Bolivian Consul General at New York, and shall be sufficiently given if addressed to said Trustee and delivered at its office in the City of New York, and the Trustee shall be protected in relying upon any notice or communication purporting to have been sent from the Bolivian Legation or said Consul General.

Any notice to the Bankers shall be given in writing addressed to Stifel-Nicolaus Investment Company, Spencer Trask & Company, and The Equitable Trust Company of New York, and delivered at their offices or at the offices of the two last mentioned in the City of New York.

ARTICLE ELEVENTH

GENERAL PROVISIONS

SECTION 1. The provisions of this Contract shall apply to and in respect of the firm of Spencer Trask & Company, one of the Bankers herein mentioned, as such firm shall from time to time be constituted, without reference to any change of membership, as well as the successors in business of said firm.

SECTION 2. In all matters in which the Bankers shall be called upon to act, the concurrent action of any two of them shall be sufficient, and shall be binding upon all three.

IN WITNESS WHEREOF, the Republic has caused this Contract to be subscribed on its behalf by Señor Don Carlos Gumucio, Consul General of the Republic in New York, thereunto duly authorized; and The Equitable Trust Company of New York has caused this Contract to be subscribed in its name by one of its Vice-Presidents, and its Corporate Seal to be hereunto affixed and attested.

This Contract is executed in several counterparts.

REPUBLIC OF BOLIVIA
By C. GUMUCIO
Consul General of the Republic of Bolivia

In the presence of:
HUGO KOHLMANN
LAWRENCE BENNETT

THE EQUITABLE TRUST COMPANY OF NEW YORK,
[CORPORATE SEAL] By SAMUEL ARMSTRONG
Vice-President.

Attest:
O. P. FARWELL JR.
Assistant Secretary.

In the presence of:
GERALD D. EGGLESTON
FREDERIC J. ALBERT

STATE OF NEW YORK }
County of New York } ss.:

On this 26th day of June, 1922, before me came CARLOS GUMUCIO, to me known to be the individual described in a certain power of attorney executed at La Paz, Bolivia, on June 5th, 1922, by the President of the Republic and the Council of Ministers, a copy of which power of attorney is set forth in a telegram dated June 7, 1922, from the Secretary of State of the United States to Messrs. Curtis, Mallet-

Prevost & Colt, and said Carlos Gumucio acknowledged that he executed the foregoing instrument on behalf of the Republic of Bolivia pursuant to said authority.

(Signed) JOHN BYRNE
Notary Public
N. Y. Co. Clerk's No. 440
[NOTARY'S SEAL] N. Y. Co. Register's No. 4242
Certificate filed Kings Co. No. 128
Register's No. 4130
Commission expires March 30, 1924

STATE OF NEW YORK }
County of New York } ss.:

On this 26th day of June, 1922, before me came SAMUEL ARMSTRONG, to me known, who being by me duly sworn, deposes and says that he resides in Westfield, Union County, New Jersey; that he is a Vice-President of THE EQUITABLE TRUST COMPANY OF NEW YORK, the corporation described in and which executed the foregoing instrument and knows the seal of said corporation; that the seal affixed to said instrument is said corporate seal; that it is so affixed by order of the Board of Trustees of said corporation, and that he signed his name thereto by like order.

(Signed) JOHN BYRNE
Notary Public
N. Y. Co. Clerk's No. 440
[NOTARY'S SEAL] N. Y. Co. Register's No. 4242
Certificate filed Kings Co. 128
Register's No. 4130
Commission expires March 30, 1924.

SCHEDULE A

STATISTICAL INFORMATION

REVENUES:

The Republic's total ordinary general revenues (exclusive of proceeds of any loans or sales of capital assets) for each of the fiscal years ending December 31st given hereunder were:

1911	Bs. 16,911,777
1912	" 20,161,184
1913	" 22,028,824
1914	" 15,840,212
1915	" 12,824,478
1916	" 15,906,501
1917	" 19,104,719
1918	" 25,828,031
1919	" 24,976,525
1920	" 27,885,323
1921 incomplete returns approximately	" 21,900,000

COLLECTIONS FROM PLEDGED SECURITIES:

During the same period, the Republic's total collections and revenues and/or income from dividends on its holdings of shares of the Banco de la Nación Boliviana and from the taxes, revenues, and profits pledged as security for this Loan under Section Two of Article Fourth of this Trust Contract were:

1911	Bs. 14,201,335
1912	" 16,864,629
1913	" 16,460,040
1914	" 11,570,725
1915	" 9,515,948
1916	" 11,781,720
1917	" 14,556,237
1918	" 17,643,154
1919	" 16,291,928
1920	" 18,899,429
1921 incomplete returns approximately	" 13,200,000

The Republic has never owned a larger number of shares of the Banco de la Nación Boliviana than it now holds and consequently the dividends above referred to have not been derived from any larger number of such shares.

DEBT STATEMENT:

The Republic's outstanding debt as of January 1st, 1922, was:

External Funded Debt:	
Sterling 6% Loan of 1909	£334,400
Yungas Dollar 6% Loan 1917	$2,158,500
Sanitation Dollar 6% Loan of 1920	$1,972,000
Railroad Dollar 8% Loan of 1922	$3,000,000
Internal Funded Debt:	
Customs Notes of 1915, 1920 and 1921	Bs. 19,485,475
Various other internal issues	Bs. 12,681,825
Floating Debt:	
Equitable Trust Company Loan	$1,000,000
Other foreign bank loans	Bs. 49,125
Various Bolivian bank loans	Bs. 27,995,963

The Republic's contingent liabilities by reason of guarantees of principal and/or interest of other than direct Government obligations are as follows:

Guarantee of interest on the Bolivia Railway Company's First Mortgage 5% Bonds which mature on January 1, 1927. The original issue of these bonds was £3,750,000, all of which are outstanding.

Guarantee of the yearly service of £24,000 on the Electric Light & Power Company of Cochabamba's 6% Bonds, which, it is expected, will all have been paid off on or before June 15, 1936 through the operation of the yearly sinking fund. The original issue of these bonds was £300,000 and the present outstanding amount is £188,780.

BIBLIOGRAPHY

CHAPTER II

AMERICAN BANKERS ASSOCIATION. *The South American West Coast.* An economic and financial survey of Chile, Bolivia and Peru. 1925.

BALLIVIÁN, ADOLFO. *Bolivia: her resources and future.* (*La Bolivie: ses resources, son avenir.*) London, 1920. "Compiled in compliance with the request of the secretary-general of the League of Nations."

Bolivia en el primer centenario de su independencia. La Paz, 1925.

BOLIVIAN PORT RESTORATION LEAGUE. *La opinión en los Estados Unidos sobre el problema de Pacífico.*

BORGOÑO, LUIS BARROS. *The problem of the Pacific and the new policies of Bolivia, together with two juridical reports by John W. Davis.* Baltimore, 1924.

BOWMAN, ISAIAH. *Desert trails of Atacama. Amer. Geogr. Soc., Spec. Pub. No. 5,* 1924.

BOWMAN, ISAIAH. "Results of an expedition to the Central Andes under the auspices of the American Geographical Society." *Bull. Amer. Geog. Soc.,* Vol. XLVI, 1914, pp. 161-183.

BOWMAN, ISAIAH. *The Andes of Southern Peru: Geographical reconnaissance along the 73rd meridian.* New York, 1916.

BOWMAN, ISAIAH. "The distribution of population in Bolivia." *Bull. Geogr. Soc. of Philadelphia.* Vol. VII, 1909, pp. 28-47.

BOWMAN, ISAIAH. "The highland dweller of Bolivia: An anthropogeographic interpretation." *Bull. Geogr. Soc. of Philadelphia,* Vol. VII, 1909, pp. 159-184.

BOWMAN, ISAIAH. "Trade routes in the economic geography of Bolivia." *Bull. Amer. Geogr. Soc.,* Vol. XLII, 1910, pp. 22-37, 90-104, 180-192.

BRABANT, WILLIAM VAN. *La Bolivie.* Paris and Brussels, n. d.

BRAVO, CARLOS. *La patria boliviana, estado geográfico.* La Paz, 1894.

BRESSON, ANDRÉ. *Bolivia: Sept années d'explorations, de voyages et de séjours dans l'Amérique australe.* Paris, 1886. Parts III-V.

BRYCE, JAMES. *South America: Observations and impressions.* New York, 1912. Chapters iii-v.

CARRASCO, JOSÉ. *Bolivia's case for the League of Nations.* London, 1920.

CONSULATE (LONDON). *Official handbook to Bolivia.* London, 1924.

CONWAY, WILLIAM MARTIN. *The Bolivian Andes; record of climbing and exploration in the Cordillera Real in 1898-1900.* New York and London, 1901.

CRESPO, LUIS S. *Geografía de la República de Bolivia.* La Paz, 1911.

DAWSON, THOMAS. *The South American Republics.* Vol. II. London, 1905.

DEPARTMENT OF COMMERCE (U. S.). *Commercial Travelers' Guide to Latin America. Revised Edition.* Washington, 1922. pp. 498-521.

DEPARTMENT OF STATE (U. S.). *Economic information concerning Bolivia.* January, 1923. (mimeographed).

DIEZ DE MEDINA, EDUARDO. *La cuestión del Pacífico y la política internacional de Bolivia.* La Paz, 1923.

ENOCK, REGINALD C. *Republics of South and Central America.* 1922.

Foreign Securities Investor. Bolivian Number. Vol. II, No. 9, April 14, 1926.

HAENKE, TADEO. "Histoire naturelle de la province Cochabamba et des environs, et description de ses productions." In Felix de Azara, *Voyages dans l'Amérique meridionale,* Vol. II, pp. 391-541. Paris, 1809.

HARMS, ESPEJO CARLOS. *Bolivia en sus diversas fases, principalmente económica.* Santiago de Chile, 1922.

INTER AMERICAN HIGH COMMISSION. *Bolivia: Financial and economic conditions and public debt.* Report prepared for the Central Executive Council, December, 1919. Washington. (Unpublished).

La Bolivian Company: *Sociedad de explotación, colonización y vialidad en la región de Caupolicán.* La Paz, 1901.

Latin American Year Book, 1920.

McBride, George McCutchen. "The agrarian Indian communities of highland Bolivia." *Amer. Geogr. Soc. Research Ser. No.* 5. New York, 1921.

Mather, Kirtley F. "Along the Andean front in southeastern Bolivia." *Geogr. Mag.,* New York, Vol. XII, pp. 358-374.

Mather, Kirtley F. "Eastern Bolivia: A land of opportunity." *Bull. Geogr. Soc. of Philadelphia,* 1920, Vol. XVIII, pp. 49-55.

Molins, W. Jaime. *El despertar de una nación (Bolivia).* Buenos Aires, 1925.

National Foreign Trade Council. *South American handbook: A compilation of information and statistics regarding public indebtedness, foreign commerce and railway development.* 1915.

Nunn, J. H. "Development of northeastern Bolivia and western Brazil." *Commerce Reports,* No. 66, March 20, 1918, pp. 1050-59.

Ogilvie, Alan G. "Geography of the Central Andes: A handbook to accompany the La Paz sheet of the map of Hispanic America on the millionth scale. With an introduction by Isaiah Bowman." *Amer. Geogr. Soc., Map of Hispanic America, Pub. No.* 1. New York, 1922.

Pan American Union. *Bolivia: General Descriptive Data.* Washington, 1925.

Paz, D. R. *Bolivian-Chilean question. The port problem of the South Pacific.* Washington, 1925.

Pfannenschmidt, Ernst. *Boliviens land-und volkswirtschaft.* Berlin, 1916.

Reid, William A. *Bolivia, the heart of a continent.* A few facts about the country and its activities. Prepared for the Bolivian legation. Washington, 1919.

Rojas, Casto. "Arica y la política comercial de Bolivia: El 'Puerto Potosí' durante la Colonia y en los cien años de la República." *El Diario,* August 6, 1925 (centennial number). La Paz.

Schurz, W. L. *Bolivia: A commercial and industrial hand-*

book. Washington, 1921. Department of Commerce, Special Agents Series. No. 208.

SIEVERS, WILHELM. *Die Cordillerenstaaten,* Vol. I. Berlin and Leipzig, 1913.

SIEVERS, WILHELM. *Süd-und Mittelamerika: Die mittleren Kordilleren.* Leipzig and Vienna, 1914.

South American Handbook, 1924. London.

The South American. "The low lands of Bolivia," Feb. 1917; "The unparalleled resources of Bolivia," March, 1917.

The South American Journal. "Northeastern Bolivia." Vol. LXXXIV, No. 18, May 4, 1918, pp. 277-278.

UZARSKI, JULIUS. *Bolivia: Natür und wirtschaftliche Verhältnisse.* Bonn, 1911.

VISCARRA HERREDIA, R. *Guía general de Bolivia, comercial, industrial, geográfica y administrativa.* La Paz, 1918.

WALLE, PAUL. *Bolivia, its people and its resources, its railways, mines, and rubber-forests.* London, 1914.

WAMBAUGH, SARAH. *A monograph on plebiscites, with a collection of official documents.* Publication of the Carnegie Endowment for International Peace. New York, 1920. (pp. 156-165 for statement of Tacna-Arica question; pp. 985-1050 for extracts from official correspondence).

WRIGLEY, GLADYS M. "Fairs of the Central Andes." *Geogr. Rev.,* Vol. VII, 1919, pp. 65-80.

ZAMORA, JULIO. "Republic of Bolivia. Official data concerning its economical situation." Address at the 2nd Pan American Commercial Conference, 1919.

Official Publications

CÁMARA DE DIPUTADOS. *Redactor de las sesiones en gran comisión,* 1922-1924.

DELEGATION TO THE LEAGUE OF NATIONS, 1921. *Bolivia's claim for the revision of the treaty of peace of 1904. Letter and memorandum from the Bolivian delegation.* Geneva, 1921.

DIRECCIÓN GENERAL DE ADUANAS. *Comercio de Bolivia en el primer semestre de* 1926. La Paz, 1926.

MINISTERIO DE COLONIZACIÓN Y AGRICULTURA. Sección de inmigración. *Indicaciones sumarias para el inmigrante á Bolivia, por Luis S. Crespo.* La Paz, 1907.

Ministerio de Colonización y Agricultura. *Guía sinóptica para el viajero inmigrante en Bolivia.* La Paz, 1907.

Ministerio de Guerra y Colonización. *La Colonización en Bolivia durante la primera centuria de su independencia, por J. Lavadenz. Apendice: Las riquezas de Bolivia, por Cristian Suarez Arana.* La Paz, 1925.

Ministerio de Industria. *Estudios e informes del Ingeniero Jorge Wannag sobre varias materias primas e industrias explotables en Bolivia.* La Paz, 1920.

Ministerio de Relaciones Exteriores. *Chile y la aspiración de Bolivia á puerto en el Pacífico.* La Paz, 1922.

Ministerio de Relaciones Exteriores. *El problema del Pacífico y la fórmula de solución del secretario de Estado de los Estados Unidos.* La Paz, 1927.

Ministerio de Relaciones Exteriores. *Las pretensiones de Bolivia sobre Arica.* La Paz, 1920.

Ministerio de Relaciones Exteriores. *The Republic of Bolivia: official information and statistics regarding the development of the country during 1916 and the first half of 1917.* Summarized by Sr. Julio Zamora, minister of foreign relations. New York, 1918.

"Resumen general de importaciones y exportaciones por vías de ingreso y salida en 1925." Official figures published in *Boletín Comercial.* 11 julio, 1926. La Paz.

Second Pan American Financial Conference. Reports and other documents of the Bolivian Delegation. Washington, 1920.

Periodicals

Boletín Comercial. (published weekly in La Paz).

Bolivia: A Bi-monthly Survey of Bolivian Activities. (published by the Bolivian Consulate in New York. Commenced publication in September, 1926 as a quarterly; became a bi-monthly beginning January, 1927).

Commerce Reports (for monthly cabled report from American consul in La Paz, etc.).

Commercial and Financial Chronicle.

El Diario (La Paz).

La Razón (La Paz).

La República (La Paz).
Pan American Union Bulletin.
West Coast Leader (Lima, Peru).

Maps

AMERICAN GEOGRAPHICAL SOCIETY. La Paz, Pilcomayo, Iquique and El Beni sheets, 1:1,000,000. South America, 1:2,000,000, and 1:4,000,000.

GERMANN, FRANZ. Mapa de la República de Bolivia, 1:2,000,000. Shows mines, railroads, borax and sulphur deposits, etc. Hamburg, 1904.

MAYER, RICHARD. Commercial map of northern Chile, Bolivia and southern Peru, showing railways, mineral deposits, mines, borax and nitrate deposits, volcanoes, altitudes, etc. Scale, 1:1,000,000. London, 1914.

PHILIPS (C. S. HAMMOND, PUB.). Commercial and Railway Map of South America. Scale, 1:8,500,000.

REYNOSO, JAVIER VALDEZ. Mapa de Bolivia: tomado de la Carta General y compilación de datos hecha por el Ingeniero auxiliar de Obras Públicas. Scale, 1:2,400,000. La Paz, 1920.

CHAPTER III

ADAMS, ALEXANDER A. *The plateau peoples of South America, an essay in ethnic psychology.* New York, 1915.

ARGUEDAS, ALCIDES. *Raza de Bronce.* Valencia, 1923.

BALLIVIÁN, JOSÉ S. Ideario Aimará. La Paz, 1926.

BANDELIER, ADOLPH F. *The Islands of Titicaca and Koati.* New York, 1910.

BINGHAM, HIRAM. *Inca Land: Explorations in the highlands of Peru.* Boston and New York, 1922.

BOWMAN, ISAIAH. "Regional population groups of Atacama." *Bull. Amer. Geogr. Soc.*, Vol. XLI, 1909, pp. 142-154, 193-211.

BOWMAN, ISAIAH. "The highland dweller of Bolivia: an anthropogeographic interpretation." *Bull. Geogr. Soc. of Philadelphia*, 1909, Vol. VII, pp. 159-184.

CALDERÓN, F. GARCIA. "Dictatorship and Democracy in Latin America." *Foreign Affairs*, April, 1925.

CHERVIN, ARTHUR. *L'Anthropologie bolivienne.* Vol. I, Ethnology, demography, metric photography; Vol. II, Anthropometry; Vol. III, Craniology. Mission Scientifique: G. de Crequi Montfort et E. Senechal de la Grange. Paris, 1908.

INMAN, SAMUEL GUY. *South America Today.* New York, 1920.

JORDAN, W. F. *Glimpses of Latin America.* New York, 1923.

MCBRIDE, GEORGE MCCUTCHEN. "The agrarian Indian communities of highland Bolivia." *Amer. Geogr. Soc. Research Ser. No.* 5, New York, 1921.

MCBRIDE, GEORGE MCCUTCHEN. "Social and religious organization of the plateau Indians." Appendix A to Ogilvie, *Geography of the Central Andes.* New York, 1922.

MARKHAM, CLEMENTS R. *The Incas of Peru.* New York, 1910.

PAREDES, MANUEL RIGOBERTO. *Mitos, supersticiones y supervivencias populares de Bolivia.* Prólogo del Dr. Belisario Diaz Romero. La Paz, 1920.

PARKER, W. B. *Bolivians of today.* New York, 1922.

POSNANSKY, ARTHUR. *Eine praehistorische Metropole in Süd-amerika.* Berlin, 1914.

POSNANSKY, ARTHUR. *Templos y vivendas prehispánicas.* La Paz, 1921.

PRESCOTT, WILLIAM H. *History of the conquest of Peru, with a preliminary view of the civilization of the Incas.* Philadelphia, 1868.

QUESADA, ERNESTO. *La faz definitiva de la sociología spengleriana.* La Plata, 1923.

QUESADA, ERNESTO. *La sociología relativista spengleriana; curso dado en el año académico de 1921.* Buenos Aires, 1921.

ROMERO, CARLOS. *Las taras de nuestra democracia.* La Paz, 1919.

ROSS, EDWARD ALSWORTH. *South of Panama.* New York, 1915. (Chapters 2 and 3 deal especially with Peru and Bolivia).

VACANO, MAX JOSEF VON. *Aus dem Erbe der Inkas—Bolivien, eine geographischethnographische Studie.* Berlin, 1912.

WRIGLEY, GLADYS M. "The traveling doctors of the Andes; the Callahuayas of Bolivia." *Geogr. Rev.*, Vol. IV, 1917, pp. 183-196.

WRIGLEY, GLADYS M. Fairs of the Central Andes. *Geogr. Rev.*, Vol. VII, 1919, pp. 65-80.

CHAPTER IV

ARNOLD, RALPH. "Conservation of the oil and gas resources of the Americas." *Proceed. 2nd Pan Amer. Sci. Cong.*, 1916-1917, Vol. III, pp. 207-37.

BALL, C. LEONARD. "Mining in Bolivia in 1925." *Boletín Comercial* (La Paz), May 23, 1926.

BANCROFT, HOWLAND. "Bolivian tin and its relation to the United States." *Proceed. of 2nd Pan Amer. Sci. Congr.*, 1916-1917, Vol. VIII, Sec. VII, pp. 294-309.

BLANCO, PEDRO ANICETO. *Monografía de la industria minera en Bolivia.* La Paz, 1910.

CLAPP, F. G. "Review of present knowledge regarding the petroleum resources of South America." *Trans. Am. Inst. Min. Eng.*, Vol. LVII, 1917, pp. 914-967.

CLAPP, F. G. *South America, a big field for petroleum development.* (Pamphlet reprint from the *New York Commercial*, 1919).

CLAPP, F. G. "The oil resources of Brazil and Bolivia." *Petr. World*, Vol. XV, 1918, pp. 333-335.

COMMERCE REPORTS. "Bolivian tin for the United States." Daily Consular and Trade Reports, Jan. 6, 1916.

DAVENPORT, E. H. AND COOKE, S. R. *The oil trusts and Anglo-American relations.* New York, 1924.

DAY, DAVID T. (ED.). Handbook of the petroleum industry. New York, 1922.

FARRAR, F. P. "Tin in its natural setting." *West Coast Leader*, Aug. 17 and Aug. 24, 1926.

FARRAR, F. P. "Oil in Bolivia." *West Coast Leader*, Aug. 24, 1926.

HARMS, ESPEJO CARLOS. *Bolivia en sus diversas fases, principalmente económica.* Santiago de Chile, 1922.

HEROLD, S. C. "The economic and geologic conditions pertaining to the occurrence of oil in the North Argentine-Bolivian field of South America." *Trans. Am. Inst. Min. Eng.* Vol. LXI, 1919, pp. 544-564.

IMPERIAL INSTITUTE. *Petroleum.* Prepared jointly with H. M. Petroleum Department, with the cooperation of H. B. Cronshaw. Monographs on mineral resources with special reference to the British Empire. London, 1921.

IMPERIAL MINERAL RESOURCES BUREAU. *The Mineral Industry of the British Empire. Tin.* Monograph. 1913-1919.

IVEY, J. H. "Some Bolivian tin mines." *Min. Mag.*, Oct. 1925, Vol. XXXIII, pp. 220-223.

JONES, W. R. *Tinfields of the world.* London, 1925.

LOAYZA, HIRAM. *La riqueza petrolífera de Caupolicán y norte de Bolivia.* La Paz, 1920.

LOPEZ, PEDRO N. *Bolivia y el petróleo.* Prólogo del H. Diputado Dr. Franz Tamayo. La Paz, 1922.

MARSTERS, V. F. "The physiography of the Peruvian Andes, with notes on early mining in Peru." *Annals, N. Y. Acad. of Science,* Vol. XXII, 1912, pp. 225-258.

MILLER, B. L., AND SINGEWALD, J. T., JR. *The mineral deposits of South America.* New York and London, 1919.

MOUSNIER, LEON. *Apuntes relativos á los aceites minerales en Bolivia.* Buenos Aires, 1913.

O'SHAUGHNESSY, MICHAEL. "Bolivia as an oil country." *Bolivia: A Quarterly Survey of Bolivian Activities,* Sept. 1926, Vol. I, pp. 21-22.

PAN AMERICAN UNION. *Commerce of Bolivia: Latest reports from Bolivian official sources.* Washington, 1924.

PAN AMERICAN UNION. "Director General de minas y petróleo. Personnel of the bureau." *Bull.* Vol. LIX, Sept. 1925, p. 937.

PATIÑO MINES AND ENTERPRISES CONSOLIDATED, INC. *Annual report,* Dec. 31, 1925.

PENBERTHY, JOHN. "Tin in Bolivia." *Royal Cornwall Polytechnic Soc.*, 76th annual report, new series, Vol. I, 1909, pp. 127-142.

POGUE, JOSEPH E. *The economics of petroleum.* New York, 1921.

REID, WILLIAM A. "A brief talk about tin." Pan American Union. Washington, 1925.

ROUNSEVELL, NELSON. "Millions being invested in Bolivian oil fields." *Bull.* Pan American Union, Nov. 1924, pp. 1110-1119.

ROUNSEVELL, NELSON. "The copper mines of Corocoro." *West Coast Leader*, Bolivian number, March, 1924.

ROUSH, G. A. (ED.). *The mineral industry during 1923: Its statistics, technology and trade.* New York, 1924.

SCHURZ, W. L. *Bolivia: A commercial and industrial handbook.* Washington, 1921. Dept. of Commerce, Special Agents Series, No. 208.

SINGEWALD, J. T. Among Bolivia's highest tin mines. *Bull.* Pan American Union, Vol. LII, 1921, pp. 217-235.

SMITH, GEORGE OTIS. The strategy of minerals. New York and London, 1919.

The South American. The Bolivian tin industry. Oct. 1916.

Times (London), *Trade and Engineering Supplement.* Prospects of the tin industry: Production and prices. Reprinted in *West Coast Leader*, Nov. 2, 1926.

VENABLES, H. L. AND HOWARD-WRIGHT, E. J. "Mining in Bolivia." *Min. Mag.*, Dec., 1924, Vol. XXXI, pp. 350-355.

VOGE, LAW. "Antimony in Bolivia." *West Coast Leader*, May 18, 1926. Reprinted from *Min. Jour. Press.*

VOGE, A. LAW. "The prospect for Bolivian antimony." *Bolivia: A Quarterly Survey of Bolivian Activities*, Vol. I, Sept. 1926, pp. 16-18.

WALLE, PAUL. *La Bolivie et ses mines.* 1913.

WARSHAW, J. *The new Latin America.* New York, 1922.

WEED, WALTER HARVEY. *The Mines Handbook*, 1924, Vol. XVI.

WILE, RAYMOND S. "Tin Mining in Bolivia." *Bolivia: A Quarterly Survey of Bolivian Activities*, Vol. I, Dec. 1926, pp. 7-13, 32.

WORLD ATLAS OF COMMERCIAL GEOLOGY, PART I., DISTRIBUTION OF MINERAL PRODUCTION. Dept. of the Interior, U. S. Geological Survey. Washington, 1921.

Official Publications

Anuario geográfico y estadística de Bolivia.

Boletín Comercial, Nov. 22 and Dec. 27, 1925, for official statistics regarding the Bolivian mining industry.

Comisión Fiscal Permanente, Segunda Memoria, 1925, pp. 52-61.

Comisión Fiscal Permanente, Tercera Memoria, 1926, pp. 30-43.

Dirección General de Estadística y Estudios Geográficos. *Vademecum del minero en Bolivia, por Enrique Mallea Balboa.* La Paz, 1912.

Memoria de Hacienda e Industria. Every year publishes a section on the mining industry.

Ministerio de Hacienda e Industria. *Minas: by de 11 de abril de 1900. Tierras baldías: proyecto de ley sobre su adjudicación.* La Paz.

Ministerio de Hacienda. *Impuesto sobre las utilidades líquidas de la explotación minera.* La Paz, 1920.

Ministerio de Industria. *Estudios e informes del Ingeniero Jorge Wannag sobre varias materias primas e industrias explotables en Bolivia.* La Paz, 1920.

Ministerio de Justicia e Industria. *Bolivia minera, artículos de propaganda e información publicados en la prensa del extranjero.* La Paz, 1916.

Oficina Nacional de Inmigración, estadística y propaganda geográfica. *El estaño en Bolivia, seguido de un apendice y de apuntes sobre el bismuto, por Manuel V. Ballivián y Bautista Saavedra.* La Paz, 1900.

Oficina Nacional de Inmigración, estadística y propaganda geográfica. *Monografías de la industria minera.* La Paz.

Oficina Nacional de Inmigración, estadística y propaganda geográfica. *Estadística minera: Instrucciones para su formación.* La Paz, 1902.

Periodicals

Boletín Comercial (La Paz).
The Mining Journal (London).
The Mining Magazine (London).

CHAPTER V

Arnous de Rivière, Henri. "Explorations in rubber districts of Bolivia." *Jour.* Amer. Geog. Soc., Vol. XXXII, pp. 432-440.

Bolivia y la Empresa Church, Folleto escrito por Luis Ortis, médico y cirujano. Sucre, 1873.

BOLIVIA DEVELOPMENT AND COLONIZATION COMPANY. *Propuesta ferrocarrilera de.* La Paz, 1912.

BOLIVIA RAILWAY COMPANY. *Extracts from manager's report,* 1921-1922. (typewritten copy in Pan American Union library).

BOLIVIA RAILWAY COMPANY. *Informe del inspector fiscal de los ferrocarriles de.* 1907-1908.

BOLIVIA RAILWAY COMPANY. *Informe del inspector fiscal de contabilidad, Sr. Enrique Gutierrez. Relativo á los gastos de construcción por* 1911. La Paz, 1912.

BOWMAN, ISAIAH. "Geographical aspects of the new Madeira-Mamoré Railroad. *Bull.*, Amer. Geog. Soc., Vol. XLV, 1913, pp. 275-281.

BOWMAN, ISAIAH. "Trade routes in the economic geography of Bolivia." *Bull.*, Amer. Geog. Soc. Vol. XLII, pp. 22-37, 90-104, 180-192.

CHURCH, GEORGE EARL. The route to Bolivia via the river Amazon. A report to the governments of Bolivia and Brazil. London, 1877.

Contract and concession for the construction and operation of railways (and supplements). The Republic of Bolivia with the National City Bank and Messrs. Speyer and Company. May 22, 1906.

Contrato ferroviario, National City Bank-Speyer y Cía. Artículos publicados en El Diario. Texto del contrato. La Paz, 1906.

CRAIG, NEVILLE B. *Recollections of an ill-fated expedition to the headwaters of the Madeira River in Brazil [written] in cooperation with members of the Madeira and Mamoré Association of Philadelphia.* Philadelphia and London, 1907.

D., M. W. "The search for rubber. New prospects in South America." *Foreign Affairs,* January 1926.

DE SANTA CRUZ, ANDRES. "El problema de la vialidad en Yungas." *Bol. de la Sociedad de Ingenieros de Bolivia.* October, 1925, pp. 8-28.

FARRAR, F. P. "Roads versus railroads in Bolivia: A question of means of communication." *West Coast Leader,* July 13, 1926.

Ferrocarriles en Bolivia: Propuesta presentada ante el Supremo Gobierno para la construcción de una red ferrocarrilera en la República, 1904.

GONZALEZ, FORMERIO. "Ferrocarriles en Bolivia." *Bol. de la Sociedad de Ingenieros de Bolivia.* October, 1925, pp. 29-51.

HALSEY, F. M. *Railways of South and Central America.* A manual containing statistical and other information concerning the important railways of South and Central America, Mexico and the West Indies. Washington, 1914.

JERRMANN, LUDWIG. "Reise in die Gummidistrikte Ost-Boliviens." *Petermanns Mitteil.* Vol. L, pp. 188-195.

Las tarifas de ferrocarriles y la ley de patrón-oro. Cuestiones de "The Antofagasta and Bolivia Railway Company" ante el supremo gobierno. La Paz, 1915.

MATTHEWS, EDWARD D. *Report to the directors of the Madeira and Mamoré Railway Company, Ltd., upon his return from Brazil and Bolivia in* 1875. London, 1875.

MEISSNER, WALTHER. *Das wirtschaftliche Vordringen der Nordamerikaner in Südamerika.* Cothen (Anhalt) 1919.

OVANDO, ALEJANDRO. "Bolivia negotiates a $14,000,000 loan for railroad works." *Bolivia: A Bi-Monthly Survey of Bolivian Activities.* January, 1927, pp. 28-30.

Papers and documents relating to Bolivian loan, National Bolivian Navigation Company, and the Madeira and Mamoré Railway Company, Ltd. London, 1873.

RIVERO, JUAN R. "La comisión panamericana de carreteras y los problemas de vialidad moderna." *Bol. de la Sociedad de Ingenieros de Bolivia.* October, 1925, pp. 53-63.

SCHURZ, WILLIAM L. *Bolivia: A commercial and industrial handbook.* Dept. of Commerce, Special Agents Series, No. 208, Washington, 1921, pp. 55-101.

SCHURZ, WILLIAM L. *Rubber production in the Amazon Valley.* Washington, 1925.

SCHURZ, WILLIAM L. "International communications in South America." *Foreign Affairs,* July, 1925, Vol. III, No. 4, pp. 624-636.

SISSON, W. LEE. *Reconnaissance report upon proposed system of Bolivian railways, May,* 1905. La Paz, 1905.

"The Bolivian loans and the contract of the Public Works Construction Company for building of the Madeira-

Mamoré Railway." Speech of A. W. Ray, Chairman of Bolivian Bondholders' Committee to the bondholders, July 30, 1873.

TEJADA, CARLOS. "The Pan American Railway in Bolivia." *Bull.*, Pan Amer. Union, Vol. LIV, 1922, pp. 123-129.

TEJADA, J. L. *El ferrocarril de La Paz á Yungas.* La Paz, 1918.

TEJADA, J. L. *Las emergencias del contrato Speyer.* La Paz, 1926.

WOODROFFE, J. F. AND SMITH, H. H. *The rubber industry of the Amazon and how its supremacy can be maintained.* London, 1915.

ZALLES, JORGE E. *Quinientas leguas á través de Bolivia. Relación del viaje de reconocimiento practicado para establecer un sistema de ferrocarriles en Bolivia,* 1904-1905. La Paz, 1906.

Official Publications

ALTA COMISIÓN INTERNACIONAL DE LEGISLACION UNIFORME. *Informes de la delegación boliviana. Abril,* 1916. La Paz, 1916.

ALVES, RODRIGUES. *Treaties, etc.* 1902—. *Brazil and Bolivia boundary settlement, treaty for the exchange of territories and other compensations, signed November* 17, 1903; *with report of Brazilian minister of foreign relations.* New York, 1904.

BALLIVIÁN, MANUEL V. *Monografía de la industria de la goma elástica en Bolivia. Dirección general de estadística y estudios geográficos.* (Edición oficial). La Paz, 1912.

CÁMARA DE DIPUTADOS. *Informe de las comisiones de hacienda e industria sobre el contrato ferroviario con el City Bank y los Srs. Speyer & Co.* La Paz, 1906.

DELEGACIÓN, SEGUNDO CONGRESO FINANCIERO PANAMERICANO, 1920. *Informe de la delegación.*

DIRECCIÓN DE OBRAS PÚBLICAS Y CUERPO NACIONAL DE INGENIEROS. *Proyecto para la construcción de ferrocarriles presentado al Señor ministro de fomento e instrucción pública, Dr. Andres S. Muñoz, por el director general de obras públicas, T. Clive Sheppard.* La Paz, 1903.

GUTIERREZ, ENRIQUE, AND MARTINEZ VARGAS, RICARDO.

Legislación ferroviaria, leyes y disposiciones vigentes, compilación. (*Edición oficial.*) La Paz, 1913.

MINISTERIO DE FOMENTO Y COMUNICACIONES. *Memoria presentada al honorable Congreso por el Ministro del Ramo, agosto de 1924 á agosto de 1925.* La Paz, 1925.

MINISTERIO DE FOMENTO E INDUSTRIA. *Ferrocarriles en Bolivia.* La Paz, 1904.

MINISTERIO DE GOBIERNO Y FOMENTO. *Ley general de ferrocarriles.* La Paz, 1910.

OFICINA NACIONAL DE INMIGRACIÓN, ESTADÍSTICA Y PROPAGANDA GEOGRÁFICA. *Compilación de leyes y supremas disposiciones relativas á concesiones ferrocarrileras años* 1880-1904. La Paz, 1904.

The Acre territory. Documents concerning the controversy between Brazil and Bolivia over a contract with American citizens. 1902.

CHAPTER VI

CALDERÓN, Y. "Bolivia. A country without a debt." *National Geographic Magazine*, Vol. XVIII, 1907, p. 573.

DEPARTMENT OF COMMERCE: Finance and Investment Division. *Latin American Financial Notes, No.* 5. May 23, 1925.

DUNN, ROBERT W. *American foreign investments. Contracts and concessions edited by Adrian Richt.* New York, 1926, pp. 65-67, 240-284.

EDWARDS, GEORGE W. *Investing in foreign securities.* Written under the auspices of the Investment Bankers Association of America—Education Committee. New York, 1926.

Hearings before the Subcommitte of the Committee on Foreign Relations, U. S. Senate, 68 Cong., 2 sess., pursuant to S. Con. Res. 22. Relative to engaging the responsibility of the Government in financial arrangements between its citizens and sovereign governments. February 25 and 26, 1925, Vol. I. Washington, 1925. Contract of loan, Republic of Bolivia and Equitable Trust Company of New York, May 31, 1922, pp. 130-152.

INTER AMERICAN HIGH COMMISSION. *Bolivia: Financial and economic conditions and public debt.* Report prepared for the Central Executive Council, December, 1919. Washington. (Unpublished).

McQueen, Charles A. *Bolivian public finance.* Dept. of Commerce. Washington, 1925.

McQueen, Charles A. *Chilean public finance.* Dept. of Commerce. Washington, 1924.

McQueen, Charles A. *Foreign exchange in Latin America: A survey of conditions since* 1914. Dept. of Commerce Trade Information Bulletin, No. 316, February, 1925, pp. 33-35.

McQueen, Charles A. *The Bolivian fiscal system: revenue, expenditure, and taxation.* Dept. of Commerce, Trade Information Bulletin, No. 201, March, 1924.

McQueen, Charles A. *Peruvian public finance.* Dept. of Commerce. Washington, 1926.

McQueen, Charles A. *The Bolivian public debt with a survey of Bolivian financial history.* Dept. of Commerce, Trade Information Bulletin, No. 194, February, 1924.

McQueen, Charles A. "The present Bolivian debt." *Commerce Reports,* June 15, 1925.

Memorandum presented by Stifel-Nicolaus Investment Company, Spencer Trask & Company, and The Equitable Trust Company of New York (as Bankers) in answer to the Memorandum presented by Srs. J. Saenz and José Mendieta, Commissioners of the Republic of Bolivia, July 30, 1923. (Strictly confidential).

Moody's Analyses of Investments and Security Rating Books. New York.

Rivera, José. *Los empréstitos extranjeros y la política americana.* La Paz, 1925.

Rojas, Casto. *Historia financiera de Bolivia.* La Paz, 1916.

Sherwell, G. Butler. *Budgets of Latin American countries.* Dept. of Commerce, Trade Information Bulletin, No. 281, October, 1924, pp. 11-14.

Standard Bond Book, 1926. New York.

Tejada, J. L. *Después de la crisis: Estudio referente á Bolivia.* 1909.

Tejada, J. L. *La reforma bancaria en Bolivia... Cuestiones económicas.* La Paz, 1913.

Tejada, J. L. *Report on the development of commercial*

relations between the United States and Bolivia. Address on international credit. Address on banking cooperation. Second Pan American Financial Conference. Washington, 1920.

Téllez, J. Guzmán. "Problemas económicos y legales de Bolivia con respeto a los Estados Unidos." *Bol.* de la Unión Panamericana, Vol. LVIII, November, 1924.

Official Publications

Anuario Legislativo, 1921-1922.

Banco de la Nación Boliviana. *Leyes orgánicas y estatutos,* 1922. The Banco de la Nación Boliviana also publishes a *Memoria* twice a year.

Comisión Fiscal Permanente. *Memoria, 15 de Julio,* 1924. La Paz.

Comisión Fiscal Permanente. *Segunda Memoria,* 1925. La Paz.

Comisión Fiscal Permanente. *Tercera Memoria,* 1926. La Paz.

Cuenta General.

Dirección General de Aduanas. *Comercio de Bolivia en el primer semestre de* 1926. La Paz, 1926.

Elías, Manuel A. *Finanzas, prácticas: Leyes orgánicas de presupuesto. Bancos. Cheques. Tratados y convenciones comerciales. Consulados.* (*Publicación autorizada*). La Paz, 1915.

Empréstito Nicolaus: *Conclusiones de la comisión especial para solicitar modificaciones del contrato,* 14 *de marzo,* 1923 (unpublished).

Memoria del Ministerio de Hacienda e Industria. Published annually, in August.

Mensaje del Presidente de la República. At the opening session of the Bolivian National Congress in August.

Ministerio de Hacienda e Industria. *Empréstito de* £500,000. *Datos e informes para su contratación.* La Paz, 1908.

Oficina Nacional de Inmigración Estadística y Propaganda Geográfica. *La empresa Church y el empréstito boliviano de* 1872 (*Sentencias judiciales—extinción de la dueda*). *Edición oficial.* La Paz, 1902.

PRESIDENTE, 1909-1913 (VILLAZÓN). *Empréstito externo por £1,500,000. Mensaje especial del poder ejecutivo.* La Paz, 1909.

PRESUPUESTO GENERAL.

ROJAS, CASTO. *Cuestiones económicas y financieras (artículos publicados en la revista ministerial Hacienda e Industria).* La Paz, 1909.

TESORO NACIONAL DE BOLIVIA. *Cuenta del empréstito celebrado con the Equitable Trust Company of New York.* December 18, 1922.

Trust Agreement between the Republic of Bolivia, the New York Trust Company as trustee, and the Ulen Contracting Corporation, made April 28, 1921.

TRUST CONTRACT. *Republic of Bolivia and The Equitable Trust Company of New York.* New York, May 31, 1922.

Periodicals

Annalist

Commerce Reports. (Also monthly summary of foreign commerce).

Commercial and Financial Chronicle

Journal of Commerce

Pan American Union Bulletin.

CHAPTER VII

(No attempt has been made in the following list of references to cover the extensive material on modern economic imperialism, foreign investments, and American imperialism that has appeared within recent years in Europe and Latin America as well as in the United States).

BITTER, WILHELM. *Die wirtschaftliche Eröberung Mittelamerikas durch den Bananen-Trust.* Hamburg, 1921.

BRAILSFORD, HENRY NOEL. *The war of steel and gold: A study of the armed peace.* London, 1917.

BRUÈRE, HENRY. "Constructive versus dollar diplomacy." *American Economic Review,* March, 1923.

BUELL, R. L. "International capitalism and its control." *Current History,* December, 1923.

Buell, Raymond Leslie. *International relations.* New York, 1925.

Drascher, Wahrhold. *Das Vordringen der Vereinigten Staaten im westindischen Mittelmeergebiet: Eine Studie über die Entwicklung und die Methoden des amerikanischen Imperialismus.* Hamburg, 1918.

Dulles, John Foster. "Our foreign loan policy." *Foreign Affairs.* October, 1926.

Dunn, Robert W. *American foreign investments. Contracts and concessions edited by Adrian Richt.* New York, 1926.

Edwards, George W. *Investing in foreign securities.* Part III. New York, 1926.

Feis, Herbert. "The export of American capital." *Foreign Affairs,* July, 1925.

Foreign Policy Association. "The international credit position of the United States." *Information Service,* Vol. II, No. 14, September 15, 1926.

Halsey, Frederic M. *Investments in Latin America and the British West Indies.* Dept. of Commerce. Special Agents Series, No. 169. Washington, 1918.

Halsey, Frederic M. *Manuscript in Dept. of Commerce on Bolivia.*

Hearings before the Subcommittee of the Committee on Foreign Relations, U. S. Senate, 68 Cong., 2 sess., pursuant to S. Con. Res. 22. Relative to engaging the responsibility of the Government in financial arrangements between its citizens and sovereign governments. February 25 and 26, 1925, Vol. I. Washington, 1925.

Hearings before the Subcommittee of the Committee on Foreign Relations, U. S. Senate, 69 Cong., 2 sess., pursuant to S. Con. Res. 15. Relative to engaging the responsibility of the Government in financial arrangements between its citizens and sovereign governments. January 25, 26 and 27 and February 16, 1927. Washington, 1927.

Hobson, C. K. *The export of capital.* London, 1914.

Hobson, J. A. *Imperialism, a study.* New York, 1902.

Ingalls, W. R. *Wealth and income of the American people: A survey of the economic consequences of the War.* New York, 1922.

KIMPEN, EMIL. *Die Ausbreitungspolitik der Vereinigten Staaten von Amerika.* Berlin, 1923.

MEISSNER, WALTHER. *Das wirtschaftliche Vordringen der Nordamerikaner in Südamerika.* Cothen (Anhalt), 1919.

MOON, PARKER THOMAS. *Imperialism and world politics.* New York, 1926.

MOON, PARKER THOMAS. *Syllabus on international relations.* New York, 1925.

NEARING, SCOTT & FREEMAN, JOSEPH. *Dollar diplomacy.* New York, 1925.

PEFFER, NATHANIEL. *The white man's dilemma.* New York, 1927.

PLEBS LEAGUE. *An outline of modern imperialism.* Plebs Textbooks No. 2. London, 1922.

SEOANE, MANUEL A. *Con el ojo izquierdo: Mirando á Bolivia.* Buenos Aires, 1926.

THOMAS, DAVID Y. *One hundred years of the Monroe Doctrine,* 1823-1923. New York, 1923.

UGARTE, MANUEL. *El destino de un continente.* Madrid, 1924. *The destiny of a continent.* New York, 1926.

VIALLATE, ACHILLE. *Economic imperialism and international relations during the last fifty years.* New York, 1923.

REFERENCE NOTES BY CHAPTERS

CHAPTER I

1 (Page 1). *Raza de Bronce* is the title of a novel by the modern Bolivian writer, Alcides Arguedas, describing the life of the highland Indian of Bolivia.

2 (Page 7). Thomas, *One Hundred Years of the Monroe Doctrine*, p. 299.

CHAPTER II

1 (Page 8.) A really scientific census of Bolivia has never been taken. The published population statistics are based upon the 1900 census. The total population is now estimated at about two and a half million. *Comisión Fiscal Permanente, Tercera Memoria*, 1926, p. 112. See also Chervin, *Anthropologie Bolivienne*, I, 248-249; Schurz, *Bolivia: A Commercial and Industrial Handbook*, pp. 25-31; Ogilvie, *Geography of the Central Andes*, pp. 136-148; Bowman, "The Distribution of Population in Bolivia" in *Bulletin*, Geographical Society of Philadelphia, VII, 28-47.

2 (Page 9). See Dawson, *The South American Republics*, Part II.

3 (Page 9). McBride, *The Agrarian Indian Communities of Highland Bolivia*, p. 2. Bowman estimated in 1910 that less than 12 percent of Bolivia's population lived on the Eastern tropical and sub-tropical plains. See his article, "Trade Routes in the Economic Geography of Bolivia" in *Bulletin*, American Geographical Society, XLII, 23.

4 (Page 9). Crespo, *Geografia de la República de Bolivia*, pp. 366-367; Chervin, *op. cit.*, I, 260.

5 (Page 9). According to Crespo, cited above, who is considered one of the leading Bolivian authorities in geography and statistics.

6 (Page 9). An inhabitant of the Yungas, the fertile region directly east of La Paz.

7 (Page 10). 186 different kinds according to an article in *Bolivia*, December, 1926. For the role of the potato in the life of Bolivia and Peru see Sievers, *Die Cordillerenstaaten*, pp. 23-64.

8 (Page 11). Bowman, "The Highland Dweller of Bolivia: An Anthropogeographic Interpretation," *Bulletin*, Geographical Society of Philadelphia, Vol. VII, No. 4; McBride, *op. cit.*, pp. 1-4; Ogilvie, *op. cit.*, pp. 17-30.

9 (Page 11). McBride, *op. cit.*, and Chervin, I, 255-259.

10 (Page 11). For the peonage system and the social basis of agriculture and stock-raising in Bolivia see Ogilvie, *op. cit.*, pp. 157 et seq.; Schurz, *op. cit.*, pp. 154 et seq.

11 (Page 12). McBride, who has made a very careful study of these agrarian communities, estimates that in 1877 about 67 percent of the highland Bolivian Indians were living in communities. Although conditions have changed somewhat in the last fifty years, the different censuses do not show any great variation in the Indian population on the plateau. The number of the communities becomes less every year, however. For this see pp. 26-27 of McBride.

12 (Page 12). McBride, p. 7.

13 (Page 12). The so-called Palacios scheme, named after the former consul-general of Bolivia in New York. See the inaugural address of President Hernando Siles, reprinted in part in *The Foreign Securities Investor,* Bolivian number, April 14, 1926.

14 (Page 12). See *La Colonización en Bolivia durante la primera centuria de su independencia,* by J. Lavadenz, *Ministerio de Guerra y Colonización;* also Schurz, *op. cit.,* p. 194.

15 (Page 12). Mr. David Weeks, professor of rural economics at the University of California, in 1926 spent several months in Bolivia investigating the practicability of this scheme from the point of view of soil and other natural conditions. See *Bolivia,* the publication of the Bolivian consulate in New York, for March and May, 1927, for articles by Prof. Weeks on opportunities for agricultural development and colonization in Bolivia. Ogilvie, pp. 107-8, asserts that, except for the Yungas and the region around Cochabamba, most of the soil in Western Bolivia is poor for agricultural development.

16 (Page 12). See Ogilvie, *op. cit.,* pp. 149-157.

17 (Page 13). The milling of the Cochabamba flour is so poorly done that flour is imported from abroad for the fastidious whites even into this wheat-growing area.

18 (Page 13). Half a boliviano, or about sixteen or seventeen cents.

19 (Page 13). To those who would advise not meddling in politics the Bolivian adds, "And go live on the planet Mars." *Ideario Aimará,* by José S. Ballivián, p. 189.

20 (Page 13). See Schurz, *op. cit.,* p. 154 et seq.

21 (Page 13). See Schurz, p. 162, and June, 1926, report of the U. S. Vice Consul in La Paz; also *Commerce Reports,* Supplement, Trade and Economic Review for 1922, No. 25. The price demanded was Bs. 2,000,000.

22 (Page 14). For the resources of this region see report, *"Las Riquezas del Oriente Boliviano"* in the Government report, *La Colonización en Bolivia, op. cit.,* pp. 86-108; also "Northeastern Bolivia" in *The South American Journal,* May 4, 1918, and Schurz, *op. cit.,* pp. 148, 165-172.

23 (Page 14). U. S. Consul's report in 1924 to the State Department on the Bolivian Colonization Association of Portland, Oregon. Col. Miguel Alaiza, writing in the *Revista Militar,* April-May, 1925, on the livestock situation in southern Bolivia, reports the price of a young bull or ox of 4-5 years as only Bs. 25-30. He estimates 65 percent of Bolivia adapted to cattle-raising and agriculture if the problem of markets could be solved. Bowman, in 1910, said that "at Reyes, in north central Bolivia, a steer out in the field cost 50 cents gold, tied to a stake $1.25, and driven to La Paz and sold for meat $35, if he survives the arduous journey of many score miles over a difficult trail." *Bulletin,* American Geographical Society, XLII, 98.

24 (Page 14). There is a weekly aeroplane service which makes the trip in a few hours, but this is obviously of no use for getting out the produce of the east country.

25 (Page 15). Although land was so freely and wastefully distributed under the 1905 law that it was suspended in 1915, and would-be concessionaires must now go through the long and expensive process of petitioning the Bolivian Congress. Schurz, *op. cit.,* pp. 190-194. For the Bolivian land laws see a pamphlet issued in 1925 by the Pan American Union entitled "Bolivia: General Descriptive Data"; Reid, *Bolivia, the Heart of a Continent,* pp. 49-51; and Ballivián, report to the League of Nations, 1920, which also describes in some detail the elaborate project of the "Americana Syndicate" for the colonization of five million acres or more. There is no indication anywhere that this ambitious plan was ever carried out.

26 (Page 15). See *La Colonización en Bolivia,* cited above.

27 (Page 15). *Ibid,* pp. 40 and 27-28. By law of September 11, 1915, the further sale of public lands was suspended. Schurz, *op. cit.,* pp. 190-194, mentions that by 1919 final titles had been granted to 13,426,550 hectares; Lopez, in his *Bolivia y el Petroleo,* pp. 355-357, gives almost 20,000,000 hectares as the amount of land conceded, and lists the chief concessionaires, among them the Bolivia Railway Company which under the Speyer-National City Bank contract of 1905 was granted a thousand square leagues. See also Elias, *Finanzas Prácticas,* pp. 155-160.

28 (Page 15). In 1901 Sir Martin Conway organized a company to exploit a concession for 15,000 square miles which the Government had just granted him. Development did not take place within the required time and in 1909 the concession was declared null and void. *La Colonización en Bolivia,* pp. 19-20, and a pamphlet published in La Paz in 1901 under the title *"La Bolivian Company": Sociedad de explotación, colonización y vialidad en la región de Caupolicán,"* which contains text of the concession.

29 (Page 15). *The New York Times,* February 4, 1926.

30 (Page 15). *West Coast Leader,* October 5 and 12, 1926.

31 (Page 15). The Bolivian Colonization Association of Portland, Oregon, organized in 1921, has to date a disgraceful record. Not only has it sold land in the Santa Cruz section of Bolivia to which it had no title, not having as yet persuaded the Bolivian Government to grant it the concession for 350,000 hectares it has petitioned for, but with the usual boom tactics, it has led naive and disgruntled farmers of our north and middle west to expect an agricultural Utopia in eastern Bolivia—no taxes, cheap help, good markets, and fertile soil that will with little effort yield all the familiar products and exotic and alluring things as well, like sugar cane, coffee, cotton, rubber, tobacco—God's own country, in fact, for $2.50 an acre and easy payments! To overcome the pangs of nostalgia which the thought of pulling up stakes and driving them in again so many thousand miles from home might induce, a town of Los Angeles in the center of the colony is promised, and on a diagram supplied by the company you pick out your plot, measured from the flag-pole in the center of the town. The scheme was such an obvious fraud that the company was sued by the United States Post Office for fraudulent use of the mails, but the case for the Government seems to have been so carelessly prepared that the Post Office lost. And yet the nearest possible market is 300 miles by mule back, private lands in the same region were said in 1924 to be selling at 5-10 cents per acre, and the Geographical Society of Santa Cruz has declared the lands the company wants unfitted for agriculture and only on a moderate scale and at great expense suited to cattle-raising. See *La Colonización en Bolivia,* p. 52.

32 (Page 15). In 1923 a 99-year lease on 18,000 hectares of public land in southeastern Bolivia was granted to Col. William H. Murray of Oklahoma, known in Bolivia as "Alfalfa Bill." Murray agreed to bring in twenty-five North American families, to open roads, establish telephone communications, and found a modern agricultural community, designed especially for the cultivation of coffee and cotton. The land was considered close enough to the Argentine border and the railhead at Embarcación to make marketing of the produce possible. The colonists who followed Murray there found the best lands taken by squatters and had themselves to occupy the less desirable land in the hills. Drought, a plague of locusts, and the Argentine prohibition on the export of cattle from Bolivia forced a number of the families to return to the United States. The Government is still hopeful that the Murray colony may be a success but as yet the only tangible result so far as it is concerned is a meager return of Bs. 5,400 on the lease and a great deal of criticism in the Bolivian Congress and the press. See *La Colonización en Bolivia,* pp. 33, 50-51; article by Col. Alaiza in the *Revista Militar* cited above; and *Redactor de la H. Cámara de Diputados,* Tomo I, 1923, pp. 7-27.

33 (Page 15). This is just what the British syndicate mentioned above is doing. By the reopening of the port of Gaiba on the Paraguay River the proposed colony will be in touch with the Atlantic. A steamer service to Buenos Aires is to be instituted, and, reminiscent of Tomlinson's *The Sea and the Jungle,* it is reported that settlers from England will set off for the colony in a 600 ton river steamer. *West Coast Leader,* October 5, 1926.

34 (Page 15). See the report of the Ministry of War and Colonization cited above, pp. 38-39, 46-47.

35 (Page 15). *La Colonización en Bolivia, op. cit.,* p. 47.

36 (Page 16). Ogilvie, *op. cit.,* Appendix B, in a short statement of the problem of Tacna-Arica, declares that the Bolivian revolution in 1919 (1920?) was caused largely by opposing views and sympathies regarding this dispute. Free transit of goods into or out of Bolivia through Chile and Peru was assured in the Traffic Conventions of 1912-1914 and 1908 respectively. See Elias, *Finanzas Prácticas.*

37 (Page 17). *"Arica y la política comercial de Bolivia: El 'Puerto Potosí' durante la Colonia y en los cien años de la República,"* by Casto Rojas, in *El Diario,* 6 agosto, 1925.

38 (Page 17). Ogilvie, Appendix B, *op. cit.*

39 (Page 17). *El Diario,* 6 agosto, 1925, as above.

40 (Page 17). See *Resumen general de importaciones y exportaciones por vias de ingreso y salida en 1925, Boletín Comercial,* 11 julio, 1926, p. 21 and table following; also Tejada, *Las emergencias del contrato Speyer,* pp. 26-30.

41 (Page 18). For Bolivian agitation for a port see reports of the Bolivian Port Restoration League, organized by Bolivians residing in the United States (*Commercial and Financial Chronicle,* April 15, 1922), especially a pamphlet entitled *"La opinión en los Estados Unidos sobre el problema del Pacífico"*; also Diez de Medina, *La cuestion del Pacífico y la política internacional de Bolivia;* Paz, *Bolivian-Chilean question, the Port Problem of the South Pacific;* Carrasco, *Bolivia's Case for the League of Nations,* which makes a plea for the restoration of Antofagasta; *Las pretensiones de Bolivia sobre Arica, Ministerio de Relaciones Exteriores,* 1920; Letter and Memorandum from the Bolivian Delegation to the League of Nations, 1921, claiming a revision of the Treaty of Peace of 1904; and Borgoño, *The Problem of the Pacific and the New Policies of Bolivia.*

42 (Page 18). The total export of live stock from Bolivia in 1923 only amounted to Bs. 353,676. Report of Director General of Customs, February 14, 1925.

43 (Page 19). The largest single item in Bolivia's list of imports in 1925 was flour; the next from the point of view of value was white sugar, while live stock and rice were well up on the list both as to weight and value. See *Dirección General de Aduanas: Comercio de Bolivia en el Primer Semestre de 1926.* The relative importance of these imports was slightly different in 1926 but not materially, flour still constituting the great bulk of the goods imported, white sugar dropping to fourth place, rice and live stock both increasing in importance.

44 (Page 19). Wrigley, "Fairs of the Central Andes," in *Geographical Review,* VII (1919), 65-80.

45 (Page 19). *Ibid,* p. 70. See also Bowman, "The Highland Dweller of Bolivia," *op. cit.,* and "Trade Routes in the Economic Geography of Bolivia," *op. cit.*

CHAPTER III

1 (Page 21). The last report of the Permanent Fiscal Commission in a comparative table of the commercial, banking and financial development of the republic during the last decade gives the population in 1925 as 2,592,916. See *Comisión Fiscal Permanente, Tercera Memoria,* 1926, p. 112.

2 (Page 21). See Chervin, *Anthropologie Bolivienne,* Vol. I. Chervin published in 1908 a very careful, detailed study of the two important population groups of the Bolivian plateau. The first volume is largely ethnological; volumes two and three contain the results of his anthropometric and craniometric study of the Aymará and Quichua Indians of highland Bolivia.

3 (Page 21). Chervin, as above; Schurz, *op. cit.,* p. 188. The population figures given by the Permanent Fiscal Commission, as cited above, show an increase of only 63,716 in the last ten years. On the other hand the population in the quarter century 1900-1925 seems to have increased almost a million. The inadequate census statistics are to be blamed for this discrepancy. Chervin in 1908 gave the foreigners living in Bolivia as not 4 per 1,000 of the inhabitants.

4 (Page 21). The 1900 census gave the ethnical distribution as follows:

Whites	12.72%	according to Chervin;	14.64%	according to Schurz
Mestizos ..	26.75%	" " "	29.45%	" " "
Indians ..	50.91%	" " "	48.42%	" " "
Negroes ..	0.21%	" " "		Schurz gives same total (3,945) as Chervin but omits %
Unclassified	9.41%	" " "	7.31%	according to Schurz

The La Paz department is 75.6% Indian, 8.9% mestizo and 8.1% white; the department of Santa Cruz is 45.1% Indian, 21.1% mestizo and 28.3% white; Cochabamba is only 23% Indian, 51.5% mestizo and 18.4% white. The statistics show the heaviest Indian population on the plateau and in the Beni country. Chervin, I, 248-249. See also Ogilvie, *op. cit.,* pp. 136-148. Sievers, *Die Cordillerenstaaten,* pp. 29-33, gives the Indian and cholo as about 9/10 of the population.

5 (Page 21). Drascher, *Das Vordringen der Vereinigten Staaten im westindischen Mittelmeergebiet,* p. 102. The Department of Commerce's *Commercial Travelers' Guide to Latin America,* p. 177, gives the proportion of pure whites in Nicaragua as about 10 percent.

6 (Page 23). Quesada, *La sociología relativista spengleriana,* especially pp. 524, 577, 588.

7 (Page 23). Ballivián, *Ideario Aimará,* p. 169. For the incapacity of the Indians of the South American plateau for progress see also Adams, *The Plateau Peoples of South America: An Essay in Ethnic Psychology,* although unfortunately Adams seems pretty thoroughly imbued with the Nordic myth.

8 (Page 24). Called *chuño*; other native foods such as oca and the grain of quinoa or millet are found in the Indian's diet, and east of the Andes yucca and banana are commonly eaten, but of animal food or milk the Indian consumes very little. Dried meat or *charqui* is a common food of the mestizo. See Ogilvie, *op. cit.,* pp. 149-157; Schurz, *op. cit.,* p. 28.

9 (Page 24). Tilling only once in 20 or 30 years was the estimate given by Sr. A. Sanjines in a report on agricultural conditions in Oruro. The average, as has been indicated above, is about once in every five years. McBride, *op. cit.,* p. 7.

10 (Page 25). See McBride, p. 3.

11 (Page 25). Ogilvie, cited above, says that the free highland Bolivian's wealth is measured in terms of the number of llamas he owns (p. 157).

12 (Page 26). *Cholo* is the word used to designate the Bolivian mestizo or half-breed.

13 (Page 26). Paredes, *Mitos, Supersticiones y Supervivencias Populares de Bolivia,* p. 120.

14 (Page 26). See Chervin, I, 52-66; Schurz, pp. 188-189; Crespo, pp. 121-122. Chervin recognizes the numerical superiority of the mestizo over the white and stresses the necessity of educating him and tightening up his

moral standards so that he may contribute more effectively to the country's development and make up somewhat for the lack of population of European origin. He questions seriously the wholesale denunciation of the indigenous population, which has already made distinguished contributions to the professional and commercial classes.

15 (Page 26). The *corregidor,* the *ilcata* and the *alcalde* are all frequently drawn from the mestizo group. For these officials see McBride, p. 8, and McBride, *Social and Religious Organization of the Plateau Indians,* Appendix A to Ogilvie, *op. cit.*

16 (Page 26). Moreover, the distinction between the cholo and either the white or the Indian is not always sharply defined.

17 (Page 26). An attempt to portray the life of the cholo has been made in a play entitled *"La Rosita"* by Villamil, produced in La Paz in August, 1926.

18 (Page 27). "The Highland Dweller of Bolivia: An Anthropogeographic Interpretation" in *Bulletin* of the Geographical Society of Philadelphia, Vol. VII, No. 4.

19 (Page 27). *The Agrarian Indian Communities of Highland Bolivia,* p. 27.

20 (Page 29). Other reasons given were lack of program, corruption, and anti-clericalism. It was largely on the last-named ground that the Student Federation, a highly organized group in Bolivia, attacked the crusade and contributed largely to its defeat. The city of La Paz was placarded with posters *pro* and *contra,* demonstrating the typically North American money-raising campaign that was undertaken and the absurdity to which it was reduced by its opponents.

21 (Page 29). The 1927 budget sets aside 9 percent of the total revenue for public instruction; and 37 percent for service of the public debt. *West Coast Leader,* July 12, 1927. In 1924 out of a total expenditure of Bs. 41,494,949, only Bs. 3,666,353 was spent for the department of instruction and agriculture combined. See *Comisión Fiscal Permanente, Segunda Memoria,* 1925, p. 43. For the years 1915-1921 the amount spent on public instruction ranged from 8 to 11 percent of the total. See McQueen, *Bolivian Public Finance,* pp. 35-36.

22 (Page 29). See comparative statistics of all countries whose government obligations are listed on the New York Stock Exchange, in Edwards, *Investing in Foreign Securities,* p. 130.

23 (Page 29). Chervin says that of those included in the 1900 census, only 16 percent were literate, and that the proportion was inverse to the number of Indians in each department (see *op. cit.,* p. 249); Inman, in his *South America Today,* estimates the illiteracy around 1920 as 87 percent (p. 43).

24 (Page 29). For some of the superstitious beliefs, both ancient and current, of the Bolivian Indians see Paredes, cited above; also McBride, *Social and Religious Organization of the Plateau Indians,* Appendix A to Ogilvie, *Geography of the Central Andes.*

25 (Page 29). Ballivián, *Ideario Aimará,* "Los Callahuayas, Medicos Ambulantes," pp. 44-58; Paredes, *op. cit.,* pp. 221, 225-240; and especially Wrigley, "The Traveling Doctor of the Andes; The Callahuayas of Bolivia," *Geographical Review,* IV (1917), 183-196. Miss Wrigley indicates no tendency of the *Callahuaya* to disappear.

26 (Page 29). See McBride in Ogilvie, *op. cit.*

27 (Page 29). *Mitos, Superstiticiones y Supervivencias Populares de Bolivia,* p. 21.

28 (Page 30). See Ross, *South of Panama,* pp. 322-323, who, in writing of the situation in southern Peru and Bolivia, says: "A gross, ignorant half-breed *cura* up among the poor natives of this Thibet may extract an income that would do credit to a metropolitan pulpit; the *cura* of San

Pedro is said to take in $4,800 a year, while the *cura* of Sacaca, a village of 2,000, derives from this and neighboring hamlets $7,200 a year."

29 (Page 30). A frequent priestly exhortation, according to Paredes (p. 179), is, "A dog is he, and not *gente,* who does not celebrate the day of the patron saint of his village."

30 (Page 30). For the *alferazgo* see Paredes, *op. cit.* pp. 176-186; Ballivián, *"El Alferez Condori"* in *Ideario Aimará,* pp. 126-131.

31 (Page 30). "Regional population groups of Atacama," *Bulletin,* American Geographical Society, XLI (1909), 142-154, 193-211, especially p. 211 for the quotation given above.

32 (Page 31). Wrigley, "Fairs of the Central Andes," *Geographical Review,* VII (1919), 76.

33 (Page 31). Paredes asserts that one of the old pagan gods is often the real cause of the celebration.

34 (Page 32). Paredes, *op. cit.,* pp. 75-76.

CHAPTER IV

1 (Page 34). Translated from Ballivián, *Ideario Aimará,* p. 175.

2 (Page 35). Ogilvie, *op. cit.,* p. 59, says that in 1678 Oruro had about five times its present population.

3 (Page 35). See *ibid,* pp. 49-53, 175-176, where Ogilvie states that "it is probably no exaggeration to say that every square league of hilly country occupied by the Spaniards bears some sign of having been explored for its mineral wealth."

4 (Page 35). The exceedingly low tunnels, no more than three feet in height, of which many traces remain, suggest that the Indian miner of the colonial period must have had to crawl in on his hands and knees, work in this cramped position, and then crawl out later with his findings. It is currently said in Bolivia that the life of an Indian laborer in the Spanish mines was a thing of two or three weeks only. Dawson, *op. cit.,* p. 242, in writing of the Spanish exploitation of the Indians, says, "To work these mines the Spaniards ruthlessly impressed the helpless Indians. Each village was required to furnish a certain number of laborers annually. Lots were drawn as if for a proscription and the unhappy creatures who drew the bad numbers went off to meet a certain death in the dark wet pits and galleries, bidding goodbye to their wives and children like men stepping on the scaffold. The destruction of life was frightful, the official returns made by the officials charged with the impressment demonstrating that in the neighborhood of Potosí the Indian population fell within a hundred years to a tenth of its original number."

5 (Page 35). *World Atlas of Commercial Geology,* Part I, pp. 60-62; Jones, *Tinfields of the World,* pp. vi, 52, which gives Bolivia third place in the 1924 output; Schurz, *op. cit.,* p. 108; Weed, *Handbook of Mines,* 1924, p. 62; *South American Handbook,* 1925.

6 (Page 35). Except for a small production from dumps, Bolivian tin comes from lodes or veins, which means greater permanence and an increased output as compared with the Eastern deposits. See the preface to Jones, *op. cit.,* which asserts that by 1935 operations in the majority of the Eastern areas will have ceased; also *Mining Journal,* August 15, 1925, p. 652. *The New York Times* on March 10, 1926, reported that the rich tin deposits on the island of Banka in the Dutch East Indies were showing signs of exhaustion. On the other hand the *World Atlas of Commercial Geology,* published by the U. S. Geological Survey, considers that tin mining in the Dutch East Indies has a long and prosperous future ahead (p. 61).

7 (Page 35). For some of the more common uses of tin see the *World Atlas of Commercial Geology* cited above; Jones, *op. cit.;* Reid, *A Brief*

Talk About Tin, Pan American Union pamphlet; Wile, "Tin Mining in Bolivia," in *Bolivia, A Quarterly Survey of Bolivian Activities,* December, 1926; Smith, *The Strategy of Minerals,* pp. 195-197.

8 (Page 35). Jones, *op. cit.,* pp. 5-6, states that the production of 2,236,-000 lbs. in 1891 had increased to almost 850,000,000 by 1900. See also Bancroft, "Bolivian Tin and Its Relation to the United States" in *Proceedings,* Second Pan American Scientific Congress, Vol. VIII, sec. 7, pp. 294-309. A single order reported by *The New York Times,* November 20, 1926, received by the American Sheet and Tin Plate Company, a subsidiary of the U. S. Steel Corporation, called for some 300,000 tons valued at approximately $31,000,000, to be turned into tin cans by the American Can and the Continental Can Companies.

9 (Page 36). "Prospects of the Tin Industry: Production and Prices," *London Times Trade and Engineering Supplement* (reprinted in the *West Coast Leader,* November 2, 1926). For the percentage of world output consumed by the United States see also Weed and the *World Atlas of Commercial Geology* cited above. Some estimates give it nearer two-thirds.

10 (Page 36). See *The New York Times,* January 10, 1926, "Hoover Warns World of Trade Wars."

11 (Page 36). Moon, *Imperialism and World Politics,* p. 543.

12 (Page 36). The extremely small amount of tin produced by the United States comes chiefly from Alaska. See *World Atlas of Commercial Geology,* p. 62.

13 (Page 36). Ex-Secretary Redfield, in his *Dependent America,* p. 209 (cited in Moon, p. 551), lists tin among the thirty essential war materials of which the United States has an insufficient supply. The U. S. Geological Survey, in the *World Atlas of Commercial Geology* cited above (p. 61), states that "in the early stages of the war tin was not regarded as a 'war mineral,' but after the slogan 'Food will win the war' was adopted it became obvious that the food resources of the Allied and neutral nations could be properly and fully utilized only by means of an adequate supply of tin plate." Smith, *op. cit.,* states that during the war "tin became the cause of as much governmental anxiety and regulation as any other metal except platinum" (p. 196).

14 (Page 36). *Comisión Fiscal Permanente, Tercera Memoria,* 1926, p. 42. The Permanent Fiscal Commission cites as authority for the Eastern production figures the Metal Information Bureau of London, but asserts that its figure for Bolivia's 1925 output, 30,500 tons, is incorrect. It is generally held that Bolivian production now exceeds that of the Dutch East Indies, although as has been indicated above, Jones assigns Bolivia third place in 1924. The Fiscal Commission's report states that in 1925 Bolivia exported 32,740 tons, more than the London figure credits her with producing.

15 (Page 37). *Boletín Comercial,* June 6, 1926, pp. 30-31. The impurities in Bolivian tin and lead, copper, arsenic, antimony, bismuth, iron, aluminum, cal, tungsten and sulphur. These make the treatment of Bolivian concentrates very complicated in comparison with Straits concentrate, which is easily reduced, yielding a very fine metal of between 99.75 and 99.90 percent tin. The Bolivian concentrates are not as high grade as the Straits concentrates either, containing from 58-70 percent tin as compared with 70-76 percent. See also Jones, *op. cit.,* p. 47; and Agassiz, "The Unparalleled Resources of Bolivia" in *South American,* March, 1917. The impurities can be removed by electrolysis, with results quite comparable to the best Straits tin, as was done in the American Smelting and Refining Company's smelter at Perth Amboy, but the costs were considerably higher than those of the English smelters.

16 (Page 37). The form in which the tin ore, after a process of crushing and washing, is shipped abroad. Bolivian concentrate, or barrilla, usu-

ally assays about 60 percent, Straits somewhat higher. See footnote 15 above.

17 (Page 37). *Boletín Comercial,* June 6, 1926, p. 30. According to the account of Mr. Hoover's warning with regard to foreign governmental and private control over raw materials cited above (*The New York Times*, January 10, 1926), the duty consists of $15.60 for 133.4 pounds. For this and other differential export taxes see Moon, *Imperialism and World Politics,* pp. 550-551.

18 (Page 37). See Schurz, *Bolivia: A Commercial and Industrial Handbook,* pp. 105, 110-111; Pan American Union: Commerce of Bolivia, Latest Reports from Bolivian Official Sources, which contains comparative figures on shipments to Great Britain and the United States in 1920 and 1921, showing the big falling off in tin shipments to the latter in 1921; *Mining Journal,* January 24, 1925; and *Boletín Comercial,* February 28, 1926, for comparative figures, 1923-1925, from official data prepared by the *Dirección General de Aduanas.* For the American Smelting and Refining Company's smelter at Perth Amboy see *Daily Consular and Trade Reports,* January 6, 1916; "Bolivian Tin Industry," *South American,* October, 1916.

19 (Page 37). Jones, *op. cit.,* pp. 25-29. The charge in the United States Smelters was £14 per ton, whereas the English smelters charge at present only about £7.10 per ton.

20 (Page 37). See Jones, *op. cit.,* and Schurz, p. 104. A South American Electric Smelting Company was organized in 1916 with Minor C. Keith, of United Fruit Company fame, as president (see *Iron Age,* March 2, 1916), but electric smelting in Bolivia did not prove successful, and the movement for it was short-lived. During the war when it was impossible to secure jute sacks for exporting tin concentrate, Luis Soux, known as the owner of Potosí Hill, smelted his own concentrates in Potosí, using *yareta* and *taquia* as fuel, and was so successful that he was able to sell his tin on the Argentine market at a very high price, but for smelting on a large scale a more satisfactory combustible would be required.

21 (Page 38). Schurz, p. 104, reports that in 1920 a large American electrical development company made an extensive survey of the power possibilities on the eastern side of the Andes, but as yet nothing has been done toward developing them. Bolivia's great need of hydro-electric power and the possibilities of developing it were pointed out by Dr. Isaiah Bowman as far back as 1910. "For railroad, as for industrial purposes, the region possesses one unrivalled resource, its water power. Were the dynamic energy in the headwaters of Bolivia's streams properly utilized today, there would be generated sufficient electrical power to run every railroad train now operated in the Republic, everyone ever to be operated, every factory, every mine . . . the transference of electrical power from the eastern Andes to the central plateau is one of the sanest present-day possibilities and would at once eliminate that great expense of the plateau railroad, coal. The coal now burned there costs $20 to $30 per ton and the rate is ruinous. Bolivia's coal resources are practically nil. She must continue to import coal whose cost even at the centers of population is bound to suffer rapid increase in the near future. . . . What Bolivia needs to supply power and bring the products of the plains to her more densely inhabited plateau is not a great coal deposit, but dams. Coal deposits are exhaustible, but the waterpower of Bolivia's magnificently watered eastern slopes is as permanent as the slopes themselves." "Trade Routes in the Economic Geography of Bolivia," *Bulletin,* American Geographical Society, XLII (1910), 103-104.

22 (Page 38). Schurz, *op. cit.,* p. 105.

23 (Page 39). For a discussion of the unfavorable mining conditions in Bolivia see Bancroft, *op cit.,* who was on the whole interested in encouraging North American capital to invest in the Bolivian tin industry.

24 (Page 39). This loss is from 30-40 percent. See *Boletín Comercial,*

December 13, 1925, p. 15, and Venables and Howard-Wright, "Mining in Bolivia," *Mining Magazine,* December, 1924, XXXI, 350-355.

25 (Page 40). Rounsevell, "The Copper Mines of Corocoro," *West Coast Leader,* Bolivia Number, March, 1924, p. 74.

26 (Page 40). Schurz, *op. cit.,* p. 103; Ogilvie, *op. cit.,* pp. 59, 176; Bancroft, in *Proceedings,* Second Pan American Scientific Congress, cited above; Penberthy, "Tin in Bolivia," 76th report of the Royal Cornwall Polytechnic Society, Vol. I, 1909, Part I, pp. 127-142; Jones, *op. cit.,* pp. 312-330.

27 (Page 40). Ogilvie gives the heights above sea level of the principal mines as follows: Morococala, 5,000 meters; Caracoles, 4,800 meters; Araca, 4,500 meters; Uncia, 4,400 meters; Llallagua, about 4,000 meters, etc. (p. 59). The highest mine in the Caracoles group is reputed to be almost 18,000 feet high.

28 (Page 40). Ogilvie, *op. cit.,* p. 176; see also Ross, *South of Panama,* pp. 153-157, on "hooking" labor in Peru.

29 (Page 40). *Boletín Comercial,* November 22, 1925.

30 (Page 41). Schurz, *op. cit.,* p. 103.

31 (Page 42). In the summer of 1926 the exchange was about 2.92 Bs. to the dollar. The *Boletin Comercial* for December 13, 1925, gives the wages of the common laborer as 1.80 to 4 Bs. per day, of the Indian or mestizo miners, 2.50 to 6 Bs. Schurz, *op. cit.,* mentions a variation in wages for mines labor of from 1 to 7 Bs. per day, with the average near 3 Bs. A consular cable to the Commerce Department in 1922 reported that general labor gets about Bs. 1.50 to Bs. 2, without board, piece workers in the mines, Bs. 3.50 to Bs. 6 per day, and the ordinary miner Bs. 4 daily; the cable adds that although some of the largest mines operate in three eight-hour shifts, the Indians do not like the system and prefer to work twelve hours. An unpublished report of the Inter American High Commission, prepared in 1919, gives the daily wages to native employees in the mines as about .70 Bs. to women, 1.80 Bs. to men. Bancroft, *op. cit.,* in 1920, states that the wage scale for ordinary Indian labor varies from 40 cents to $2.40 per day, the average being one dollar.

32 (Page 43). Schurz, *op. cit.,* p. 103.

33 (Page 43). To be worked profitably tin ore must contain from 1 to 2 percent of tin. The veins now being worked by the Guggenheims at Caracoles run as low as 2 percent. The Llallagua and Uncia mines contain a higher grade ore, running 5.45 percent on an average. The highest grade tin ore in Bolivia carries from 18-20 percent tin but such high-grade ore is exceedingly rare.

34 (Page 44). See Annual Report, Patiño Mines and Enterprises Consolidated, Inc., December 31, 1925; circular of Lehman Brothers, December, 1926, offering for sale 200,000 shares of the company; and *The New York Times,* December 22, 1926. The production figures given on page 7 of the annual report are enlightening:

Production cost (not including depreciation) at mine and mill	£645,548. 6. 4
Other costs on concentrates	
Cartage and expenses to railroad	£38,673.11. 5
R. R. freight and shipping expense	63,207. 5. 8
Export duties	178,060. 8. 2
Additional taxes	18,952.11.11
Marine, freight and insurance	36,159.18. 6
Smelting charges	186,055. 8. 9
Commissions and other charges in Europe..	13,527. 5.10
Total	£1,180,184.16. 7

(This at $4.83 to the £, the average rate for 1925, equals .... $5,700,292.72)
Sales—10,515 tons Concentrates containing 6,837.30 tons tin at £260.11.7 .... £1,781,660.12.8
(According to these figures the total costs of production were $833.70 per ton, or 37 cents a pound.)

35 (Page 44). The story runs that the deed to the valuable Llallagua and Uncia properties was turned over to Patiño, at the time a clerk in a general merchandise store in Bolivia, in payment of a debt of $250 owed his firm. The firm refused to accept the deed and discharged Patiño. On finding signs of tin on the property, Patiño started working the mine in a very small way; later he succeeded in making a working agreement with the British commercial house, Duncan, Fox and Company, by which they advanced him capital on condition that he sell them his output. The tale of this mestizo's rapid rise to fortune is current in Bolivia. See also *The New York Times,* December 22, 1926.

36 (Page 45). Domestic capital, 35.5 percent, foreign capital 64.5 percent, according to the official figures given out after a General Register of Mines, based on declarations and balance sheets of each enterprise, had been prepared by the Permanent Fiscal Commission. This register lists 110 enterprises with almost 2,000 employees and over 27,000 laborers, and 53,567 hectares in mining concessions being worked. See *Comisión Fiscal Permanente, Segunda Memoria,* pp. 52-53; *Boletín Comercial,* November 22 and December 27, 1925.

37 (Page 45). Schurz, *op. cit.,* p. 242. It is interesting to note that of the companies listed by Schurz as Chilean, Patiño had a big interest in one of the largest and has since acquired either control of or an interest in two others, while the most important from the point of view of paid up capital has since passed into the hands of North Americans. A statement in *Commerce Reports* for March 24, 1924, to the effect that a new tin mining company with a capital of £3,000,000, largely American but incorporated in Chile, was commencing operations near Potosí, bears out this point.

38 (Page 45). For these see Weed, *The Mines Handbook,* 1924: *Boletín Comercial,* December 27, 1925; *Mining Magazine,* December, 1924, XXX, 353-354; Schurz, *op. cit.,* pp. 120-137, 242.

39 (Page 45). At the rate of 3 Bs. to the dollar, 64.5 percent of the total amount invested in Bolivian mining would be equivalent to $69,607,-243.30. This is doubtless an underestimate.

40 (Page 45). See *Comisión Fiscal Permanente, Tercera Memoria,* 1926, table facing p. 42. These five companies produced 23,648 fine tons out of a total of 36,602, or almost 2/3 of the whole output. The figures are reproduced here as of possible interest:

Company	*Output (concentrate) Tons*	*Export (concentrate) Tons*	*Grade %*	*Value in Bs.*	*Taxes collected Bs.*	*Profits Bs.*
Patiño Mines & Enterprises	† 12,129	11,089	64.42	26,885,942	2,442,430	17,850,291
‡ Caracoles	3,732	3,244	62.41	7,970,098	732,518	——
Oploca	3,468	2,377	58.78	5,832,404	534,820	3,942,238
Araca	2,395	2,340	60.36	5,475,560	499,679	2,390,292
Aramayo	1,924	1,904	57.68	4,700,586	431,539	3,075,401

† The 1925 annual report of the company gives the amount of concentrate produced as 15,827 tons; Patiño himself, in a letter of December 18, 1926, to Lehman Brothers, gives the 1925 production as only 10,039 long tons.

‡ The balance sheet of the Caracoles Company, which has been producing only since 1924, showed a loss of Bs. 1,057,274.

41 (Page 46). Weed, *The Mines Handbook,* 1924, pp. 2,283-2,284; *Boston News Bureau,* August 29, 1924.

42 (Page 46). The exact prices paid, as given by Weed, p. 2,275, were £6,250,000 for the mines and £991,667 for the railroad.

43 (Page 46). In December, 1926, there were 1,380,316 shares outstanding. See circular of Lehman Brothers of that date.

44 (Page 46). Weed, *op. cit.,* pp. 2,275-2,276.

45 (Page 46). Weed, p. 2,284; *Moody's Industrials,* 1923, p. 1,951.

46 (Page 46). *Mining Journal,* August 15, 1925, p. 652; *Mining Magazine,* December, 1924, XXXI, 355.

47 (Page 46). 15,827 tons of tin concentrate (see Annual Report of the Company for 1925) out of a total for Bolivia of 36,602 tons (see 1926 report of the Permanent Fiscal Commission) and for the world of approximately 142,000 tons. If the Permanent Fiscal Commission's production figure for Patiño be used, Patiño Mines and Enterprises produced only one-third of Bolivia's total and about 9 percent of the world output. Weed, in 1924, assigned to this company one-half of the total Bolivian output, and one-fifth of that of the world. The Department of Commerce on August 28, 1924, stated that these properties, costing $27,000,000, produced approximately 50 percent of Bolivia's tin.

48 (Page 47). December 22, 1926.

49 (Page 47). Yeatman & Berry. See extracts from their report reprinted in the circular issued by Lehman Brothers, December, 1926.

50 (Page 47). See Annual Report of the company, December 31, 1925, pp. 10-11.

51 (Page 47). Ivey, "Some Bolivian Tin Mines," *Mining Magazine,* October, 1925, XXXIII, 220-223. The Araca company is capitalized at £200,000, the Oplaca at £600,000. See also article by Venables and Howard-Wright in *Mining Magazine,* December, 1924, XXXI, 352-353.

52 (Page 48). Weed, *op. cit.,* p. 2,273; report of consul at La Paz to Department of Commerce, September, 1922; Schurz, *op. cit.,* p. 122, mentions petitions filed for about 3,000 hectares more of mining properties in the same region.

53 (Page 48). *Mining Journal,* January 3, 1925, p. 9, "Ore Handling at the Caracoles Tin Mine."

54 (Page 48). Consular report, September, 1922, cited above; Reid, *A Brief Talk about Tin,* p. 9, gives the cost as $50,000 a mile, which at 68 miles would be $3,400,000 or less than half the maximum estimate.

55 (Page 48). "Mining in Bolivia in 1925," by C. Leonard Ball, Director General of Department of Mines, *Boletín Comercial,* May 23, 1926. Wile, *op. cit.,* on the other hand, says that in some of the modern mills, thanks to the oil flotation process, recovery is now as high as 92 percent, whereas until this process was used it did not exceed 72 percent.

56 (Page 48). Early expectations of the quality of the ore in these mines were very high, Schurz stating in 1921 that the ore ran from 3 to 25 percent. As a matter of fact it is quite low grade. It has been running 4 percent and 5 percent, but is now yielding only about 2 percent ore.

57 (Page 49). Ball in *Boletín Comercial,* cited above; *Mining Magazine,* October, 1925, XXXIII, 223; *The New York Times,* September 14, 1925; Schurz, *op. cit.,* p. 136.

58 (Page 49). *Comisión Fiscal Permanente, Tercera Memoria,* 1926, p. 42.

59 (Page 49). As a result of a recent law-suit, control of this company, capitalized at $3,000,000, has now passed to London, but Americans still hold an interest in it. An interesting American veteran in Bolivian gold and tin mining has played a prominent part in the company's affairs from the beginning. Its properties cover 6,600 acres in the Huayna-Potosí

district north of La Paz. The company was incorporated in Bolivia in 1921, and did not begin production to any extent until March, 1923. See Weed, *op. cit.*, p. 2,282 and consular report to Department of Commerce, September, 1922.

60 (Page 49). A small company, capitalized at around one million dollars, with properties covering 355 hectares and an annual production of under 200 tons. See *Boletín Comercial,* December 27, 1925, and *Comisión Fiscal Permanente, Tercera Memoria,* 1926, p. 42.

61 (Page 49). Capitalized at 1,000,000 bolivianos with properties variously given as 3,500 hectares (Schurz, p. 136 and Weed, p. 2,282) and 480 hectares (*Boletín Comercial,* December 27, 1925).

62 (Page 49). Schurz, *op. cit.,* p. 137; Aniceto Blanco, *Monografía de la Industria Minera en Bolivia,* p. 67.

63 (Page 49). No record has been found of the consummation of the sale. See Weed, *op. cit.,* p. 2,272; Schurz, p. 122.

64 (Page 49). *Boletín Comercial,* December 27, 1925, and *Comisión Fiscal Permanente, Tercera Memoria,* 1926, p. 42.

65 (Page 50). See *South American Yearbook,* 1915, p. 200, and Walle, *Bolivia,* Chapter XVII for the Empresa Chuquiaguillo.

66 (Page 50). Weed, *op. cit.,* p. 2,272; *Boletín Comercial,* December 27, 1925.

67 (Page 50). See Schurz, *op. cit.,* pp. 118-119; American Bankers' Association report on Bolivia, 1925, p. 38, which gives the value in bolivianos of the principal mineral exports from 1910-1923. The 1926 report of the Permanent Fiscal Commission gives the production figures for tin, lead, copper, silver and bismuth, but says nothing about gold. *La Revista Comercial* of Valparaiso for November, 1925, gives a total gold output for the ten years 1914-1923 of only 891 kilos with a value of Bs. 1,238,456.

68 (Page 50). See Schurz, pp. 111-112; also Walle, *op. cit.,* Chapter XVIII, for the great decline in silver mining. See statement of Jesse S. Cottrell, American Ministe. to Bolivia, on the development of lead mining in Bolivia, published in the *West Coast Leader,* June 1, 1926.

69 (Page 50). *Mining Magazine,* December 1924, XXXI, 352-353; for its output 1895-1910 see Aniceto Blanco, *op. cit.,* p. 327.

70 (Page 50). Ball, "Mining in Bolivia in 1925," *Boletín Comercial,* May 23, 1926.

71 (Page 50). *Boletín Comercial,* December 27, 1925.

72 (Page 50). For detailed account of the Compañía Huanchaca de Bolivia see Schurz, pp. 125-127.

73 (Page 50). See Ball in *Boletín Comercial,* and Rounsevell in *West Coast Leader,* both cited above. The 1923 *Memoria de Hacienda,* pp. 4-5, placed copper second in Bolivia's mineral production, but by 1925 it had dropped behind lead in importance.

74 (Page 51). See McQueen, *The Bolivian Public Debt,* pp. 7-8; also *World Atlas of Commercial Geology,* Part I, for production of these minerals, and American Bankers Association, 1925, *op. cit.,* for exports during the war years; for the latter see also Schurz, pp. 114-117, and "Antimony in Bolivia," by Law Voge, *West Coast Leader,* May 18, 1926 (reprinted from *The Mining Journal Press*).

75 (Page 51). Schurz, pp. 115-116.

76 (Page 51). Weed, *op. cit.,* p. 36.

77 (Page 51). The U. S. Minister to Bolivia, in a report made June 11, 1925, on general conditions in Bolivia, stated that until recently commercial houses like W. R. Grace & Company and Duncan, Fox of London had handled about all of Bolivia's minerals, but that several independent buyers like Hochschild & Company were now entering the field, in this way stimulating small mining.

78 (Page 52). For failure of the country as a whole to benefit by the immense profits made in mining during the war see McQueen, *The Bolivian Public Debt.*

79 (Page 52). See *Comisión Fiscal Permanente, Memoria,* 1924; *Segunda Memoria,* 1925, pp. 56-61; and *Tercera Memoria,* 1926, pp. 32-40; especially the last for two decisions of the Supreme Court upholding the Permanent Fiscal Commission in its claims against the Patiño interests.

80 (Page 52). For a summary of this law and of the new export duties on tin see Roush, *The Mineral Industry during 1923,* pp. 656-660; also *Mining Magazine,* December, 1924, XXXI, 354-355.

81 (Page 52). *Comisión Fiscal Permanente, Segunda Memoria,* 1925, p. 54.

82 (Page 52). *Comisión Fiscal Permanente, Tercera Memoria,* 1926, p. 32.

83 (Page 52). *Mining Journal,* February 7, 1925, p. 120, which states that these dumps or tailings contain only about 30 percent tin. The former taxes were based upon concentrate carrying 60 percent metal.

84 (Page 53). At 35 cents per pound the cost of producing a long ton is $784, or roughly £150.

85 (Page 53). The 1925 Annual Report of the company, p. 13, asserts that Patiño Mines and Enterprises disbursed during the year within Bolivia a total of £915,097.15.7 in salaries and wages, in donations to workers' societies, hospitals, charities, etc., and in taxes, "which establishes the importance that the Corporation's existence has for the prosperity and well-being of the country in general." In this statement may be seen Patiño's defense against the oft-repeated criticism of him in Bolivia for draining the country of its greatest resource and shipping the proceeds abroad.

86 (Page 53). The Permanent Fiscal Commission gives the total commercial value of the 1925 tin exports as Bs. 79,618,768, on which export duties amounting to Bs. 7,303,338 and profits taxes of Bs. 5,971,720 were collected. See its *Tercera Memoria,* pp. 41 and 32. Some additional revenue was derived, too, from licenses, taxes on mining claims, on transfers of mining property, etc.

87 (Page 53). Of Bolivia's 1925 exports, 90.51 percent were minerals, of which 66.75 percent were tin. See *Comisión Fiscal Permanente, Tercera Memoria,* 1926, pp. 40-41.

88 (Page 53). According to the *West Coast Leader,* July 6, 1926, Bolivian imports for that period totalled £81,576,943, her exports £167,-448,249. For this illusory trade balance see also Tejada, *Después de la Crisis,* p. 35, and *Comisión Fiscal Permanente, Tercera Memoria,* 1926, pp. 87-88.

89 (Page 53). For text of this bill see the *West Coast Leader,* November 9, 1926.

90 (Page 54). See article on "Prospects of the Tin Industry: Production and Prices." *Times Trade and Engineering Supplement* (reprinted in the *West Coast Leader,* November 2, 1926), which speaks of the depletion of the Bantoong Pool in 1923 and the reduced output in the East in 1925.

91 (Page 54). The increasing price of tin has stimulated search for a chemical substitute, but for the making of tin plate none has as yet been found, although the National Canners' Association have just reported that the production of "tinless" cans would soon be possible as the result of experiments carried on by its research department. *The New York Times,* January 27, 1927. See also Smith, *The Strategy of Minerals,* pp. 181-182, for the use of cadmium in solder.

92 (Page 54). For the effect of the price of tin on Bolivian exchange see *Comisión Fiscal Permanente, Segunda Memoria,* 1925, pp. 86-90, and Tellez, *"Problemas Económicas y Legales de Bolivia con respeto á los*

Estados Unidos," *Boletín* de la Unión Panamericana, November, 1924, Vol. LVIII, No. 11.

93 (Page 54). Reproduced from Day, *Handbook of the Petroleum Industry,* I, 147; see also on Bolivia's petroleum resources pp. 146, 153-154, where Day says: "In view of the cumulative evidence it seems likely that Bolivia will some day be a great producer of petroleum;" Herold, "The economic and geologic conditions pertaining to the occurrence of oil in the North Argentine-Bolivian field of South America," *Trans. American Institute Mining Engineers,* LXI (1919), 544-564; Davenport and Cooke, *The Oil Trusts and Anglo-American Relations,* p. 235, who write that "according to the most sober geological opinion vast oilfields lie in the El Beni and Santa Cruz provinces of Bolivia;" Wannag, *Estudios e Informes,* p. 76; Lopez, *Bolivia y el Petroleo,* pp. 181-214; Schurz, *op. cit.,* pp. 139-140.

94 (Page 55). Mousnier, *Los Petroleos de Bolivia,* p. 14; *South American Year Book,* 1915, p. 201, which gives an example of the quality of some oil found twelve leagues from Santa Cruz that contained 78.2 percent kerosene, 17.5 percent lubricating oil and 4.3 percent coke. Spruille Braden, in announcing his purchase of a large oil area in Eastern Bolivia, said he expected this new field to become one of the most productive in the world as the oil is perhaps one of the highest grades of oil ever found. See in *Commercial and Financial Chronicle,* October 8, 1921, CXIII, 1,577. See also Loayza, *La Riqueza Petrolífera de Caupolicán y Norte de Bolivia,* pp. 27-29, which compares the quality of the Bolivian oil with that found in other important oil deposits of the world.

95 (Page 55). The subsoil rights have been preserved to the nation in Bolivia, Costa Rica and Venezuela, and in part in Argentina, Colombia and Ecuador. A movement to vest oil rights in the Government entirely is in progress in Colombia and San Domingo. See Davenport and Cooke, *op. cit.,* p. 163, footnote 2. For a comparison of the petroleum royalties required in the different oil-producing countries of South America see Lopez, *op. cit.,* p. 20.

96 (Page 55). For text of this law and a running commentary on it see Lopez, pp. 13-79; also *Commercial and Financial Chronicle,* July 2, 1921, CXIII, 31.

97 (Page 55). From 10 to 8 centavos per hectare. See Schurz, pp. 140-141.

98 (Page 55). For the oil policy of the Gutierrez Guerra Government see Lopez, *op. cit.*

99 (Page 55). By Supreme Resolutions of February 28 and March 8, 1920.

100 (Page 56). For criticism of this law on the grounds of its severity and its restricting effect on oil development in Bolivia, see Warshaw, *The New Latin America,* pp. 68-69.

101 (Page 56). During the exploration period there is a tax of 2½ centavos per hectare. A tax of 5 percent of the sale price is levied on the transfer of oil properties. When production has begun oil companies are liable to the profits tax paid by all mining companies. See McQueen, *The Bolivian Fiscal System,* p. 7.

102 (Page 56). Exploitation must begin within four years. Within five years the concessionaires must drill one well of 500 meters depth for each 50,000 hectares granted, and one additional well three years after for each 10,000 hectares. The penalty for not complying with this requirement is a fine of two Bs. per hectare if the wells are not drilled within three years after the time limit prescribed, cancellation of the concession if not after another three years. At least 30 percent of the employees holding skilled positions must be Bolivians, and in hiring laborers the oil companies must give natives preference.

103 (Page 57). 1,000,000 hectares secured through transfer of the

Richmond Levering concession of February 28, 1920, to the Standard Oil Company of New Jersey; 2,144,850 hectares secured through acquisition of the Braden oil interests; *ca.* 700,000 hectares secured through purchase of old titles. For these various transactions see below. The Bolivian Consul-General in New York in 1926 gave the total of the Standard Oil Company's concessions as only 1,519,039 hectares; by drilling and opening new wells it has so far consolidated ownership of 300,000 hectares. See O'Shaughnessy, "Bolivia as an Oil Country" in *Bolivia: A Quarterly Survey of Bolivian Activities,* September, 1926, p. 22, Note of the Editor.

104 (Page 57). Bs. 7,500,000, according to *La República,* April 5, 1925. Lopez, on the other hand, says that the transfer was made for $200,000 and was negotiated in New York on March 3, 1921.

105 (Page 57). For text of this concession see Lopez.

106 (Page 58). See especially *La República,* organ of the Saavedra party, for April 5, 1925, which accuses ex-president Montes, J. L. Tejada, Minister of Finance in 1920, and others prominent in the Liberal party, of working to get the concession through and of profiting thereby. The 1923 *Memoria de Hacienda* (p. 9) in turn, speaks of the bitter criticism and attacks on this concession made by the party of the opposition, which proves the purely political basis of both attacks, for in 1923 the Saavedra Government found itself in the position of defending itself against charges of erecting a Standard Oil monopoly in Bolivia.

107 (Page 59). See *Commercial and Financial Chronicle,* October 8, 1921, CXIII, 1,577; *Journal of Commerce,* October 4, 1921; Schurz, *op. cit.,* pp. 141-142, who gives as the price paid for the Braden interests $3,-649,875; Lopez, *op. cit.,* p. 289, on the other hand, states as the price $1,500,000.

108 (Page 59). Lopez, *op. cit.,* pp. 257 and 273-274.

109 (Page 59). Schurz, p. 141.

110 (Page 59). The so-called *"Pensilvania"* concession made to Sr. Jorge de la Reza, for 50 years with a 12½ percent State royalty proviso. See Lopez, pp. 91-98, 289. This went finally to Gibbs & Company, of London. *Memoria de Hacienda,* 1923, pp. 9-14.

111 (Page 60). For text of this concession, granted March 8, 1920, see Lopez, *op. cit.,* pp. 83-90.

112 (Page 60). *Memoria de Hacienda,* 1923, pp. 9-14; Schurz, *op. cit.,* p. 142.

113 (Page 60). *Memoria de Hacienda,* 1924, p. 107.

114 (Page 60). Lopez, *op. cit.,* pp. 357-359.

115 (Page 60). *The New York Times,* October 8, 1923, mentions a decree declaring all oil concessions except those of the Standard Oil Company and of J. Backus lapsed for failure to comply with their terms. This measure, it was said, affected more than 80 concerns and 2,000,000 hectares of oil lands.

116 (Page 60). *Memoria de Hacienda,* 1924, pp. 104-105.

117 (Page 60). At a price of $3.50 per share. The authorized capital is 1,000,000 shares, of no par value, of which it is proposed to issue 905,000. This company is being organized under the laws of Nevada to acquire one-half the capital stock of the Bolivian Petroleum Corporation, the other half of which will be owned by the Atlantic Refining Company. The directors proposed include former or present officers of the Venezuela Petroleum Corporation, the Lago Petroleum Company, the Creole Syndicate, the Consolidated Oil Company and the Pioneer Petroleum Corporation. O'Shaughnessy, cited above, mentions the Cosden interests and J. B. Shearer, a pioneer in the Venezuelan oil fields and formerly Vice-President of the Louisiana Oil Refining Company, as being identified with the enterprise. See advertisement of the stock in *The New York Times,* February 23, 1927.

118 (Page 60). Pogue, *The Economics of Petroleum,* p. 218.

119 (Page 61). For a brief account of the history of oil development in Bolivia, see Schurz, *op. cit.,* pp. 138-142; Clapp, "South America a Big Field for Petroleum Development" (pamphlet reprint from the *New York Commercial,* 1919); and Lopez throughout.

120 (Page 61) For an account of this reconnaissance work and early drilling, see Rounsevell, "Millions being invested in Bolivian oil field," *Bulletin,* Pan American Union, November, 1924.

121 (Page 61). Moody's, 1924, p. 2,402.

122 (Page 61). The most important one is Bermejo No. 2, with a capacity of about 500 bbls. a day. This has been capped. The cost of opening a well in Bolivia is estimated at from $300,000 to $400,000. President Siles' message to the Bolivian Congress on August 6, 1927, mentioned five wells drilled by the Standard Oil, and seven in preparation.

123 (Page 62). In the United States the proportion of wild cat wells in unproven areas is said to be about 3-1.

124 (Page 62). See Davenport and Cooke, *op. cit.,* p. 235.

125 (Page 62). In 1922 Sr. Lopez, a member of the Chamber of Deputies, proposed the appropriation of Bs. 2,000,000 to begin a State-controlled oil venture. His solution for the development of Bolivia's oil is a mixed company in which foreign and domestic capital and the State would all share. But with the mere drilling of a single well costing in the neighborhood of $400,000 his two million bolivianos would be but a drop in the bucket. See Lopez, *op. cit.,* pp. 282-285, in which he expresses his fear of the Standard Oil's monopolizing the Bolivian oil industry; also Chapter VII of Part IV, pp. 360 et seq.

126 (Page 63). Paredes, *Mitos, Supersticiones y Supervivencias Populares de Bolivia,* pp. 19-20.

127 (Page 64). *South America: Observations and Impressions,* pp. 192-193.

CHAPTER V

1 (Page 67). "Trade Routes in the Economic Geography of Bolivia," in *Bulletin,* American Geographical Society, XLII (1910), 31.

2 (Page 69). The Bolivian delegation to the Second Pan American Financial Conference, in approving the Conference's resolution with regard to the Pan American Railroad, made the following reservation: "That in order to give to the Pan American Railroad all the scope of the high purposes which inspired its construction and bind together by land all the nations of the Americas, a transverse line to cross South America from east to west, utilizing insofar as possible the sections of the main line already constructed, is considered an integral part of the same." See *Reports and Other Documents of the Bolivian Delegation,* pp. 59 and 43-45.

3 (Page 69). See Gonzalez, *"Ferrocarriles en Bolivia,"* in *Boletín de la Sociedad de Ingenieros de Bolivia,* October, 1925, for unfavorable comment on this latitudinal interoceanic railway. Gonzalez points out that from Arica to Santos, Brazil, is a distance of 3,963 kilometers, whereas from Buenos Aires to Arica is only 3,114, to Antofagasta 2,792. More significant, 1,300 kilometers in Bolivia, and 50 in Brazil, are lacking to complete it, an extremely important item in view of the heavy cost of railroad-building in Bolivia, the country's lack of capital, and the sparsely-settled regions it would traverse.

4 (Page 70). A mail and passenger air service recently established between Santa Cruz and Yacuiba covers the distance of 1,000 kilometers in seven hours and puts Santa Cruz within two days of Buenos Aires. The *West Coast Leader* (November 16, 1926) is of the opinion that this should stimulate the Bolivian Government to build the Cochabamba-Santa Cruz

line since the new air service will draw closer the bond between the Argentine and Eastern Bolivia which has "always in the past felt more inclined to adopt the traditions and customs of its southern neighbor than those of the Bolivian altiplano."

5 (Page 70). For a description of Bolivia's railway system, built and projected, see *Memoria de Fomento y Comunicaciones,* 1925; Schurz, *op. cit.,* pp. 58-87; *Bolivia: General Descriptive Data,* pp. 19-25 (pamphlet issued by Pan American Union, 1925); Zamora, address before the Second Pan American Commercial Conference, June 5, 1919; Report of the Bolivian Delegation concerning theme IV of the program of the Second Pan American Financial Congress, January 20, 1920; President Siles' Inaugural address in *Foreign Securities Investor,* April 14, 1926, and his message at the opening of Congress, August 6, 1926, in *West Coast Leader;* Bowman, "Trade Routes in the Economic Geography of Bolivia" and Gonzalez, *Ferrocarriles en Bolivia,* both cited above.

6 (Page 70). Gonzalez, *op. cit.*

7 (Page 70). Bowman speaks of the enormous cost of transporting materials and provisions in the construction of the Mollendo-La Paz line, involving for the Bolivian section five separate handlings from the time they were loaded on steamers in the United States until they reached their destination. "The locomotives, steel rails, ties, in fact all the material for the railroads now building in Bolivia, must be unloaded into barges from the ocean steamers, after the voyage from the United States, then to the freight trains on the wharf, by rail to Puno, by steamer to Guaqui, and again by rail to the construction camps at the end of the line. What this means in the case of heavy machinery and steel rails so awkward to handle can better be imagined than described." He also adds that the ties in the Viacha-Oruro line, imported from Oregon and California, cost $2 gold each (p. 30). The Southern Railway of Peru, built by the British, was contracted for at £29,500 per mile. (Bowman, *op. cit.* p. 29).

8 (Page 70). Taken from Gonzalez, *op. cit.,* p. 50. The legal gauge in Bolivia is one meter.

9 (Page 70). The 1925 *Memoria de Fomento y Comunicaciones,* pp. 7-8, gives the railways in operation, with and without State guarantee, on July 31, 1925, as follows:

With guarantee

The Bolivia Railway Company		
Viacha-Oruro	202 kms.	
Rio Mulato-Potosí	174 "	
Oruro-Cochabamba	204 "	
Uyuni-Atocha	90 "	
		670 kms.
Empresa Luz y Fuerza de Cochabamba		
Cochabamba-Vinto	18 kms.	
Cochabamba-Arani	60 "	
		78 "
State-owned		
Corocoro-Tarejra branch	8.5 kms.	
Potosí-Sucre (remainder under construction)	102 "	
Atocha-Villazón	198 "	
La Paz-Beni (via the Yungas)	53.5 "	
		362 "

Without guarantee

Antofagasta (Chile) & Bolivia Ry. Co.	
Antofagasta-Oruro (Bolivian section)	488 kms.
Viacha-La Paz	41 "
	529 "
Arica-La Paz Railway (Bolivian section)	231 "
Patiño Mining Consolidated, Inc.	
Machacamarca-Uncia Railway	96 "
Peruvian Corporation, Ltd.	
Guaqui-La Paz	96 "
Cia. Huanchaca de Bolivia	
Uyuni-Huanchaca branch	38 "
	2,100 "

10 (Page 71). Schurz, *op. cit.*, pp. 74-76.

11 (Page 71). *Ibid*, p. 84.

12 (Page 72). For the details of the Bolivian loan of 1871 which Col. Church, as special agent of Bolivia, placed in London in that year, the Government's default, and the subsequent suit brought against the National Bolivian Navigation Company, organized in the United States by Church, see chapter on loans which follows.

13 (Page 72). *South American Year Book,* 1915, pp. 282-283. Also Bowman, "Geographical Aspects of the New Madeira-Mamoré Railroad," *Bulletin,* American Geographical Society, XLV (1913), 275-281.

14 (Page 72). For an account of this ambitious syndicate see Meissner, *Das wirtschaftliche Vordringen der Nordamerikaner in Südamerika;* for its relation to the Madeira-Mamoré Railway, pp. 59, 65, 69, 104-106. Meissner surmises that after the collapse of the syndicate its interests were taken over by the American International Corporation, organized by the National City Bank (p. 69). Meissner cites for a detailed description of the organization of the Farquhar Trust, Lufft, *Die nordamerikanischen Interessen in Südamerika vor dem Kriege.*

15 (Page 72). Schurz, *op. cit.*, pp. 86-87.

16 (Page 73). Church, "Bolivia and Brazil in the Amazon Valley," *Fortnightly Review,* November, 1870, reprinted in Papers and Documents relating to the Bolivian Loan, the National Bolivian Navigation Company, and the Madeira and Mamoré Railway Company, Ltd.; also Church, *The Route to Bolivia via the River Amazon: A Report to the Governments of Bolivia and Brazil,* 1877.

17 (Page 73). McQueen, *Bolivian Public Finance,* p. 111; see also Walle, Bolivia, Chapter XVI, for the collapse of the Bolivian rubber industry. For the recent revival of interest in South American rubber see Schurz, "Rubber Production in the Amazon Valley," Department of Commerce, *Trade Promotion Series No. 23;* Preliminary Report on Crude Rubber, Coffee, etc., House of Representatives, 69th Congress, 1st Session, March 13, 1926; "The Search for Rubber: New Prospects in South America," by M. W. D. in *Foreign Affairs,* January, 1926. Bolivian and British interests, notably the Suarez Brothers, dominate the Bolivian rubber industry at present. Schurz, *op. cit.*, pp. 170-174, and Halsey, MS in Dept. of Commerce.

18 (Page 73). Schurz, p. 87.

19 (Page 73). See *Ferrocarriles en Bolivia: Propuesta presentada ante el Supremo Gobierno para la construcción deuna red ferrocarrilera en la República,* 1904.

20 (Page 74). Sisson, *Reconnaissance Report upon Proposed System of Bolivian Railways.*

21 (Page 74). See below; also address of Mr. Ricardo Martinez Vargas, Financial Representative of Bolivia, at the Ritz-Carlton Hotel, December 29, 1926, published in *Bolivia: A Bi-Monthly Survey of Bolivian Activities,* January, 1927, p. 17.

22 (Page 75). For criticism of the Speyer contract, which it describes as *"más leónino,"* on the grounds of the enormous cost to the Government of this perpetually private enterprise, see *Memoria de Hacienda,* 1922, pp. 32-35. Estimating that for five years more, up to 1927, Bolivia must pay £130,000 annually, or about £650,000, on the first mortgage bonds, this Treasury report says, "To draw from our scanty national income an annual amount of £130,000 is like bleeding an anaemic body to leave it destroyed. In 1927, when no more payments have to be made, we will begin to breathe more freely." For arguments of Sr. Rafael Urquidi against the contract see *Contrato Ferroviario, National City Bank—Speyer y Cia., articulos publicados en El Diario,* 1906.

23 (Page 75). The law of December 27, 1905, called for bids on railways built for account of the Government, but was held not to apply to these lines which were to be built for account of the concessionaires. See Resolution of acceptance of the contract, signed May 21, 1906, by President Montes and others, printed as a supplement to the contract.

24 (Page 75). Tejada, *Las Emergencias del Contrato Speyer,* pp. 4-7.

25 (Page 75). J. Pierce Hope was Director General pro. tem. of Public Works. See his report of May 19, 1906, approving the plan, published as a supplement with the text of the contract.

26 (Page 75). See Text of Contract and Concession for the Construction and Operation of Railways in the Republic of Bolivia with the National City Bank and Messrs. Speyer & Company, May 22, 1906, with Supplements.

27 (Page 75). Criticism of this twenty percent discount was expressed in a number of articles published in *El Diario* and reprinted, in 1906, under the title *Contrato Ferroviario, National City Bank-Speyer y Cia.*

28 (Page 76). See Bowman, "Trade Routes in the Economic Geography of Bolivia," *op. cit.,* pp. 184-187, who attributes much of the growth of W. R. Grace and Company's business in Bolivia to its association with this railway project.

29 (Page 76). *Informe del Inspector Fiscal de los Ferrocarriles de "The Bolivia Railway Company,"* 1908, which contains the text of incorporation of the company, and the text of the contract between the Bolivia Railway Company and the South American Construction Company, signed March 22, 1907. The directors of the former company at that time were Edward W. Burdick, Aloysius C. Gahan, Jacob G. Metcalfe, Arthur Starke and Frank L. Sullivan.

30 (Page 76). See Tejada, *op. cit.,* p. 8.

31 (Page 76). The right to select these lands was to be in force for two years and by the payment of a certain amount might be extended over twenty years. Lopez, *Bolivia y el Petroleo,* p. 356, speaks of 2½ million hectares conceded to the Bolivia Railway Company in the department of Santa Cruz. There is no indication that this concession has ever been developed. For other privileges of the concessionaires under the Speyer contract see the contract itself: e.g., free use of fiscal lands and of state forests and of public waters, exclusive privilege of railroad building for 30 years in a zone of 40 kilometers on each side of railway, right to construct piers on lakes and rivers and establish navigation on same, etc.

32 (Page 76). See footnote 29 for its contract with the Bolivia Railway Company.

33 (Page 76). Tejada, *op. cit.,* pp. 10, 12.

34 (Page 77). See Schurz, *op. cit.,* pp. 61-62, who gives the lines constructed by the company with the cost of each section as follows:

Oruro-Viacha	125 miles	£1,063,608 or	$5,176,048
Oruro-Cochabamba .	127 "	2,747,721	13,371,784
Rio Mulato-Potosí ...	108 "	1,518,716	7,390,831
Uyuni-Atocha	56 "	532,154	2,589,727
	416 "	£5,862,199	$28,528,390

The additional expense went into studies for other lines (Potosí-Sucre and La Paz-Puerto Pando) and materials.

35 (Page 77). *The New York Times,* December 16, 1926.

36 (Page 77). Bowman, *op. cit.,* pp. 36-37, who states that the change in the original concession providing for the lease was made at the request of the Speyer syndicate which received from the Antofagasta and Bolivia Railway Company payment for a majority of the Bolivia Railway Company's stock.

37 (Page 77). Tejada, *op. cit.,* p. 29, mentions a 25 percent rebate on minerals shipped to Antofagasta, with the result that 40,000 tons are deflected annually from the Oruro-Viacha line, on which the Government must pay an annual guarantee of 5 percent because the earnings of the Bolivia Railway Company are not sufficient to cover the service of its bonds. This, Tejada estimates, represents a loss of $100,000 per year to the Bolivia Railway Company.

38 (Page 77). *Ibid,* pp. 26-30; also *Boletín Comercial,* July 11, 1926, table 10, for share of exports and imports handled at Bolivia's various ports of exit and entry in 1925.

39 (Page 77). Gonzalez, *op. cit.,* p. 46, estimates the earning capacity at from 8 to 10 percent on the capital invested, although he admits he has no basis for his surmise. Tejada, p. 14, gives the income in 1924 as only 1.18 percent.

40 (Page 77). See *Memoria de Hacienda,* 1922, pp. 32-35, and Schurz, *op. cit.,* pp. 62-63, on the resources from which the annual service has been met; see Elias, *Finanzas Prácticas,* p. 167, for Chile's quota of the guarantee as provided by the Treaty of Peace, 1904, and by protocol of May 26, 1908. The interest account on these bonds has been handled by the National City Bank, Speyer & Company, and J. Henry Schroeder & Company of London, representing the Antofagasta & Bolivia Railway Company. See *Memoria de Fomento,* August, 1924-August, 1925, pp. 28-30.

41 (Page 78). *West Coast Leader,* September 21, 1926; *The New York Times,* December 16, 1926.

42 (Page 78). See Tejada, *op. cit.*

43 (Page 78). *West Coast Leader,* August 23, 1927, annual message of President Siles to the Bolivian Congress, August 6; also the *West Coast Leader* for July 26, 1927.

44 (Page 79). Schurz, *op. cit.,* pp. 76-79. In addition to this 10 percent discount, the Bolivian Government had to pay a commission of about $62,000 (Bs. 187,488), making the net proceeds barely over $2,000,000. See *Memoria de Fomento, Apendice,* 1918, p. 29.

45 (Page 79). *Memoria de Hacienda,* 1919, p. 262.

46 (Page 79). See Schurz, p. 77, and Gonzalez, cited above.

47 (Page 80). See Gonzalez, *op. cit.,* and Andres de Santa Cruz, *"El Problema de la Vialidad en Yungas," Boletín de la Sociedad de Ingenieros de Bolivia,* October, 1925.

48 (Page 80). Rivero, *"La Comisión Panamericana de Carreteras y los Problemas de Vialidad Moderna, ibid,* and *West Coast Leader,* January 4 and 11, 1927. See *Bolivia* for December, 1926, which reports that two auto roads, one to Coroico in North Yungas, the other to Chulumani in South Yungas, will be built, for which a loan of Bs. 7,000,000 will be raised.

49 (Page 80). In addition to the lack of funds the Yungas Railway is handicapped by the fact that the Liberal party, in which are to be found many of the Yungeño finca-owners and indeed the moving spirit in the construction so far, Carlos Tejada Sorzano, has had very little influence with the Government since 1920.

50 (Page 80). Bowman, *op. cit.*, p. 90.

51 (Page 81). The bonds were taken by the Credit Mobilier at 90. Schurz, *op. cit.*, p. 81.

52 (Page 81). *Commercial and Financial Chronicle,* September 24, 1921; *West Coast Leader,* November 23, 1926, which states that the American International Corporation is the largest shareholder, owning fifty percent of the preferred and about forty-two percent of the common stock; the remainder of the stock is divided among three groups: Stone & Webster, Marshall Field, Glore, Ward & Company, and Henry Ulen and his associates.

53 (Page 81). *Commercial and Financial Chronicle,* July 23, 1921.

54 (Page 81). *Journal of Commerce* and *The New York Times,* July 14, 1921.

55 (Page 81). For the security pledged to these bonds see the following chapter.

56 (Page 81). *Memoria de Hacienda,* 1924, pp. 75-76.

57 (Page 81). *Empréstito Nicolaus: Conclusiones de la Comisión Especial para solicitar modificaciones del contrato.*

58 (Page 81). At a cost to the Government of $150,000, which the Ulen Company demanded as compensation. See *Empréstito Nicolaus,* cited above. This report estimates the total cost of this conversion, including the difference in the price of these and of the other bonds of the refunding loan issue, the difference in redemption rate, certain interest losses and the cost of engraving and issuing two sets of bonds, at more than a million dollars on the $7,000,000 issue; at not less than $1,600,000 on $10,000,000.

59 (Page 82). See Ovando, "Bolivia Negotiates a $14,000,000 Loan for Railroad Works," in *Bolivia: A Bi-Monthly Survey of Bolivian Activities,* January, 1927, p. 28.

60 (Page 82). The actual construction costs amounted, by the end of the Saavedra administration, to Bs. 28,872,554, or roughly $8,850,000. The balance is accounted for by the discount at which the Government had to issue the Atocha-Villazón Railway bonds. See *Comisión Fiscal Permanente, Segunda Memoria,* 1925, p. 10, and *Memoria de Fomento,* August, 1924-August, 1925, pp. 42-50.

61 (Page 82). See footnote 58.

62 (Page 83). Schurz, pp. 82-83.

63 (Page 83). *West Coast Leader,* September 21, 1926.

64 (Page 84). *Memoria de Fomento,* August, 1924-August, 1925, pp. 56-63; *Comisión Fiscal Permanente, Segunda Memoria,* 1925, p. 25.

65 (Page 84). *Boletín Comercial,* April 18, 1926, for text of law authorizing this loan.

66 (Page 84). *West Coast Leader,* September 21, 1926.

67 (Page 84). Schurz, *op. cit.*, p. 83.

68 (Page 85). See *Memoria de Hacienda,* 1922, Memorandum of Ramón Rivero.

69 (Page 85). Confidential report of the American Consul in Bolivia, September 2, 1922.

70 (Page 85). *West Coast Leader,* December 28, 1926, which reports that the *Sociedad Boliviana de Cemento* has just secured free importation of the machinery needed in the industry, and the levy of a surcharge of 10 percent on all cement imported into Bolivia.

71 (Page 85). The *West Coast Leader* (January 18, 1927) states in no uncertain terms its belief that the work will go to American contractors since the Government will need to turn to the bankers soon again for more money

for this road and will hence be careful to follow out their wishes. "It is believed," said the *Leader,* "that the bankers, as is usual in these cases, will insist that the construction be given to American contractors." This prediction is borne out by the report in *The New York World,* March 19, 1928, that the award had gone to the American firm of Kennedy and Carey.

72 (Page 85). *Memoria de Fomento,* August, 1924-August, 1925, pp. 53-55; also *West Coast Leader,* December 6, 1927.

73 (Page 86). The engineer, Dr. Hans Grether, who conducted the surveys and drew up the plans for the Cochabamba-Santa Cruz line, estimated the cost at about $30,000,000. Other estimates have put it at between $40,000,000 and $50,000,000, or more than $100,000 per mile. See Ovando, in *Bolivia, op. cit.,* and Schurz, p. 84.

74 (Page 86). See *West Coast Leader,* January 4 and 11, 1927; also Farrar, "Roads vs. Railroads in Bolivia: A Question of Means of Communication," in the same, July 13, 1926. The American expert on railroads attached to the Kemmerer Commission estimated that 1,200 kilometers of motor roads could be built with the money already at the disposal of the Government, which is more than twice the distance from Cochabamba to Santa Cruz. By this means Santa Cruz could be brought in touch with the Argentine country to the south, as well as with the Bolivian plateau, and without further indebtedness. *West Coast Leader,* July 12, 1927.

75 (Page 88). Gonzalez, *op. cit.,* p. 46.

76 (Page 88). *Ibid.*

CHAPTER VI

1 (Page 90). McQueen, *Bolivian Public Finance,* p. 39.

The following summary of Bolivia's public debt, taken from a circular issued by Imbrie and Company, outlining the history of Bolivia from the Inca Empire to 1918, approximates the truth and suggests the fluctuation in the size of the debt during the past five decades:

1870	debt	none			
1880	"	$27,100,000	per	capita	$13.84
1890	"	5,072,121	"	"	4.24
1900	"	1,901,225	"	"	1.08
1910	"	13,311,000	"	"	5.79
1913	"	19,369,000	"	"	7.75
1918	"	27,079,821	"	"	9.67

2 (Page 90). According to the Permanent Fiscal Commission, Statement of the Public Debt of the National Treasury of Bolivia on December 31, 1925 (No. 47), the total external debt was $32,426,280. This was reduced by July 1, 1926, to $31,640,951.20. See *Comisión Fiscal Permanente, Tercera Memoria,* 1926, p. 9. To this must now be added the $14,000,000 issued through Dillon, Read & Company on February 2, 1927. See *The New York Times* of that date.

3 (Page 90). This so-called Patiño loan, placed at par and bearing 8 percent interest and accumulative amortization at a rate to pay it in five years, was secured by 50 percent of the tax on mining profits payable by the Patiño Mines and Enterprises Consolidated. The money was loaned by the Anglo-South American Bank and the banking house of Glyn, Mills & Company. The purpose was the construction of the Potosí-Sucre Railway. See *Comisión Fiscal Permanente, Segunda Memoria,* 1925, p. 25. The loan was considered an infraction of the contract for the refunding loan of 1922 since the income from the tax on mining profits had been pledged to the latter. It is rumored in Bolivia that Patiño was rewarded for floating this loan in London by an assurance that the taxes on his tin would not be raised for five years.

4 (Page 90). For example, Switzerland, the Netherlands and Denmark, with respective per capita debts of $251, $174 and $100, sums equivalent to 1/8, 1/7 and 1/10 of the estimated per capita wealth respectively, as compared with Mexico and Poland, whose per capita debts of $37 and $13.5 are equivalent to 1/13 and 1/33 of their respective per capita wealth. The enormous per capita debts of the belligerent countries in the Great War are not fair illustrations, although among these are the most advanced industrial nations of the world, as a great share of their present indebtedness was incurred for military purposes rather than for national development.

5 (Page 90). With the new $14,000,000 bond issue, made February 2, 1927, Bolivia's per capita indebtedness is nearer $21.

The following table shows the comparative indebtedness and wealth of the countries of South America:

	National debt	*Debt per capita*	*Estimated national wealth*	*Wealth per capita*
Argentina	$922,394,000	$96.6	$13,800,000,000	$1,445
Bolivia	42,232,000	14.0	1,000,000,000	334
Brazil	852,058,000	27.0	16,000,000,000	522
Chile	307,500,000	81.0	3,372,000,000	887
Colombia	48,754,000	7.4	1,464,000,000	221
Peru	57,821,000	10.5	1,615,000,000	293
Uruguay	189,435,000	118.0	1,750,000,000	1,100

See comparative statistics of all countries whose government obligations are listed on the New York Stock Exchange in Edwards, *Investing in Foreign Securities*, p. 131. The relation of national debt to national wealth in the case of these particular countries is, hence, as follows: Argentina, 6.7 percent; Bolivia, 4.2 percent; Brazil, 5.1 percent; Chile, 9.1 percent; Colombia, 3.3 percent; Peru, 3.6 percent; Uruguay, 10.7 percent.

6 (Page 91). For examples see *Financial America*, May 19, 1916; *Memoria de Hacienda, Apendice*, 1919, p. 283; *Empréstito Nicolaus: Conclusiones de la Comisión Especial para solicitar modificaciones del contrato*, 1923 (unpublished).

7 (Page 91). See annual message of President Siles to the Bolivian Congress, August 6, 1927, published in the *West Coast Leader*, August 23, 1927; also *The New York Times*, February 2, 1927.

8 (Page 91). Republic of Bolivia 6 percent Gold Loan of 1917, due 1940, amortization at 2 percent.

9 (Page 91). *Memoria de Hacienda*, 1919, p. 262, and *Apendice*, pp. 228-229; also *Journal of Commerce*, June 20, 1917. The three year contract with Chandler & Company expired in January, 1920, when, as this report of the Treasury states, Bolivia would "recover full independence of action in transacting her business in North America." In giving notice that the contract would not be renewed, the Bolivian Government declared that it was "not agreeable to the national interests to continue the restrictions and options which the contract provided for the negotiation of loans." Yet the loan from Imbrie & Company, contracted for in 1920 but never made because of the revolution in that year, named Imbrie & Company fiscal agents for the three years following. See *Commerce Reports*, May 8, and July 25, 1920, and Legation Report No. 32, April 21, 1920.

10 (Page 91). *Comisión Fiscal Permanente, Tercera Memoria*, 1926 (see table, p. 138); Schurz, *Bolivia: A Commercial and Industrial Handbook*, p. 77.

11 (Page 91). MS of a report on Bolivia by F. M. Halsey, Department of Commerce.

12 (Page 94). See circular of W. G. Souders & Company advertising the

loan; also *Memoria de Hacienda,* 1918, *Apendice,* p. 426; McQueen, *op. cit.,* p. 43, and Schurz and *Journal of Commerce* as above.

13 (Page 94). Equitable Trust Company's Security List for April, 1926.

14 (Page 94). *Comisión Fiscal Permanente, Tercera Memoria,* 1926 (see table, p. 138). An interesting forerunner of the State Department's request of March, 1922, for information with regard to foreign loans is seen in the letter of Secretary Lansing to the Bolivian Minister, dated May 11, 1917, with reference to this loan. The letter, which was quoted in Souder's circular, runs as follows:

> "My dear Mr. Minister:
>
> I beg to acknowledge receipt of your note of April the 13th, in which you state that bankers in New York have agreed to make your Government a loan for use in railroad construction, and have asked you to obtain from me a declaration, which you accordingly request me to make, that the loan is approved by the Government of the United States, and that there is no objection to its being granted.
>
> In reply I wish to say that the Department is glad that a satisfactory arrangement for this loan has been consummated between the Government of Bolivia and the New York bankers."

15 (Page 94). *Commercial and Financial Chronicle,* November 12, 1921, and January 7, 1922; also circular issued by Hemphill, Noyes & Company, November, 1921.

16 (Page 94). For revenues pledged see Trust Agreement between Republic of Bolivia, the New York Trust Company as trustee, and the Ulen Contracting Corporation, made April 28, 1921; also McQueen, *op. cit.,* pp. 43-44.

17 (Page 94). *Comisión Fiscal Permanente, Tercera Memoria,* 1926 (see table, p. 138).

18 (Page 94). *Commercial and Financial Chronicle* as above; also circulars of Hemphill, Noyes and Company, and John Nuveen & Company, and MS Report on Bolivia by F. M. Halsey, Department of Commerce, cited above.

19 (Page 94). *Comisión Fiscal Permanente, Tercera,* 1926 (see table, p. 138).

20 (Page 95). McQueen, *The Bolivian Public Debt, with a Survey of Bolivian Financial History.* Trade Information Bulletin No. 194, February 18, 1924.

21 (Page 95). Exclusive of the ill-fated Madeira-Mamoré Railway loan of 1871, when the Government's 6 percent 25 year bonds, to the amount of £1,700,000, were floated in London by Erlangers at a price of 68. The net proceeds of the loan were only £853,286. The companies formed by Col. G. E. Church, an American, to build a railway 153½ miles long and to establish navigation on these rivers, were paper organizations and the whole project chimerical. The bonds went into default in 1875. By a judicial settlement in London in 1879 the bondholders got £45 per bond, having paid £68 for them. See Loan for Madeira-Mamoré Railway, Collection of Papers relating to the Bolivian Loan; *La Empresa Church y el Empréstito Boliviano de 1872; Sentencias Judiciales-Extinción de la Deuda; Money Market Review,* July 26, 1879; *London Times,* May 20-24 and 31, 1879; *Boletín de la Unión Panamericana,* November, 1924, article by J. Guzmán Tellez.

22 (Page 95). J. Speyer & Company, and a London group of bankers competed for this loan, the London group offering 6 percent and a price of 85.

23 (Page 95). See Casto Rojas, *Cuestiones Económicas y Financieras,* pp. 3, 125, 206; Luis Tejada, *Después de la Crisis,* especially pp. 14 and 18;

and unpublished MS report on Bolivia, dated 1919, prepared by the Inter American High Commission.

24 (Page 95). *Ministro de Hacienda e Industria: Mensaje Especial del Poder Ejecutivo, Empréstito Externo por* £1,500,000.

25 (Page 95). For a good brief history of the Bolivian public debt see McQueen, *Bolivian Public Finance,* Chapter II; also Trade Information Bulletin No. 194, February 18, 1924, by the same author.

26 (Page 95). The *Journal of Commerce,* June 20, 1917, states that over $4,000,000 of this loan was still on deposit in Paris.

27 (Page 96). The credit from the Bolivian banks was advanced for a two-year period at 8 percent, the interest rate to be increased to 10 percent if the obligations were not met at the end of that time. As security the Government pledged 100,000 of its shares of the Banco de la Nación. If the Government should default on its interest payments the creditor banks could collect the taxes on mineral and oil concessions, the dividends of corporations and the profits of these, of mining companies and of banking institutions. Of the total Bs. 11,600,000 loaned, the Banco de la Nación paid half, the Banco Nacional de Bolivia and the Banco Mercantil each a quarter. See text of official decree of November 10, 1920, in Appendix, III-d to the Inter American High Commission's unpublished report on Bolivia.

28 (Page 96). The balance of the $10,000,000 contracted for with Imbrie & Company was to be used for railways. *Commerce Reports,* May 8 and July 25, 1920; Legation Report No. 32, April 21, 1920; *New York Evening Post,* June 12, 1920.

29 (Page 96). *Comisión Fiscal Permanente,* 1925, *Segunda Memoria,* p. 18. It was estimated that the entire French loan, normally equivalent to $11,320,000, could be liquidated for approximately $6,000,000. The debt in 1920 amounted to 43,500,000 francs. Conversion was made at the rate of four francs to the boliviano. See unpublished report of the Inter American High Commission on Bolivia.

30 (Page 96). It is idle to reproach the Bolivian Government for not waiting until the franc dropped even lower. True, there was no need of rushing the liquidation, as the French bonds would not have expired until 1940 (Report of S. Ballivián to the League of Nations, 1920), but the continued collapse of the franc could not have been altogether foreseen in 1920.

31 (Page 96). $7,000,000 was to be issued by 1924, another $3,000,000 was authorized if needed to complete the railroad.

32 (Page 96). $3,000,000 had been issued but not publicly offered; $2,000,000 was to be issued January 1, 1923; in June, 1922, this $5,000,000 was exchanged for bonds of the new loan. McQueen, *Bolivian Public Finance,* p. 42.

33 (Page 97). See *Memoria de Hacienda,* 1919, pp. 227-230, and *Apendice,* p. 539; also McQueen, *op. cit.,* p. 51. Negotiations for the Ulen Sanitation Bonds, for which a contract ad referendum had been signed in 1919, seem not to have been affected by the Revolution. See *Bulletin,* Pan American Union, October, 1920, p. 426.

34 (Page 97). 1924 is the only year in the recent history of Bolivia with a surplus. In 1925 there was again a deficit, amounting to some Bs. 3,000,-000. See *Comisión Fiscal Permanente, Tercera Memoria,* 1926, pp. 21-25; also its *Memoria* of July 15, 1924, pp. 45-55; Sherwell, "Budgets of Latin American Countries," in *Trade Information Bulletin No. 251,* October, 1924; "Latin American Financial Notes, No. 5," Department of Commerce, Finance and Investment Division, May 23, 1925. José Rivera in his *"Los Empréstitos Extranjeros y la Política Americana"* says that when Bolivia approached J. P. Morgan and Company in 1919 for a loan, the bankers pointed significantly to the budget deficits of the past ten years, at which he wisely comments "reputable banking houses will not accept legislative fantasies nor consular propaganda" (p. 79).

35 (Page 97). See report on the 1922 refunding loan in *Memoria de Hacienda,* 1924, pp. 68-74.

36 (Page 97). See *Anuario Legislativo,* 1921-1922, p. 5, for Law of December 5, 1921, authorizing this preliminary loan.

37 (Page 97). The special Bolivian commission appointed in 1923 to seek some modification of the contract charged, in its report, that this preferential option would hold whether the immediate refunding loan were concluded or not. See *Empréstito Nicolaus: Conclusiones de la Comisión Especial para solicitar modificaciones del contrato,* 1923; Memorandum of Ramón Rivero on the 1922 loan in *Memoria de Hacienda,* 1922, pp. 43-64; and Dunn, *American Foreign Investments,* pp. 251 and 255. In an appendix to Dunn, pp. 249-284, are reprinted texts of the preliminary contract of November 12, 1921, the Agreement of December 5, 1921 for the short-term loan, and the Trust Contract of May 31, 1922.

38 (Page 97). Exchange stood at the time Bs. 4 to the dollar; with the improved exchange of the following year the possibility of any such enormous reduction of the principal disappeared. As a matter of fact the actual saving on the principal of the obligations converted was over a million and a half dollars less than the National City Bank plan anticipated. Nor was Bolivian exchange restored to par, although its condition steadily improved. The substitution of internal for external obligations calling for payment in gold dollars thus offset somewhat the reduction in the principal.

39 (Page 98). In connection with the loss to Bolivia in serving her external obligations while her currency is below par see *Comisión Fiscal Permanente, Memoria,* July 15, 1924, pp. 36-45 and *"Problemas económicas y legales de Bolivia con respeto á los Estados Unidos,"* por J. Guzmán Tellez, *Boletín de la Unión Panamericana,* November, 1924.

40 (Page 98). See Dunn, *American Foreign Investments,* pp. 249, 251.

41 (Page 98). *Anuario Legislativo,* 1921-1922, pp. 15-17, 55-59, for the covering laws of February 10, 1922, and May 24, 1922.

42 (Page 98). The *Memoria de Hacienda* for 1922, p. 39, reports that the loan had many adversaries because of its size; some thought it should not have exceeded $15,000,000; others that it should have been for only $10,000,000 to cancel back loans and complete railways begun. "The North Americans, who are more practical than we in business, point out that only by placing a loan of $33,000,000 could we finish the railways, convert the customs notes and the floating debt, and establish our finances on a sound basis." The first law, that of February 10, 1922, authorized a loan of only $15,000,000. The report of the special commission appointed in 1923 to secure modifications of the contract asserts that the sum was far in excess of the country's present economic capacities. Rivera, *op. cit.,* p. 28, states that the idea of a large loan originated not in Bolivia but abroad. This assertion is substantiated by the records of the preliminary discussions and the plan for a blanket mortgage loan advanced by the National City Bank.

43 (Page 98). Of a total income of Bs. 23,055,848 in 1922, Bs. 12,554,839 was pledged to the refunding loan of 1922. Computed from tables in McQueen, *The Bolivian Fiscal System,* pp. 15-16. The 1926 report of the Permanent Fiscal Commission gives the returns from the securities pledged in 1922 as Bs. 12,600,810 (p. 28).

44 (Page 98). Schedule A, appended to the Loan Contract, shows a total revenue for 1920 of Bs. 27,885,323, of which Bs. 18,899,429 would represent the yield from the items pledged.

45 (Page 98). For these see *Comisión Fiscal Permanente, Memoria,* July 25, 1924.

46 (Page 99). Bs. 27,945,511 out of a total revenue of Bs. 41,956,630. *Comisión Fiscal Permanente, Tercera Memoria,* 1926, p. 27.

47 (Page 99). See appendix for full text of the *Trust Contract.*

48 (Page 100). *Comisión Fiscal Permanente, Tercera Memoria,* 1926, p. 108.

49 (Page 101). Article V of the Trust Contract; *Anuario Legislativo de 1921-1922,* pp. 32-33, for text of the Law of March 27, 1922, authorizing the Permanent Fiscal Commission.

50 (Page 101). See *Comisión Fiscal Permanente, Memoria,* July 15, 1924, and *Segunda Memoria,* 1925, p. 64.

51 (Page 101). *Comisión Fiscal Permanente, Segunda Memoria,* 1925, pp. 12-13; McQueen, *Bolivian Public Finance,* p. 52. The actual amount in bolivianos refunded was Bs. 19,137,800.75.

52 (Page 104). For the proceeds of the refunding loan of 1922, and their distribution, see table on pp. 102-103, compiled from the *Segunda Memoria de la Comisión Fiscal Permanente,* 1925, pp. 1-16, and from the *Cuenta del Empréstito celebrado con the Equitable Trust Company of New York, Tesoro Nacional de Bolivia,* December 18, 1922.

53 (Page 104).

For the Potosí-Sucre Railway.......	$916,731
For the Yungas Railway...........	464,106
For the Cochabamba-Santa Cruz Ry.	102,379
For the Villazón-Tarija highway....	155,008

54 (Page 104). Trust Contract, Art. III, Sec. 1.

55 (Page 105). Edwards, *Investing in Foreign Securities,* p. 196.

56 (Page 105). For full report of the negotiations see Memorandum of Ramón Rivero on this loan in *Memoria de Hacienda,* 1922, pp. 43-64.

57 (Page 105). See footnote 37 above; also Art. IV, Sec. 7 of the Trust Contract. The special Bolivian commission in its report of March, 1923, called this provision "an alienation of Bolivia's economic sovereignty, which imposes upon our institutions and upon the popular will the absolute discretion of a group of foreign bankers whose actions do not and cannot have any other guide than profit. . . . Such regulations try to impose on this part of America the imperialist sentiments of some bankers. Contracts of this nature help very little in developing political and economic *rapprochement* between the United States and the Latin American countries."

58 (Page 105). Memorandum of Ramón Rivero, cited above.

59 (Page 105). In September, 1922, President Saavedra asked the North American members of the Permanent Fiscal Commission whether Art. IV, Sec. 7 of the contract might not be modified so that Bolivia might accept this loan. The reply was that the commissioners could see no security for such a loan even if the terms of the contract permitted it. See confidential letter from the United States Minister to Bolivia to our Secretary of State, September 16, 1922.

60 (Page 106). 90 minus a commission of 2½ percent.

61 (Page 106). *Memoria de Hacienda,* 1922.

62 (Page 107). According to the special commission appointed in 1923 to study the loan, the Bankers, on April 27, 1922, offered to extend this earlier loan three months so that the arrangement with Bernheim was unnecessary.

63 (Page 107). The Bankers claim that this arrangement was wholly unnecessary as when it was made a price of 90 had already been offered. The cable offering the higher price was declared by the Saavedra Government never to have been received. The cost to Bolivia of Bernheim's services was $316,654.

64 (Page 107). See *Memoria de Hacienda,* 1922, for these details regarding the negotiations and final terms.

65 (Page 107). *Commercial and Financial Chronicle,* June 3, 1922.

66 (Page 107). See letter of R. Villanueva, Minister of Finance, to the Bolivian Minister in Washington, May 26, 1924, which was distributed to the bondholders. Published in *Commercial and Financial Chronicle,* June 7, 1924.

67 (Page 107). *The New York Times,* January 1, 1927, and throughout the month.

68 (Page 108). See report on the loan in *Memoria de Hacienda,* 1924, pp. 68-74.

69 (Page 108). Notably the Morgan Bonds and the alcohol monopoly. See below.

70 (Page 108). *Memoria de Hacienda,* 1924, pp. 68-74.

71 (Page 108). *Empréstito Nicolaus: Conclusiones de la Comisión Especial para solicitar modificaciones del Contrato,* 14 *Marzo,* 1923. In addition to this long report, two members of the Commission, Sr. J. Saenz and Sr. José Mendieta, came to New York and submitted a special memorandum to the Bankers in June, 1923, proposing definite changes in the Trust Contract. This latter memorandum the Bankers' counsel replied to point for point.

72 (Page 108). On the other hand Sr. Rivero, in his report to the Government of May 8, 1922, said: "We insist on emphasizing the favorable price obtained for the bonds. The price of 92 for those to be immediately issued and of 93 for the later ones, we consider the highest that can be obtained. These prices place us at a level with the most accredited nations of South America." See *Memoria de Hacienda,* 1922, p. 60.

73 (Page 109). Memorandum presented by Stifel-Nicolaus Investment Company, Spencer Trask & Company and the Equitable Trust Company of New York (as Bankers) in answer to the Memorandum presented by Señores J. Saenz and José Mendieta, Commissioners of the Republic of Bolivia, July 30, 1923 (strictly confidential).

74 (Page 110). The Ulen Bonds of 1922, which were included in this new issue and covered $10,000,000 of the total, had under their original contract been redeemable at par at any time.

75 (Page 111). See McQueen, *Chilean Public Finance,* pp. 35 and 37.

76 (Page 111). The Government at present owns 114,738 out of a total of 176,000.

77 (Page 112). McQueen, *Bolivian Public Finance,* p. 78.

78 (Page 113). At first Saavedra asked for the return of the shares when the loan had been 20 percent amortized. *Memoria de Hacienda,* 1922.

79 (Page 114). The $14,000,000 loan placed in 1927 with Dillon, Read & Company is to be applied in part to the continuation of the Potosi-Sucre Railway.

80 (Page 114). Trust Contract, Art. IV, Sec. 1(b) and Art. VIII, Sec. 4(a).

81 (Page 114). The Banco de la Nación had to accept Bs. 4,110,800 in 1924 State Bonds which covered the unamortized balance of the £292,000 Morgan Bonds it had loaned the Government as guarantee for the preliminary loan of $1,000,000, and which were held by the Equitable Trust Company. The Morgan Bonds that were still in the hands of the public were either converted into bonds of this new loan or redeemed out of a fund on deposit with J. P. Morgan & Company. In this way the entire Morgan loan was liquidated. See *Comisión Fiscal Permanente, Segunda Memoria,* 1925, pp. 27-29.

82 (Page 114). *Comisión Fiscal Permanente, Tercera Memoria,* 1926, p. 30. According to Sr. José Rivera they were quoted as low as 56 (see his *Los Empréstitos Extranjeros y la Política Americana* (p. 78). *Moody's Investors Service,* August, 1925, classifies them as a pure speculation.

83 (Page 114). Letter from the Bolivian Minister of Finance to the Bolivian Minister at Washington, May 26, 1924, *op. cit.*

84 (Page 115). By the issue of *notas de más cargo,* which claim for the Government larger tax payments than those returned by the companies or individuals on which they are served, the Permanent Fiscal Commission has in the last three years added about Bs. 3,500,000 to the tax receipts, with a prospect of over a million more on *notas* yet to be collected. Not only

are the tax returns to the state increased by this vigilance, but a more regular and careful procedure is established and the likelihood of fraud considerably lessened. The Commission has, moreover, covered its expenses six times over in pressing these claims against delinquent tax-payers. The total cost of the commission since June, 1923, exclusive of the expenses of the North American members was Bs. 302,241. The total expenses of the North American Commissioners, August, 1922-July, 1926, was Bs. 313,236. Subtracting the salaries of one bank director, of an inspector of banks and of the Director-General of Customs, all of which posts are filled by the representatives of the Bankers on the Commission, the cost of the North American members is reduced to Bs. 281,661, or approximately $93,887. The total cost of the Commission up to July 31, 1926, was Bs. 583,902 or about $194,634. See *Comisión Fiscal Permanente, Tercera Memoria,* 1926, p. 104; also *Segunda Memoria,* 1925, pp. 56-61.

85 (Page 115). Statement of Bankers' counsel, November 16, 1922.

86 (Page 116). The considerably better terms secured for the most recent external loan—that of $14,000,000 from Dillon, Read & Company—may be attributed in part to Bolivia's freedom to consider proposals from five different American banking houses as well as one British group. Speyer & Company, Eastman, Dillon & Company, Lehman Brothers, the Equitable Trust Company, and Dillon, Read, were the American banking groups interested. See address of Sr. Martinez Vargas and article by Sr. Alejandro Ovando in *Bolivia: A Bi-Monthly Survey of Bolivian Activities,* January, 1927.

87 (Page 117). It may also be asserted that international bankers can be expected to be their brothers' keepers in preventing poor and weak governments from committing folly in their external borrowings.

88 (Page 117).

Floating debt and administrative expenses	$4,782,454.87
Service of the refunding loan..........	1,674,485.29
Commissions	441,666.00
Loss on sale of bonds below par........	2,690,000.00
	$9,588,606.16

The first item includes repayment of the six months preliminary loan of $1,000,000, which had yielded Bs. 4,080,000, disposed of as follows:

1.	Cancellation of loan from Banco de la Nación, guaranteed by bonds	Bs. 827,000.00
2.	Cancellation of loan from Banco de la Nación, guaranteed by customs notes................................	200,000.00
3.	Interest on earlier obligations........................	36,121.78
4.	Deposit in Banco Alemán..........................	200,000.00
5.	Cable remittance to Morgan, N. Y., commission and expenses	407,409.23
6.	Remittance to Erlangers, London, for service of F. C. Eléctrico de Cochabamba...........................	161,495.32
7.	Bolivia Railway Company, arrears.....................	187,500.00
8.	Remittance to Metcalf, on account..................	307,000.00
9.	Discount on alcohol charge (10% on Bs. 1,500,000—90 days)	37,500.00
10.	Internal loan, interest on Bs. 11,600,000.............	464,000.00
11.	Arrears on instruction account........................	260,000.00
12.	Interest on bank credits to Dec. 31, 1921..............	285,371.96
13.	Internal debt—2nd half (paid to date)................	219,616.00
14.	Atocha-Villazón Railway, Ulen Contracting Co.........	170,565.00
		Bs. 3,763,579.29
	Balance applied to administrative expenses............	316,420.71

See *Cuenta del empréstito celebrado con "The Equitable Trust Company," Tesoro Nacional de Bolivia,* December 18, 1922.

89 (Page 118). In bonds of the refunding loan.......... $ 102,855.91
In bonds of the State, 1924 (Bs. 4,110,800, converted at par).................... 1,599,101.20

$1,701,957.11

The Morgan Bonds were redeemable in 1934, the 1922 bonds as a whole but not in part in 1937.

90 (Page 118). £500,000 at 6 and 2 percent would require £40,000 per year, or.................. $194,400.00
$102,856 at 8 and 2 percent will require.... 10,285.60
Bs. 4,110,800 at 8 and 1 percent will require Bs. 369,972 or at par............ 143,919.10
making a total annual charge on the refunding bonds of..................... $154,104.70

The disadvantage of the higher interest rate is further offset by the conversion of part of the Morgan loan into internal bonds not requiring service in dollars.

91 (Page 118). See footnote 27.

92 (Page 118). "These customs notes were not only burdensome because of the high rate of interest, but represented an incorrect principle of finance that had become evident after the satisfaction of the pressing needs to which they were devoted." McQueen, *Bolivian Public Finance,* p. 53.

93 (Page 119). The Bolivian commission contended that Bolivia and not the Ulen people should have benefited by the improved price of these bonds over the railway bonds contracted for earlier.

94 (Page 119). See March, 1923, report of the commission cited above.

95 (Page 119). The Ulen railway bonds were secured by a first mortgage on the Atocha-Villazón Railway and its equipment and a lien on its net earnings as well as by the revenue from the export duties on minerals and rubber, formerly pledged to the French loans of 1910 and 1913; to the Morgan Bonds had been pledged the tax on the net profits of banks, joint stock companies and mining enterprises, 90 percent of the revenue from the stamp taxes on tobacco, and the tax on income from mortgages; the customs notes were secured by the customs revenue from exports and imports. See McQueen, *Bolivian Public Finance,* pp. 42, 40, 52.

96 (Page 119). As the Government's inability to dispose of some Bs. 787,000 of what amounted to a forced loan of Bs. 10,000,000 in 1921 indicates. See American International Corporation's plan for a blanket mortgage loan cited above.

97 (Page 119). According to McQueen, interest rates on ordinary loan accommodations from the Bolivian banks vary from 7 to 12 percent, with 9 percent as the average rate under ordinary conditions. *Bolivian Public Finance,* p. 78.

98 (Page 119). For a description of this vicious circle by a Bolivian see *"Problemas económicas y legales de Bolivia con respeto á los Estados Unidos"* por J. Guzmán Tellez in *Boletín de la Unión Panamericana,* November, 1924.

99 (Page 120). By the end of 1922 the floating debt was as low as Bs. 8,753,748. On December 31, 1925, it amounted to Bs. 16,158,721, dropping again by June 30, 1926, to Bs. 14,923,380. See McQueen, *op. cit.,* p. 49, and *Comisión Fiscal Permanente, Tercera Memoria,* 1926, p. 8.

100 (Page 120). The Inter American High Commission report on Bolivia, prepared in 1919, gives the following list of projected loans showing the improvements that were considered necessary at that time. Some of these, such as the Atocha-Villazón Railway and the La Paz and Cochabamba sewerage and paving projects, have been carried out. New development plans, espe-

cially for highways, take their place, however, and if the political pressure for the construction of the Cochabamba-Santa Cruz Railway should persist, it is safe to assert that as much if not more capital will be needed to carry out the improvements contemplated by the present Government. Moreover, if Bolivia should actually buy Tacna-Arica, the existing debt would need to be more than doubled. A recent law authorizes Oruro to contract a loan for Bs. 6,000,000 for sewers, paving and water supply. (*West Coast Leader,* November 16, 1926.)

Projected loans, December 30, 1919 (from Consular Report, La Paz, of that date):

1.	Branch railway to Tarija....................	£ 550,000
2.	Atocha-Tupiza Railway	1,100,000
3.	Potosí-Sucre Railway	1,100,000
4.	Cochabamba-Santa Cruz Railway............	4,400,000
5.	" sewerage, paving and water supply	412,000
6.	La Paz " " " " "	549,370
7.	Sucre " " " " "	200,000
8.	Potosí sanitary works " " " "	200,000
9.	Oruro sewerage	200,000
	Total	£8,711,370
	or approximately	$43,557,800

101 (Page 120). *Comisión Fiscal Permanente, Tercera Memoria,* 1926, pp. 12-15.

102 (Page 120). *Comisión Fiscal Permanente, Segunda Memoria,* 1925, pp. 22-24.

103 (Page 120). Certain of the petroleum taxes or royalties have been pledged to the new $14,000,000 bond issue, but until oil production begins, it is difficult to see how these can be considered valuable security.

104 (Page 120). This complaint is a persistent note in Bolivian politics of the moment when, though the 1922 loan is accepted pretty generally as a closed chapter, its restricting effects are keenly felt.

105 (Page 120). Rivera, *op. cit.,* p. 75; see McBride, *The Agrarian Indian Communities of Highland Bolivia,* pp. 9-10, for the land taxes paid by the community Indians.

106 (Page 121). The "spread" of nine points is explained by the bankers on the ground of the heavy costs of marketing Bolivian bonds at the time. Bolivia was a little-known country and needed a great deal of advertising. It is possible, too, that the very fact that the bonds were speculative in character made it necessary to distribute them widely to brokers all over the country.

107 (Page 121). See in this connection statement of Dr. Max Winkler in Moody's Weekly Letter, June 28, 1923.

CHAPTER VII

1 (Page 123). For text of this manifesto, which contains a plea for the removal of restrictions upon European trade on the part of one hundred and sixty-five leading bankers and industrialists of fifteen different countries including the United States, see Foreign Policy Association, *Information Service,* "The International Tariff Problem," November 10, 1926.

2 (Page 124). For the comparative yield of foreign and domestic investments see Edwards, *Investing in Foreign Securities,* pp. 6-9. A study made by the *Wall Street Journal* in 1924 showed a difference in yield of 1.77 percent between forty representative domestic bonds which were selected for its index and fourteen typical foreign dollar bonds listed on the New York

Stock Exchange. The former yielded on an average 5.31 percent and the latter 7.08 percent.

3 (Page 126). Nearing and Freeman, *Dollar Diplomacy,* pp. 33-34.

4 (Page 127). See Dunn, *American Foreign Investments,* which reprints a number of loan contracts bearing out this point. See also Moon, *Imperialism and World Politics,* Chapter XVI, for an excellent summary of the Latin American policy of the United States; Nearing and Freeman, *op. cit.*; and Thomas, *One Hundred Years of the Monroe Doctrine.*

5 (Page 128). The veiled seizure of a strip of Colombian territory for the Panama Canal, although clearly an imperialistic act affecting a South American state, involves a rather different situation.

6 (Page 128). As Nearing and Freeman, in their work on dollar diplomacy, cited above, put it, "Bolivia is now in the twilight zone between peaceful migration of capital and political control by American bankers" (p. 18). McQueen, writing for our Department of Commerce, asserts that at the present stage of her development Bolivia needs foreign capital more than any other country in South America to operate her mining industry on a scale sufficient to maintain the economic balance, and to expand her transportation system. See "Foreign Exchange in Latin America," *Trade Information Bulletin No. 316,* February, 1925.

7 (Page 128). See the *Bandera Roja,* published weekly in La Paz, and Chapter IX of Seoane, *Con el Ojo Izquierdo: Mirando á Bolivia.*

8 (Page 128). See *Dirección General de Aduanas: Comercio de Bolivia en el Primer Semestre de 1926,* which gives comparative statistics for the first six months of 1925 and 1926. According to these figures, 83.06 percent of Bolivian exports in 1925 went to Great Britain, as compared with 7.66 percent to the United States; in 1926, 80.58 percent to Great Britain, 9.04 percent to the United States. With regard to imports on the other hand, in 1925, 26.36 percent came from the United States; in 1926, 28.77 percent; as compared with 21.94 percent and 22.53 percent from Great Britain. It is interesting to compare these with the statistics of Bolivia's foreign trade twenty years or so ago. According to the *Bulletin* of the International Bureau of American Republics (July, 1908 and 1909, pp. 69 and 37 respectively), 5.6 percent of Bolivia's imports came from the United States in 1906; in 1907, 6.4 percent; in 1908, 14 percent. (Cited in Bowman, "Trade Routes in the Economic Geography of Bolivia," *Bulletin,* American Geographical Society, XLII (1910), 188.)

9 (Page 128). See *Moody's Investors' Service,* August, 1925, p. 49, which gives the following distribution:

American investments..	$70,000,000	French investments..	$20-25,000,000
British	30,000,000	Chilean	22,500,000

Dunn, *American Foreign Investments,* p. 65, estimated the total American investment in Bolivia as not less than $80,000,000, while Halsey in a manuscript on file in the Department of Commerce makes the discreet statement that in a total foreign investment in Bolivia of probably more than $100,-000,000 "The United States now probably has as large interests as any other country." Sr. Jorge de la Barra, Secretary of the Bolivian Legation at Washington, in an address published in *Bolivia: A Bi-Monthly Survey of Bolivian Activities,* January, 1927, stated that the $10,000,000 of United States capital invested in Bolivia in 1912 had today increased tenfold. The Dillon, Read loan, though not all subscribed in the United States, will run Dunn's estimate up, and this with the growing mining investment brings the total close to the $100,000,000 mark.

10 (Page 130). The exact wording of the State Department's request was in part as follows: "The flotation of foreign bond issues in the American market is assuming an increasing importance and on account of the bearing

of such operations upon the proper conduct of affairs, it is hoped that American concerns that contemplate making foreign loans will inform the Department of State in due time of the essential facts and subsequent developments of importance. . . . It [the Department] will not pass upon the merits of foreign loans as business propositions, nor assume any responsibility whatever in connection with loan transactions. Offers for foreign loans should not, therefore, state or imply that they are contingent upon an expression from the Department of State regarding them, nor should any prospectus or contract refer to the attitude of this Government. The Department believes that in view of the possible national interests involved it should have the opportunity of saying to the underwriters concerned, should it appear advisable to do so, that there is or there is no objection to any particular issue." For text of the announcement see *Commercial and Financial Chronicle,* March 11, 1922, CXIV, 1,009.

11 (Page 130). See article by Dulles, "Our Foreign Loan Policy," in *Foreign Affairs,* October, 1926.

12 (Page 130). See Hearings on the Ladd Resolution (S. Con. Res. 22), February 25 and 26, 1925.

13 (Page 131). Dulles, *op. cit.*

14 (Page 131). See Buell, "International Capitalism and Its Control," *Current History,* December, 1923; Bruère, "Constructive vs. Dollar Diplomacy," *American Economic Review,* March, 1923, which advances as the two elements of a constructive financial program regarding the Latin American countries: (1) "Let the United States Government discountenance the assumption by American financial interests of specific governmental functions in any borrowing country, particularly in Latin America; (2) Let a definite stand be taken against the exaction of any form of monopoly as a condition to any loan made to any of the Latin American states." C. K. Hobson, in the introduction to his *The Export of Capital* has something to say about the question of political control over loan operations.

15 (Page 132). See Dulles' article, cited above, which argues against formal control by the State Department on the ground that time is often of the greatest importance in bidding for a loan, a feature that will become increasingly important as London returns to prominence as a market for foreign loans.

16 (Page 132). See Article 27 of the Mexican Constitution of 1917; see also "The Mexican Land and Oil Law Issue" in the Foreign Policy Association, *Information Service,* December 22, 1926.

17 (Page 133). See his *Imperialism: A Study,* p. 63; also p. 379 for what Hobson calls "The essentially illicit nature of this use of the public resources of the nation to safeguard and improve private investments."

18 (Page 133). For a discussion of this see Moon, *op. cit.;* also Hobson, *op. cit.,* pp. 78-85, in which he speaks of Cuba, the Philippines and Hawaii as "the hors d'oeuvres to whet an appetite for an ampler banquet"; and Feis, "The Export of American Capital," *Foreign Affairs,* July, 1925, who, in reviewing our policy towards foreign investments, says: "As long as present conditions continue it is almost certain, in view of our national strength and economic enterprise, that there will be an extension of our governmental obligations to private capital and frequent engagements in the same sort of semi-political, semi-financial negotiations as occupied the European nations before the war. That way lies an American empire of subordinate states."

19 (Page 134). See Moon, *op. cit.,* who ranks the American empire among the present empires of the world as sixth from the point of view of area and population, and second from the point of view of commercial value, in this last exceeded only by the British Empire. See tables, pp. 515, 516, 519 and 524. This last is sufficiently interesting to warrant reproduction:

TABLE IV

The Colonial Empire of the United States

	Area (*square miles*)	*Population*	*Commerce*† (*dollars*)
OUTLYING TERRITORIES:			
Alaska	590,884	60,000	$88,905,000
Hawaii	6,449	307,000	188,541,000
DEPENDENCIES:			
Philippine Islands	115,026	11,076,000	243,356,000
Porto Rico	3,435	1,347,000	172,478,000
Virgin Islands*	132	26,000	2,559,000*
Samoa*	58	8,000	294,000*
Guam	210	13,000	967,000
Wake and Midway Is.	29	....	....
LEASED TERRITORY:			
Panama Canal Zone, Guantanámo, Fonseca Bay, Corn Island	527	27,000	....
Total Possessions	716,750	12,864,000	$697,100,000
NOMINALLY INDEPENDENT DEPENDENCIES:‡			
Cuba	44,164	3,369,000	$724,595,000
Haiti	11,072	2,045,000	28,872,000
Dominican Republic	19,325	897,000	51,843,000
Panama	33,667	443,000	16,250,000
Nicaragua	49,200	638,000	21,797,000
Liberia	36,834	1,500,000	2,528,000*
Total nominally independent dependencies	194,262	8,892,000	$845,885,000
Grand Total	911,012	21,756,000	$1,542,985,000

* 1923.

† 1924, Commerce Year Book.

‡ Whether these should be included, and whether other Latin-American countries might also be added, must necessarily be a matter of opinion. I have selected the countries which are definitely under a form of control which Europeans might be tempted to describe as a protectorate, quasi-protectorate, or veiled protectorate. Technical classification is difficult, if not impossible, but the fact of control is indubitable.

20 (Page 136). Moon, *op. cit.*, p. 415.

21 (Page 136). Ugarte, *"El Destino de un Continente,"* quoted in *The Nation*, July 9, 1924, p. 31.